HATSUNE MIKU MIKUBON

STORY AND ART BY
ONTAMA

EDITOR
CARL GUSTAV HORN

TRANSLATOR
MICHAEL GOMBOS

LETTERER
JOHN CLARK

DARK HORSE MANGA

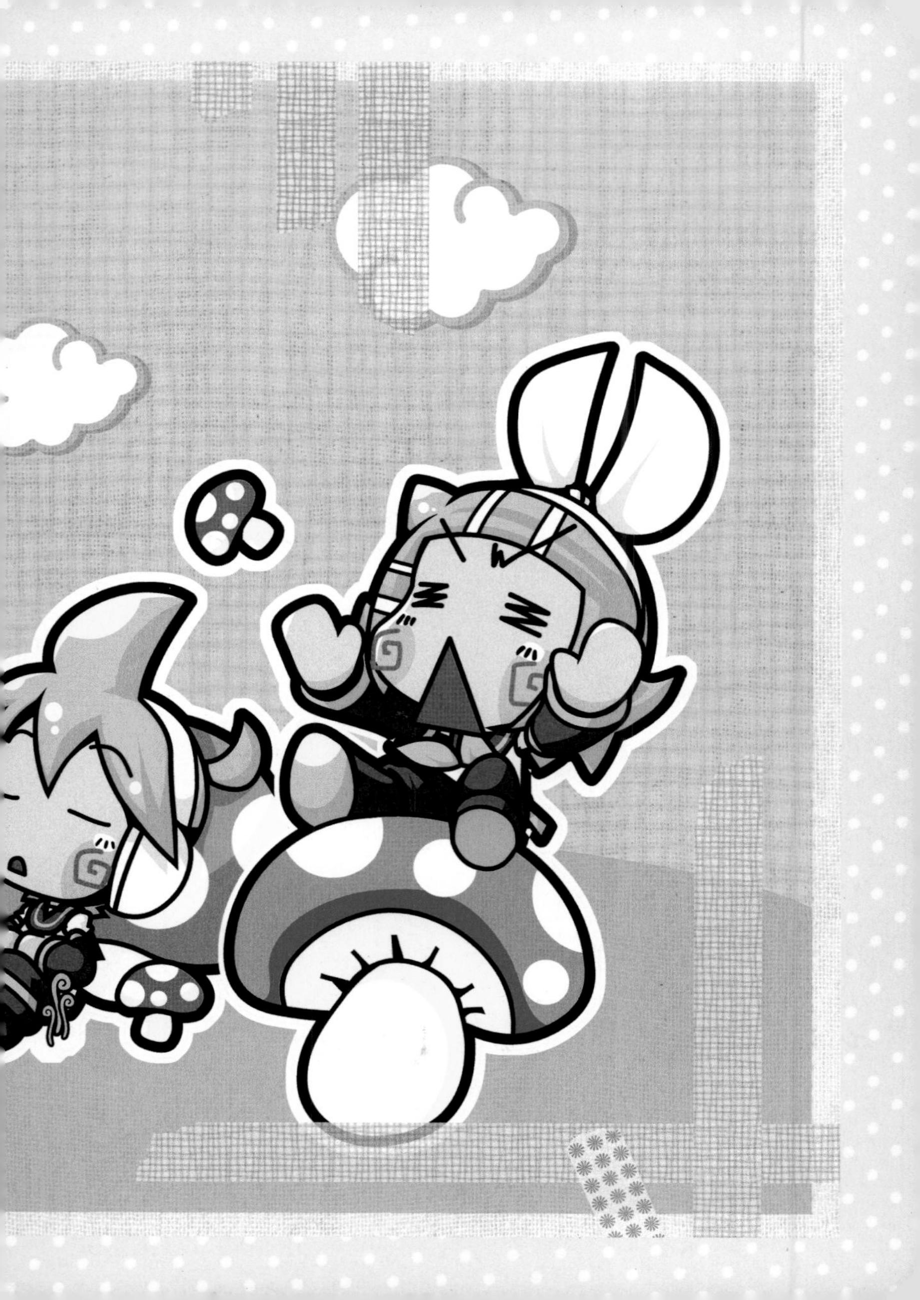

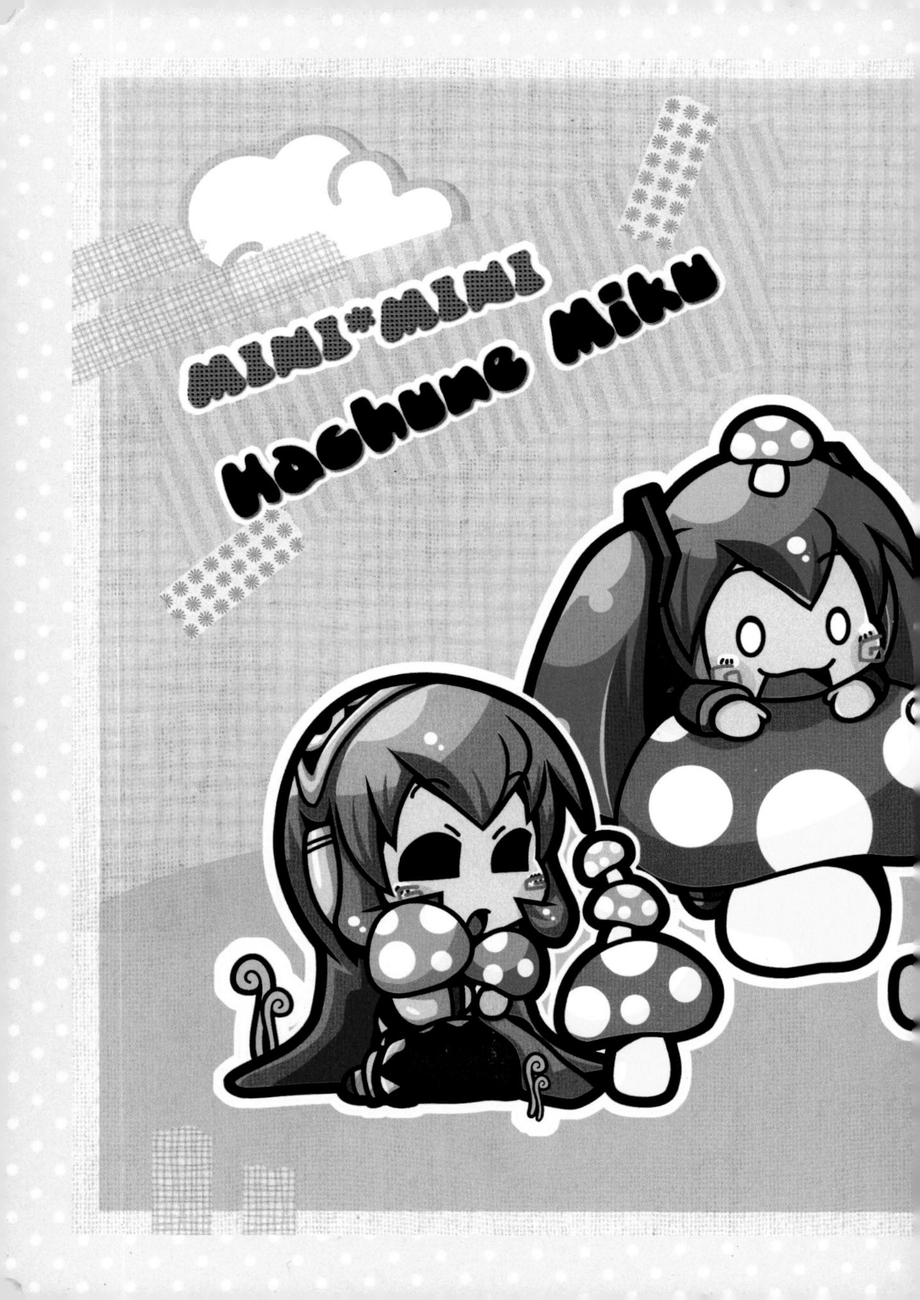
MINI*MINI
Hachune Miku

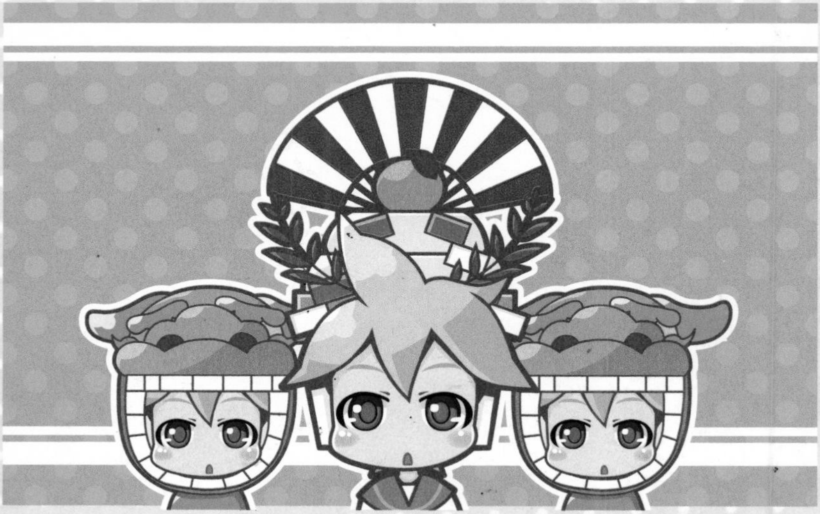

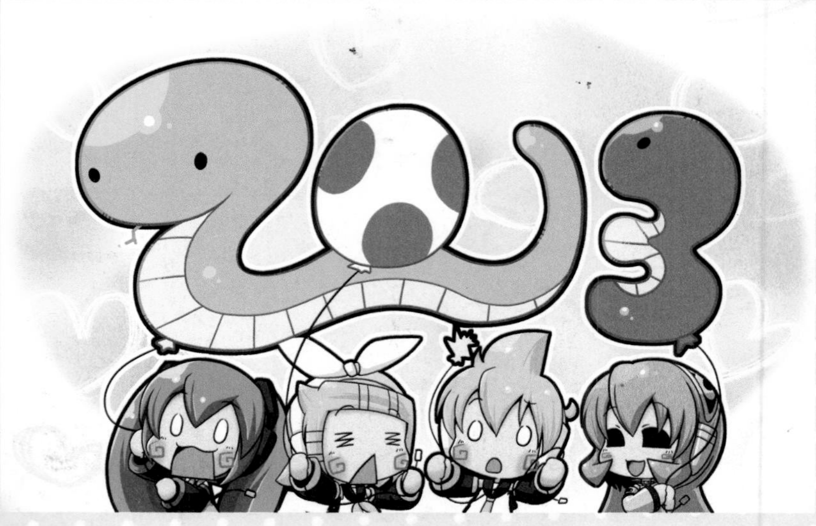

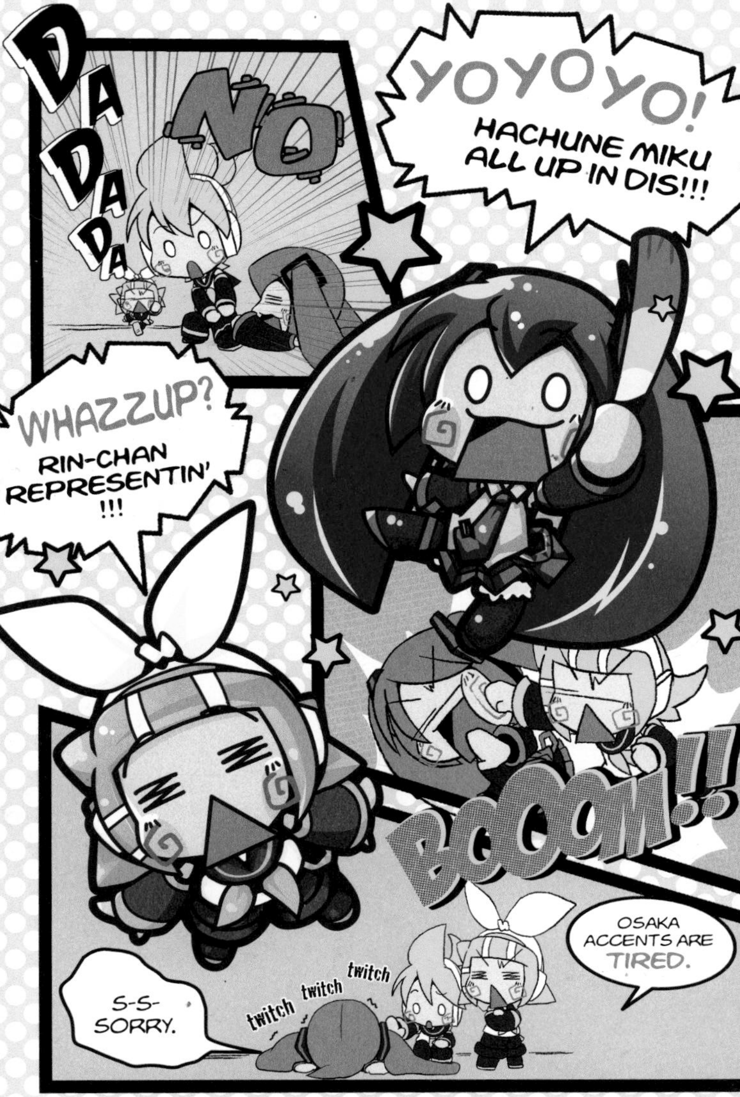
YOYOYO! HACHUNE MIKU ALL UP IN DIS!!!
DADADADA
NO
WHAZZUP? RIN-CHAN REPRESENTIN' !!!
BOOOM!!
OSAKA ACCENTS ARE TIRED.
twitch twitch twitch
S-S-SORRY.

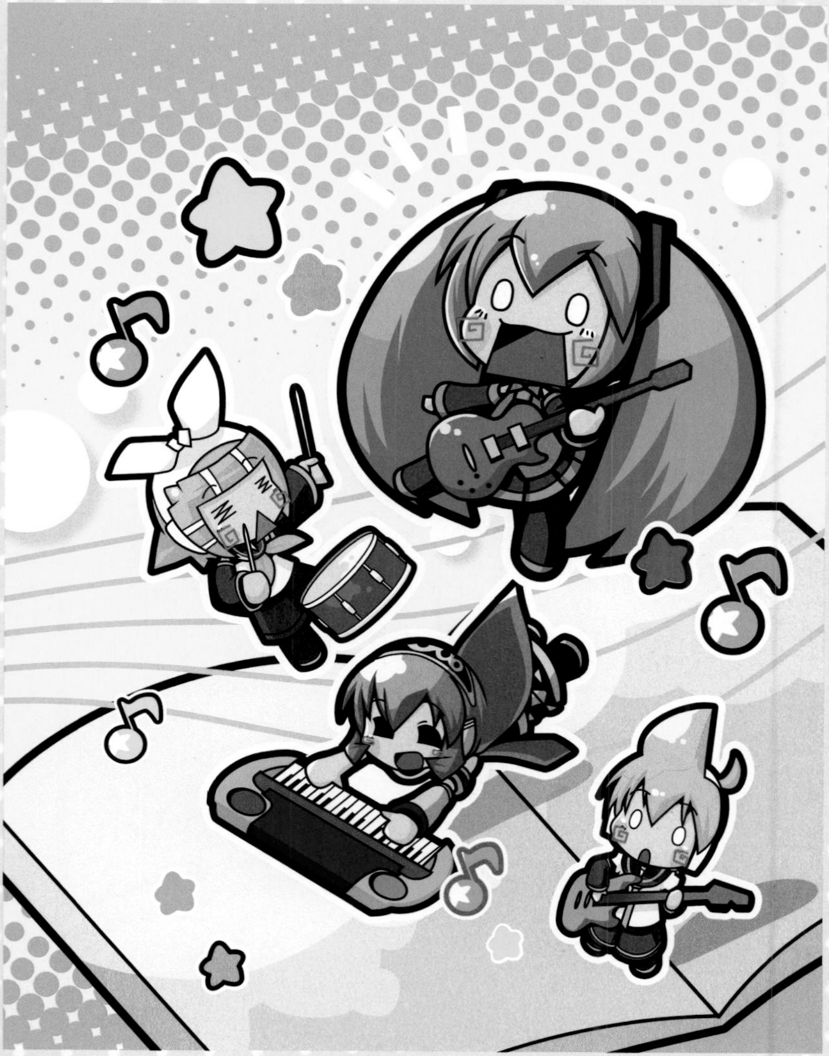

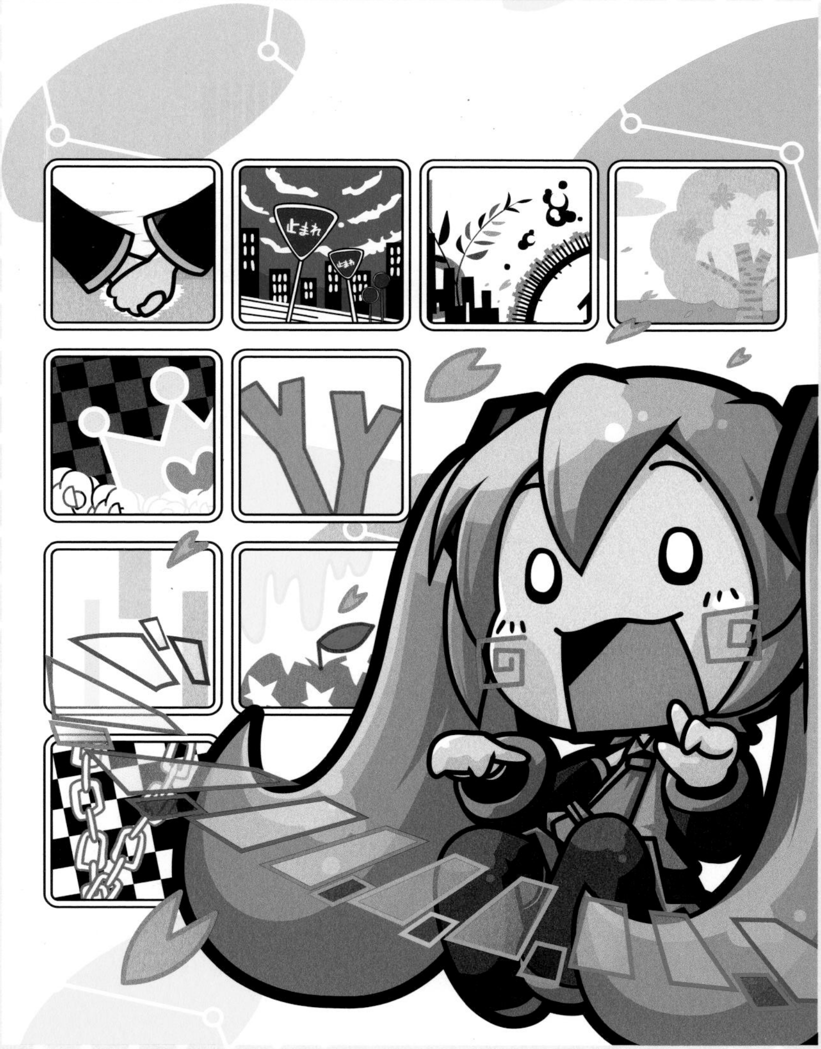
止まれ
止まれ

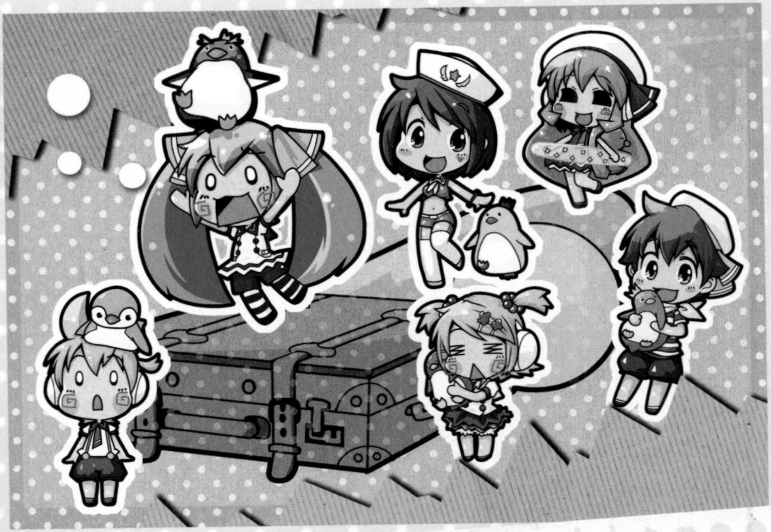

HACHUNE MIKU LAB

VOCALOID IN WONDERLAND

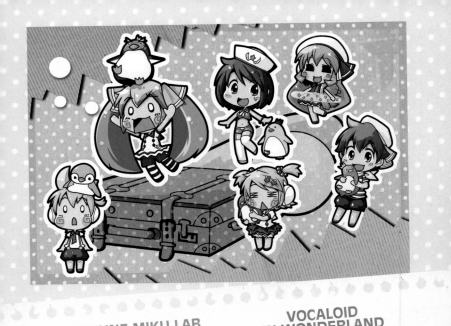

CONTENTS

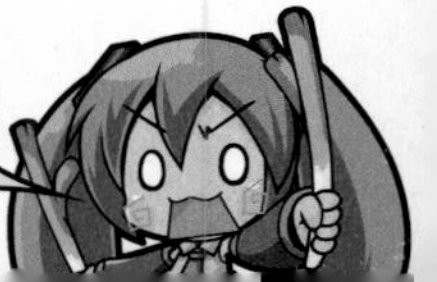

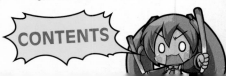

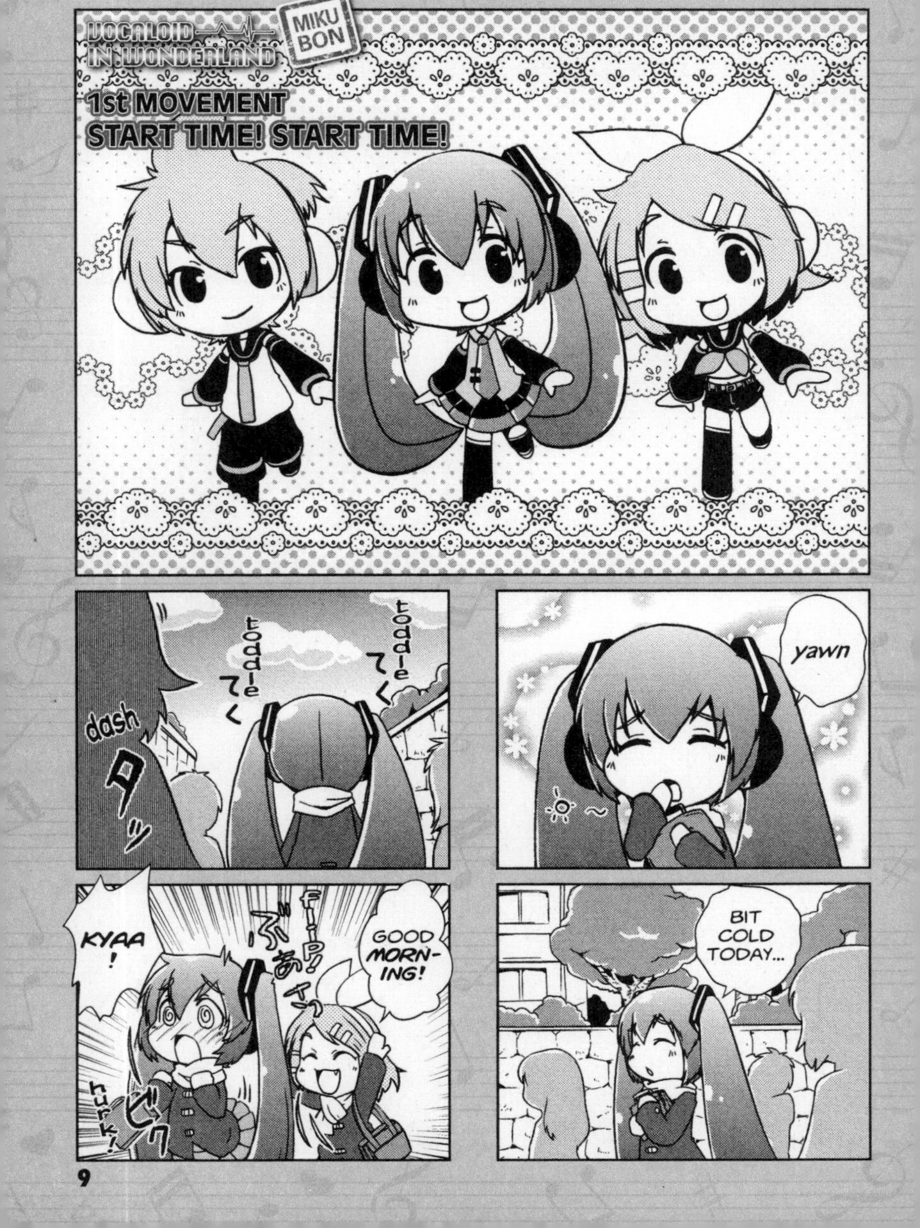
VOCALOID IN WONDERLAND
MIKU BON
1st MOVEMENT
START TIME! START TIME!
yawn
toddle てく
toddle てく
dash タッ
BIT COLD TODAY...
GOOD MORNING!
FLIP! ぶあっ
KYAA!
hurk! ビクッ

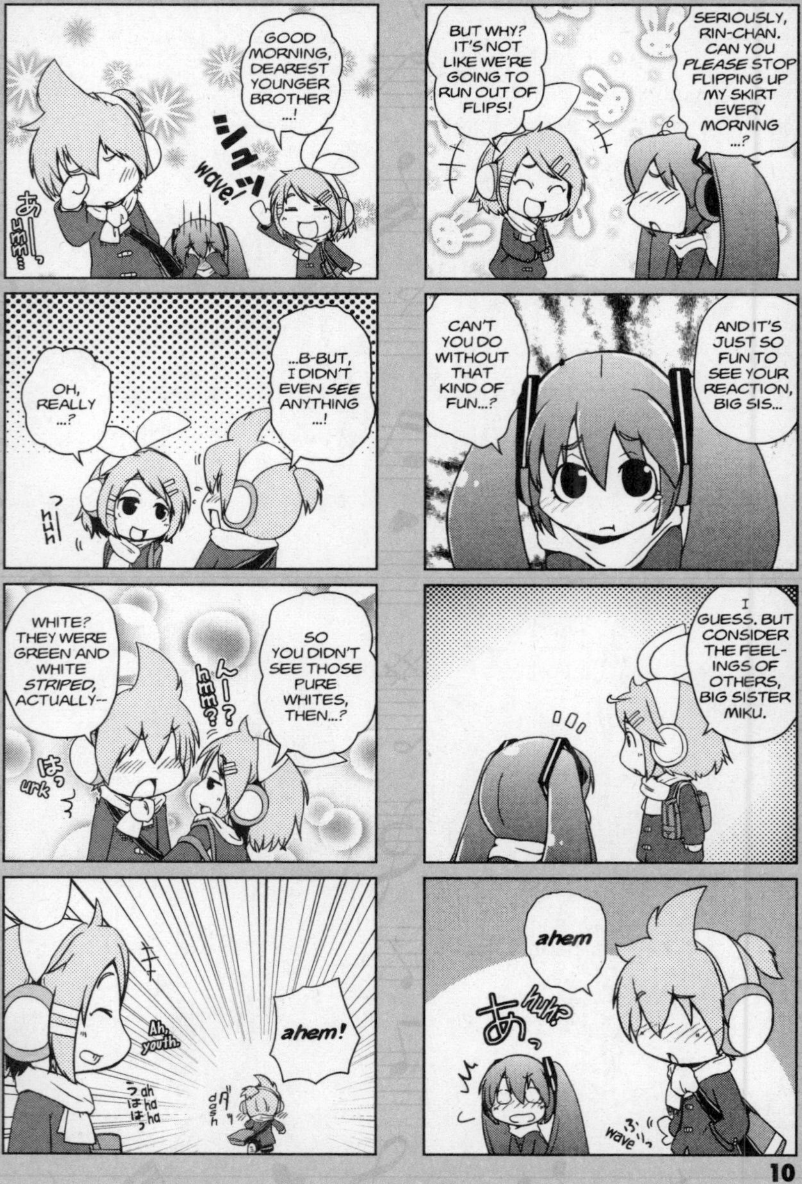
SERIOUSLY, RIN-CHAN. CAN YOU *PLEASE* STOP FLIPPING UP MY SKIRT EVERY MORNING ...?
BUT WHY? IT'S NOT LIKE WE'RE GOING TO RUN OUT OF FLIPS!
AND IT'S JUST SO FUN TO SEE YOUR REACTION, BIG SIS...
CAN'T YOU DO WITHOUT THAT KIND OF FUN...?
I GUESS. BUT CONSIDER THE FEEL- INGS OF OTHERS, BIG SISTER MIKU.
ahem
あっ huh?
wave
GOOD MORNING, DEAREST YOUNGER BROTHER ...!
wave!
あー hmm...
...B-BUT, I DIDN'T EVEN *SEE* ANYTHING ...!
OH, REALLY ...?
huh
SO YOU DIDN'T SEE THOSE PURE WHITES, THEN...?
んー? hmm?
WHITE? THEY WERE GREEN AND WHITE *STRIPED*, ACTUALLY--
はっ urk
ahem!
Ah, youth.
dash
うははっ ah ha ha

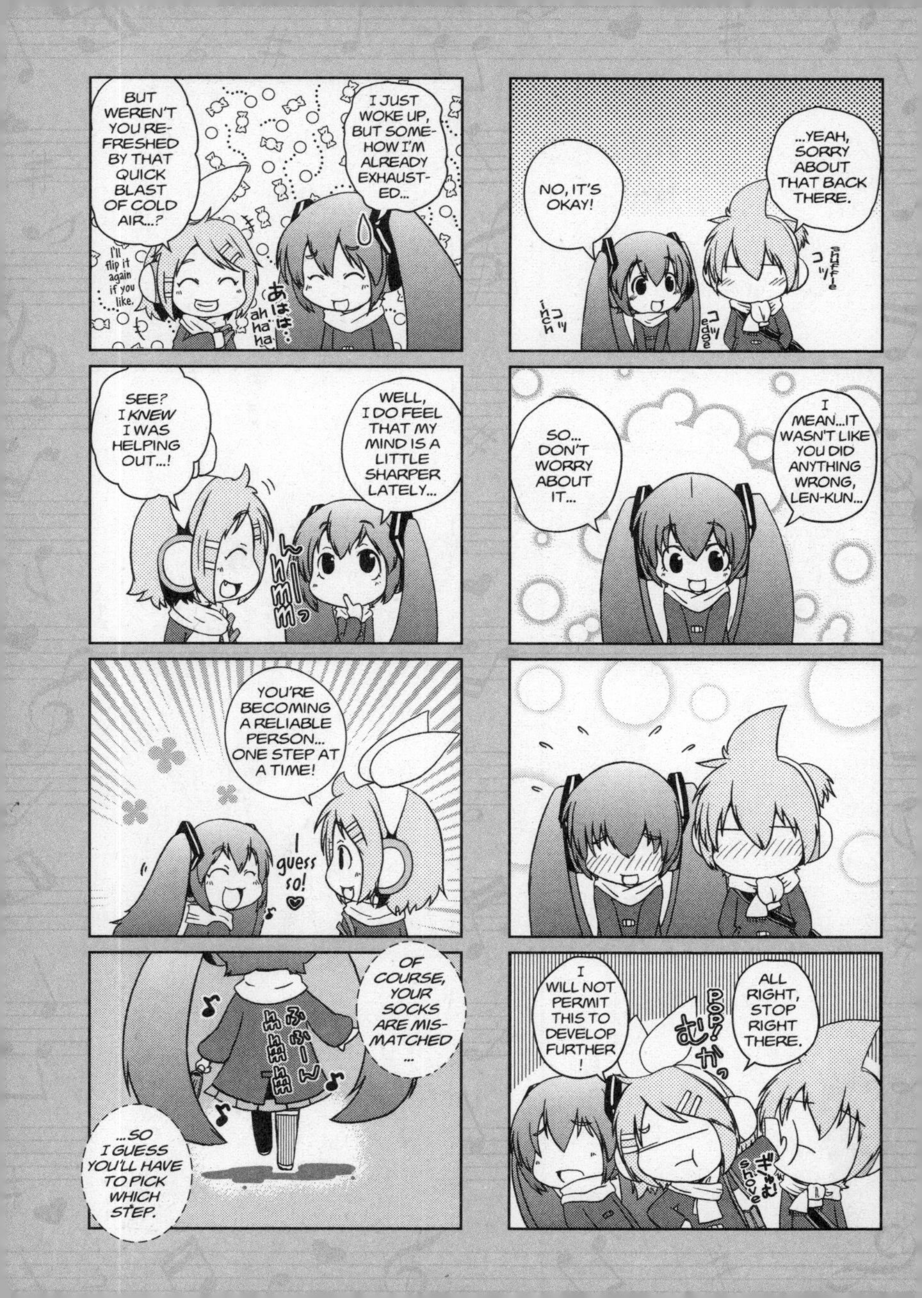
...YEAH, SORRY ABOUT THAT BACK THERE.
コッ shuffle
NO, IT'S OKAY!
コッ edge
コッ inch
I MEAN...IT WASN'T LIKE YOU DID ANYTHING WRONG, LEN-KUN...
SO... DON'T WORRY ABOUT IT...
ALL RIGHT, STOP RIGHT THERE.
むかっ POP!
I WILL NOT PERMIT THIS TO DEVELOP FURTHER!
ぎゅむ shove
I JUST WOKE UP, BUT SOMEHOW I'M ALREADY EXHAUSTED...
BUT WEREN'T YOU REFRESHED BY THAT QUICK BLAST OF COLD AIR...?
あはは... ah ha ha
I'll flip it again if you like.
WELL, I DO FEEL THAT MY MIND IS A LITTLE SHARPER LATELY...
んー hmmm
SEE? I KNEW I WAS HELPING OUT...!
YOU'RE BECOMING A RELIABLE PERSON... ONE STEP AT A TIME!
I guess so!
OF COURSE, YOUR SOCKS ARE MISMATCHED...
ふふーん
...SO I GUESS YOU'LL HAVE TO PICK WHICH STEP.

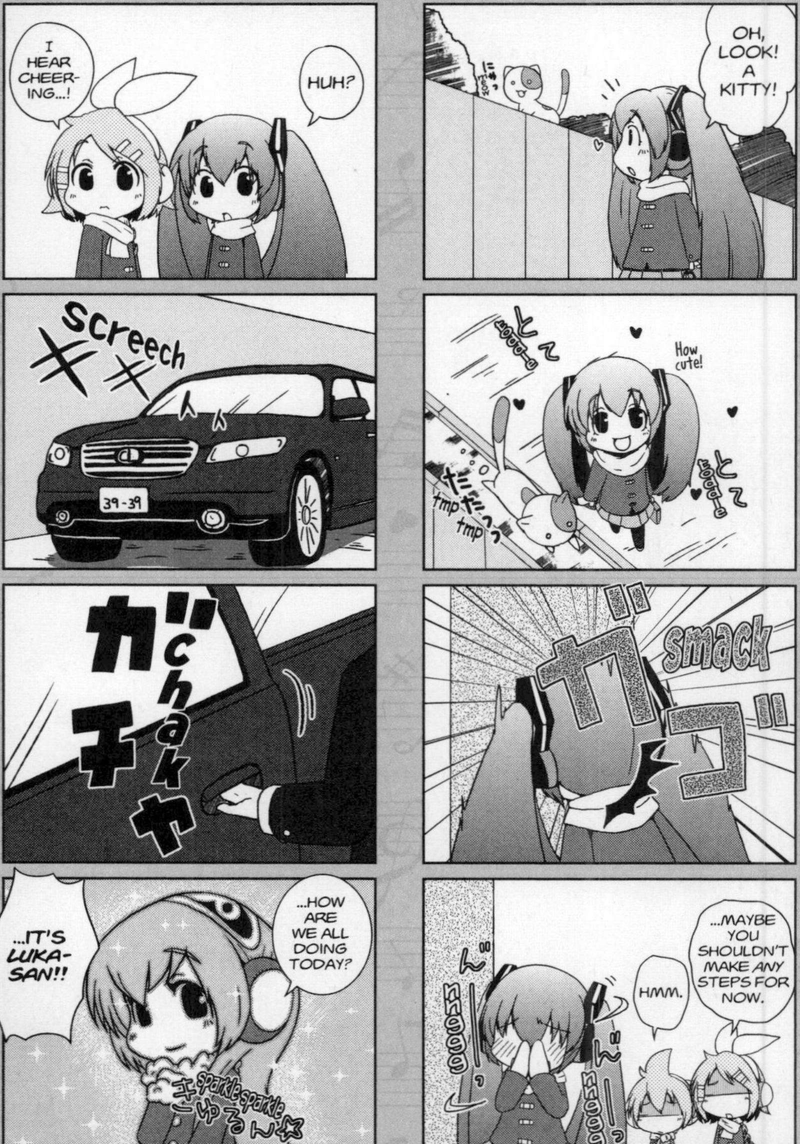

OH, LOOK! A KITTY!
How cute!
toddle
tmp tmp
toddle
smack
...MAYBE YOU SHOULDN'T MAKE ANY STEPS FOR NOW.
HMM.
nnggg
nnggg
I HEAR CHEERING...!
HUH?
screech
chak
...HOW ARE WE ALL DOING TODAY?
...IT'S LUKA-SAN!!
sparkle sparkle

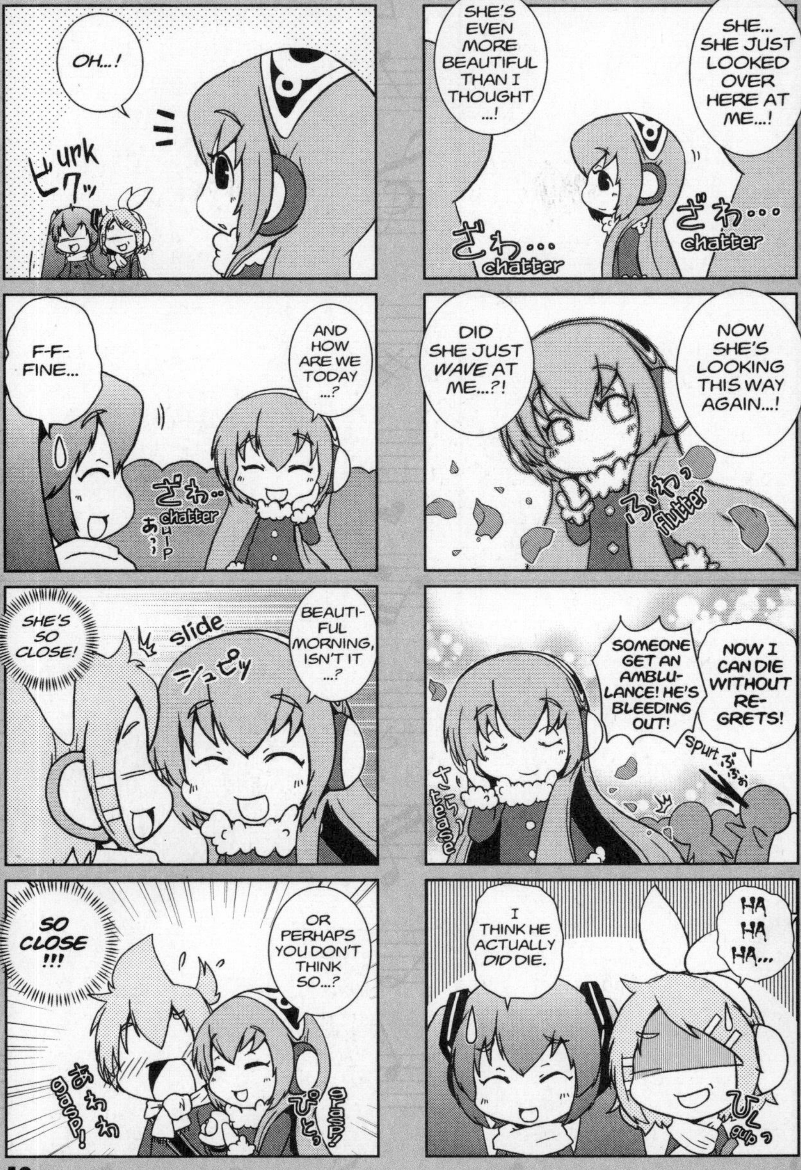
SHE... SHE JUST LOOKED OVER HERE AT ME...!
SHE'S EVEN MORE BEAUTIFUL THAN I THOUGHT ...!
ざわ… chatter
ざわ… chatter
OH...!
ビクッ urk
NOW SHE'S LOOKING THIS WAY AGAIN...!
DID SHE JUST *WAVE* AT ME...?!
ふわっ flutter
AND HOW ARE WE TODAY ...?
F-F-FINE...
ざわ chatter
NOW I CAN DIE WITHOUT RE-GRETS!
SOMEONE GET AN AMBLU-LANCE! HE'S BLEEDING OUT!
spurt
BEAUTI-FUL MORNING, ISN'T IT ...?
slide
シュピッ
SHE'S SO CLOSE!
HA HA HA...
I THINK HE ACTUALLY *DID* DIE.
OR PERHAPS YOU DON'T THINK SO...?
SO CLOSE !!!

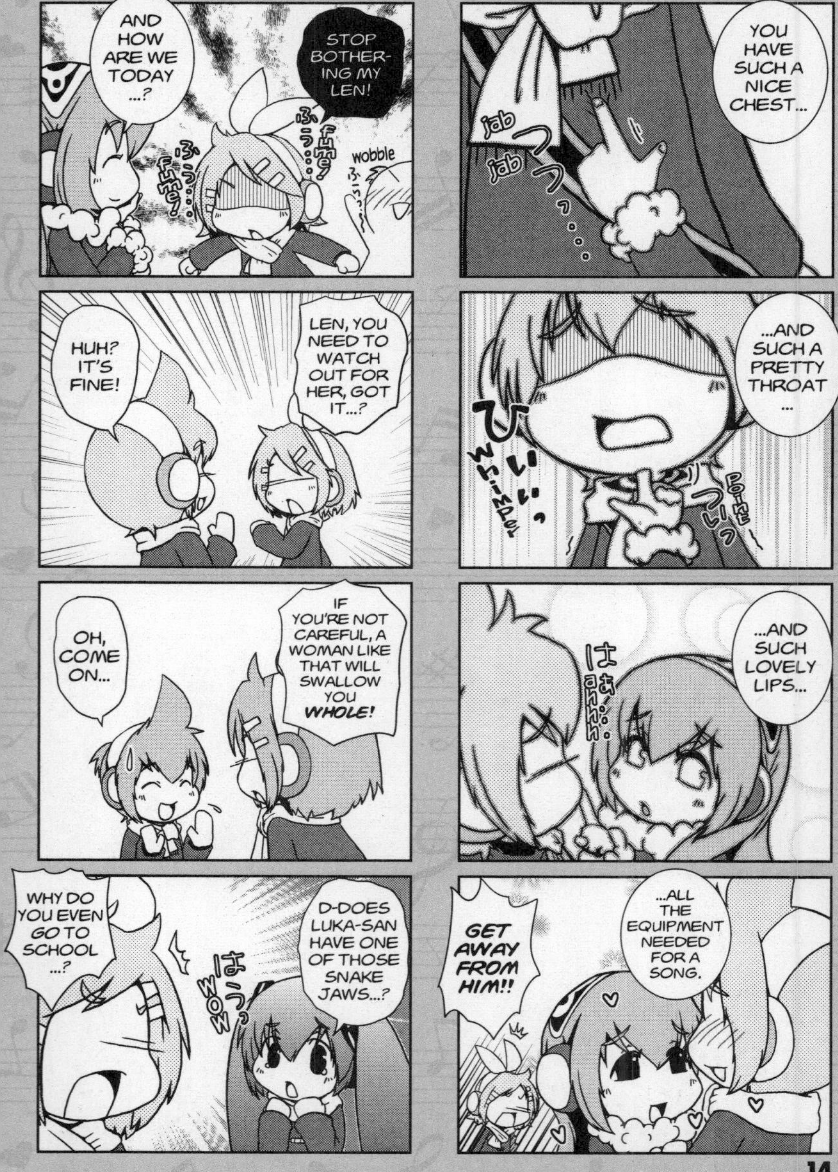
YOU HAVE SUCH A NICE CHEST...
jab jab
...AND SUCH A PRETTY THROAT ...
WHIMPER
...AND SUCH LOVELY LIPS...
...ALL THE EQUIPMENT NEEDED FOR A SONG.
GET AWAY FROM HIM!!
STOP BOTHERING MY LEN!
AND HOW ARE WE TODAY ...?
FUME!
wobble
LEN, YOU NEED TO WATCH OUT FOR HER, GOT IT...?
HUH? IT'S FINE!
IF YOU'RE NOT CAREFUL, A WOMAN LIKE THAT WILL SWALLOW YOU *WHOLE!*
OH, COME ON...
D-DOES LUKA-SAN HAVE ONE OF THOSE SNAKE JAWS...?
WOW
WHY DO YOU EVEN GO TO SCHOOL ...?

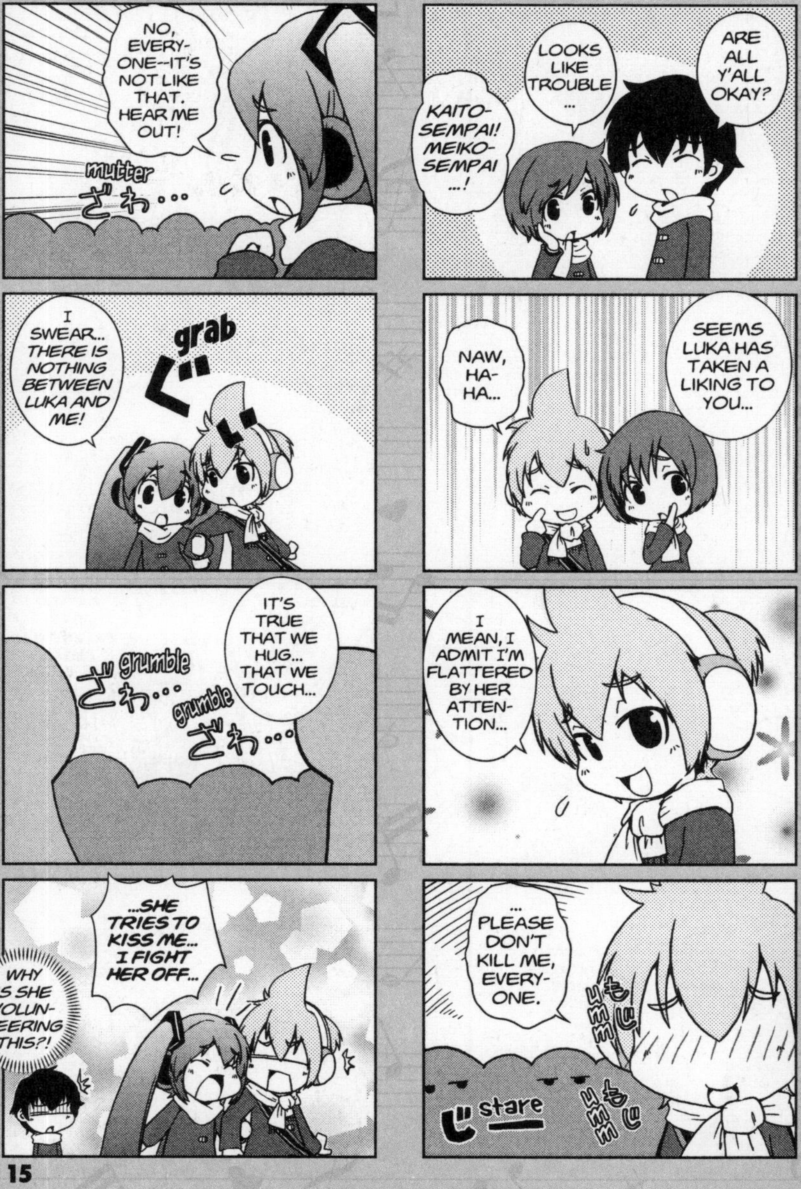
ARE ALL Y'ALL OKAY?
LOOKS LIKE TROUBLE ...
KAITO-SEMPAI! MEIKO-SEMPAI ...!
NO, EVERYONE--IT'S NOT LIKE THAT. HEAR ME OUT!
mutter
ざわ...
SEEMS LUKA HAS TAKEN A LIKING TO YOU...
NAW, HA-HA...
grab
ぐい
I SWEAR... THERE IS NOTHING BETWEEN LUKA AND ME!
I MEAN, I ADMIT I'M FLATTERED BY HER ATTENTION...
IT'S TRUE THAT WE HUG... THAT WE TOUCH...
grumble
ざわ...
grumble
ざわ...
... PLEASE DON'T KILL ME, EVERYONE.
もじ
stare
じー
もじ
...SHE TRIES TO KISS ME... I FIGHT HER OFF...
WHY IS SHE VOLUNTEERING THIS?!

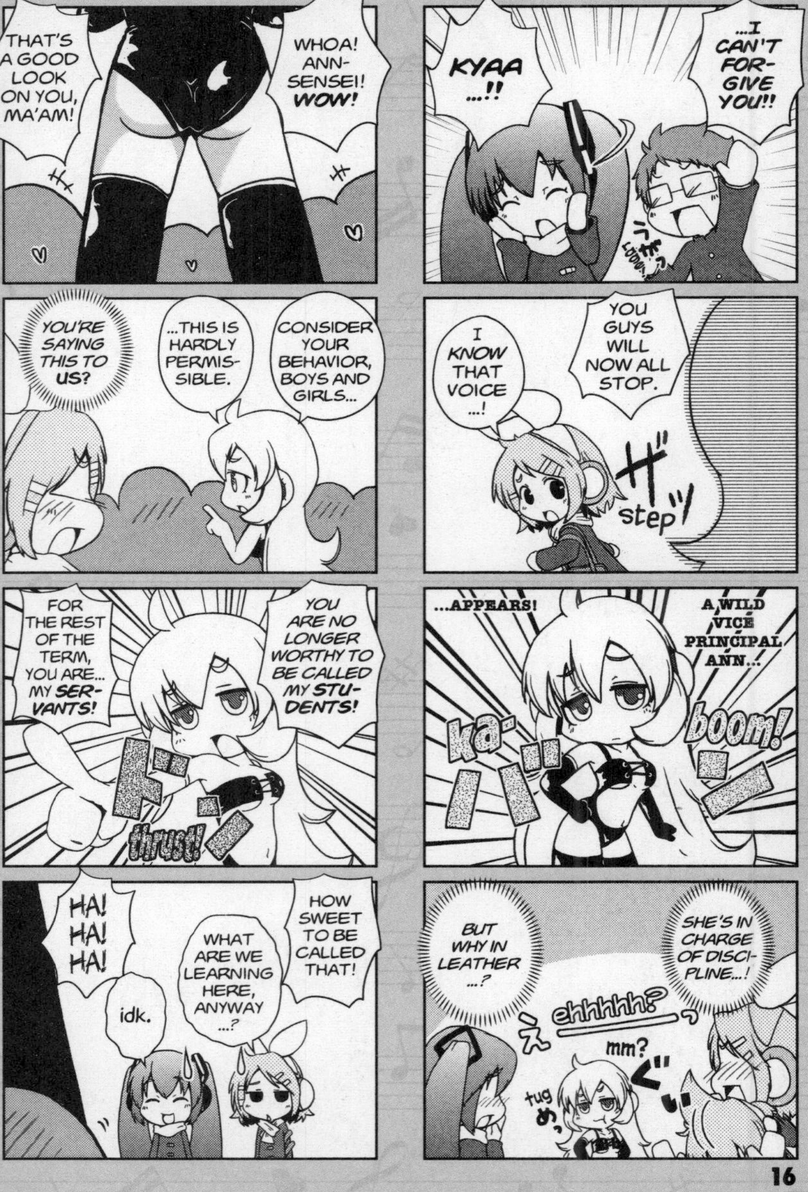

...I CAN'T FOR-GIVE YOU!!
KYAA ...!!
WHOA! ANN-SENSEI! WOW!
THAT'S A GOOD LOOK ON YOU, MA'AM!
YOU GUYS WILL NOW ALL STOP.
I KNOW THAT VOICE ...!
step
CONSIDER YOUR BEHAVIOR, BOYS AND GIRLS...
...THIS IS HARDLY PERMIS-SIBLE.
YOU'RE SAYING THIS TO US?
A WILD VICE PRINCIPAL ANN...!
...APPEARS!
boom!
ka-
YOU ARE NO LONGER WORTHY TO BE CALLED MY STU-DENTS!
FOR THE REST OF THE TERM, YOU ARE... MY SER-VANTS!
thrust!
SHE'S IN CHARGE OF DISCI-PLINE...!
BUT WHY IN LEATHER ...?
ehhhhh?
mm?
tug
HOW SWEET TO BE CALLED THAT!
WHAT ARE WE LEARNING HERE, ANYWAY ...?
HA! HA! HA!
idk.

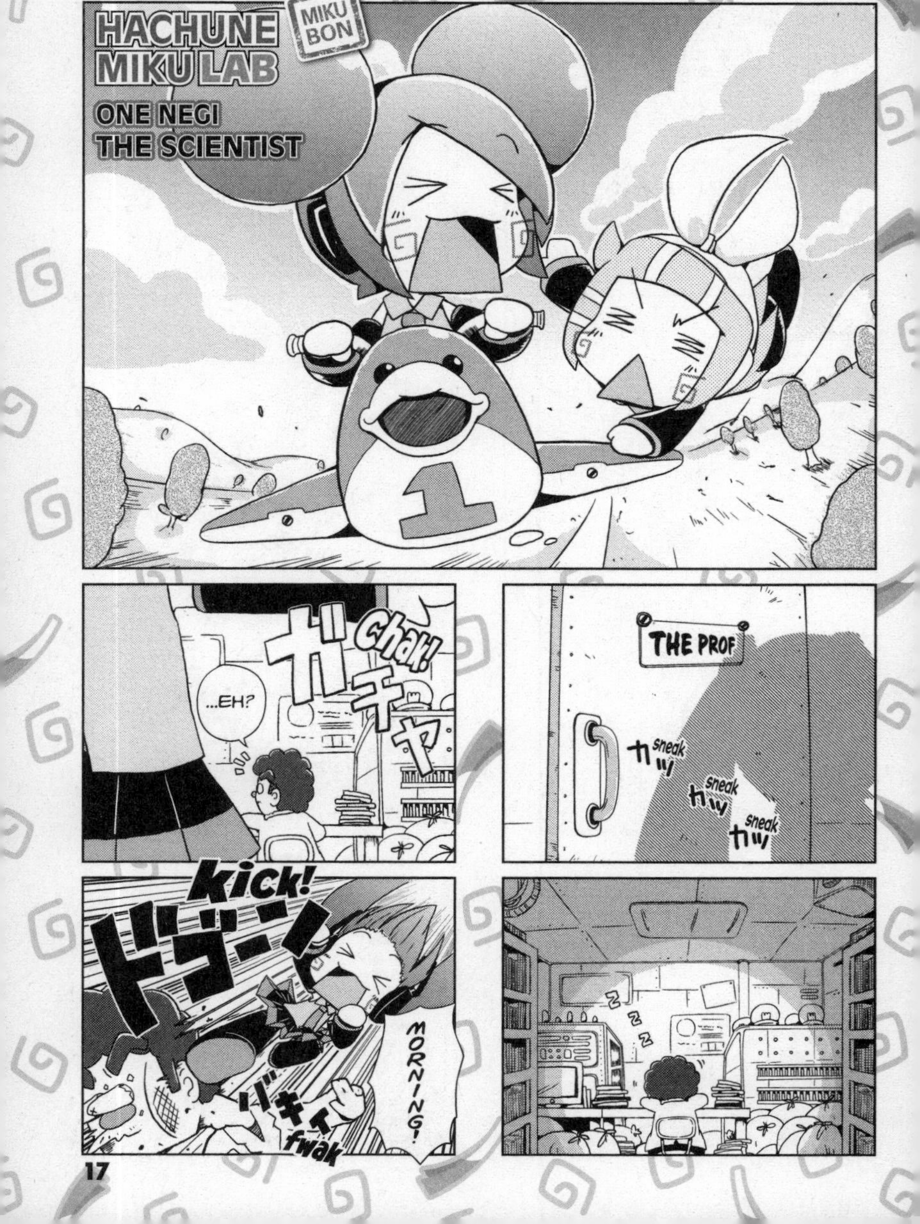
HACHUNE MIKU LAB
MIKU BON
ONE NEGI THE SCIENTIST
THE PROF
カッ sneak
カッ sneak
カッ sneak
ガチャ chak!
...EH?
Z Z Z
ドゴーー! kick!
バキィ fwak
MORNING!

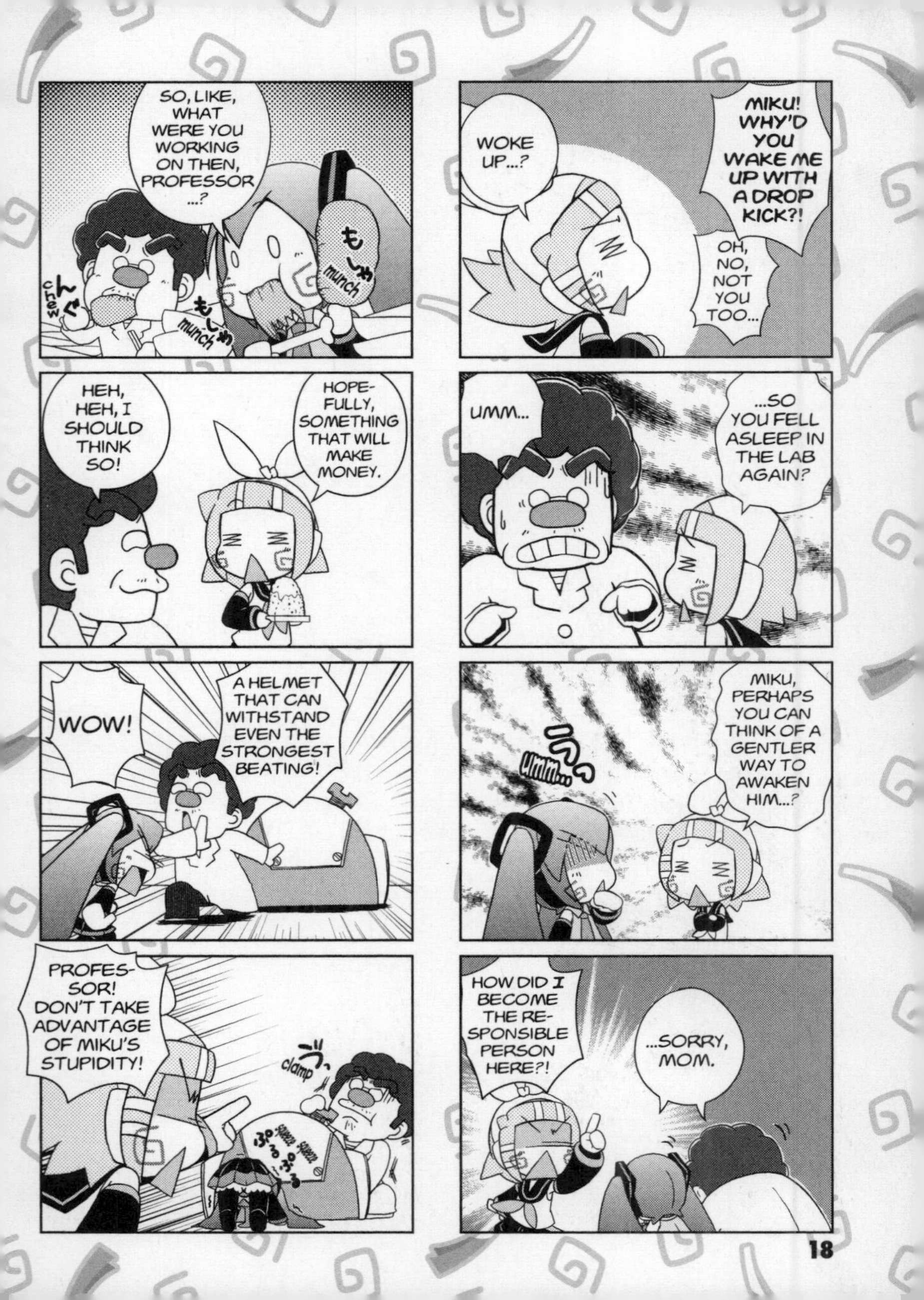
MIKU! WHY'D YOU WAKE ME UP WITH A DROP KICK?!
WOKE UP...?
OH, NO, NOT YOU TOO...
...SO YOU FELL ASLEEP IN THE LAB AGAIN?
UMM...
MIKU, PERHAPS YOU CAN THINK OF A GENTLER WAY TO AWAKEN HIM...?
HOW DID I BECOME THE RE-SPONSIBLE PERSON HERE?!
...SORRY, MOM.
SO, LIKE, WHAT WERE YOU WORKING ON THEN, PROFESSOR ...?
もしゃ munch
んぐ chew
もしゃ munch
HOPE-FULLY, SOMETHING THAT WILL MAKE MONEY.
HEH, HEH, I SHOULD THINK SO!
A HELMET THAT CAN WITHSTAND EVEN THE STRONGEST BEATING!
WOW!
clamp
PROFES-SOR! DON'T TAKE ADVANTAGE OF MIKU'S STUPIDITY!

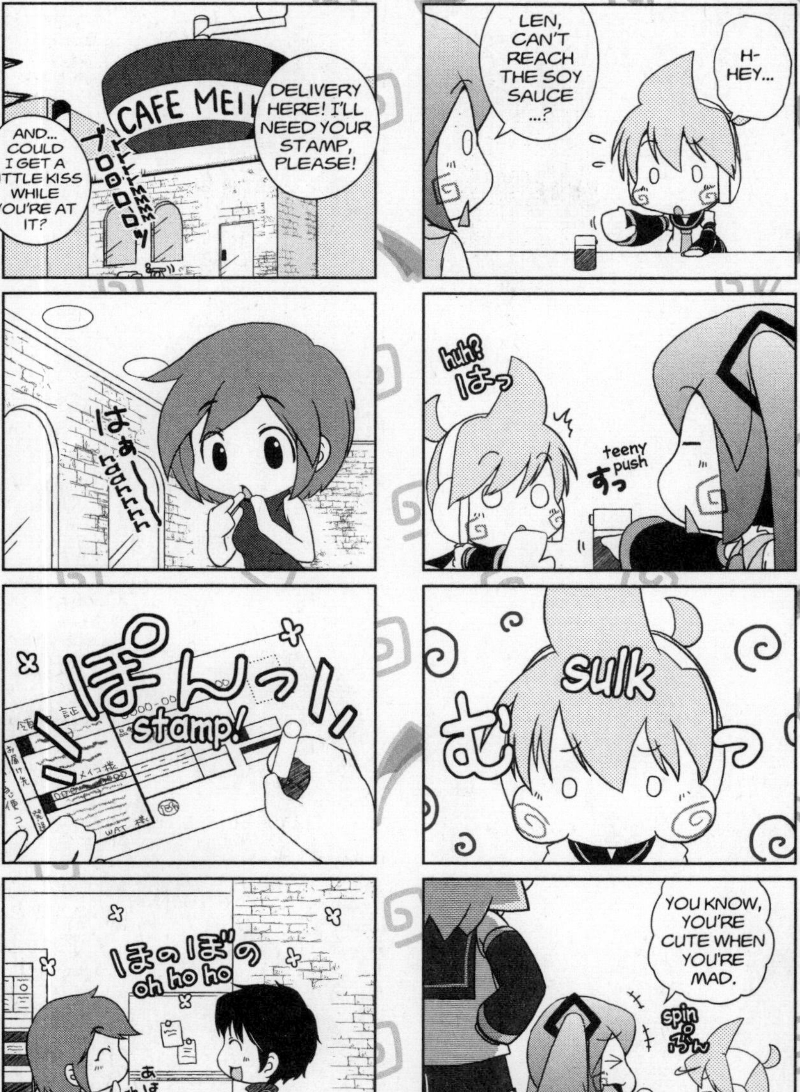
H- HEY...
LEN, CAN'T REACH THE SOY SAUCE ...?
はっ
huh?
すっ
teeny push
むっ
sulk
YOU KNOW, YOU'RE CUTE WHEN YOU'RE MAD.
ぷん
spin
DELIVERY HERE! I'LL NEED YOUR STAMP, PLEASE!
CAFE MEI
ブロロロロッ
rrrrrmmmm
AND... COULD I GET A LITTLE KISS WHILE YOU'RE AT IT?
はぁ~
haaahhhh
ぽんっ
stamp!
ほのぼの
oh ho ho
あはは
ah ha ha

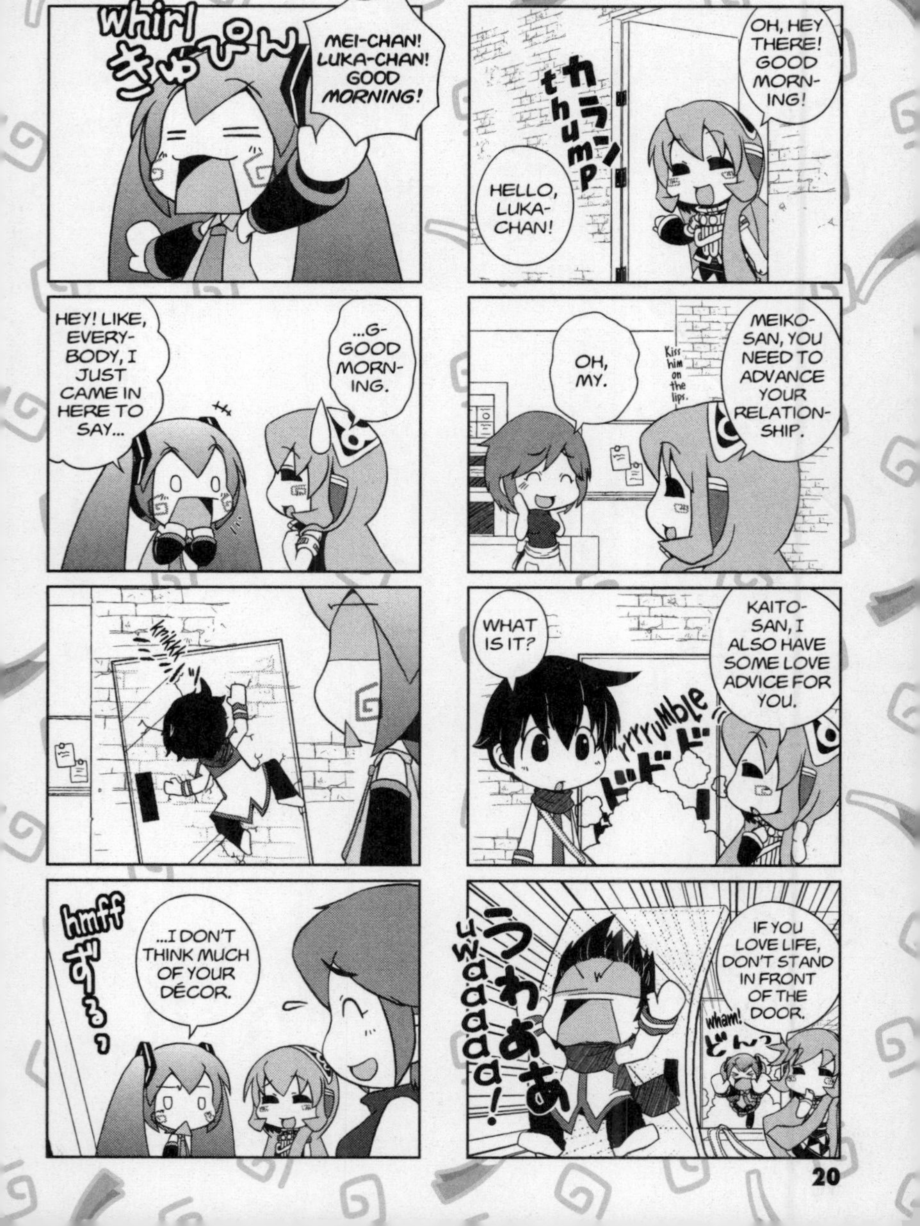
OH, HEY THERE! GOOD MORNING!
thump
カラン
HELLO, LUKA-CHAN!
MEI-CHAN! LUKA-CHAN! GOOD MORNING!
whirl
きゅぴーん
MEIKO-SAN, YOU NEED TO ADVANCE YOUR RELATIONSHIP.
Kiss him on the lips.
OH, MY.
...G-GOOD MORNING.
HEY! LIKE, EVERYBODY, I JUST CAME IN HERE TO SAY...
KAITO-SAN, I ALSO HAVE SOME LOVE ADVICE FOR YOU.
WHAT IS IT?
yrrrumble
ドドド
krikkk
IF YOU LOVE LIFE, DON'T STAND IN FRONT OF THE DOOR.
wham!
どんっ
うわあぁ
uwaaaaaa!
...I DON'T THINK MUCH OF YOUR DÉCOR.
hmff
ずるっ

HATSUNE MIKU MIKUBON

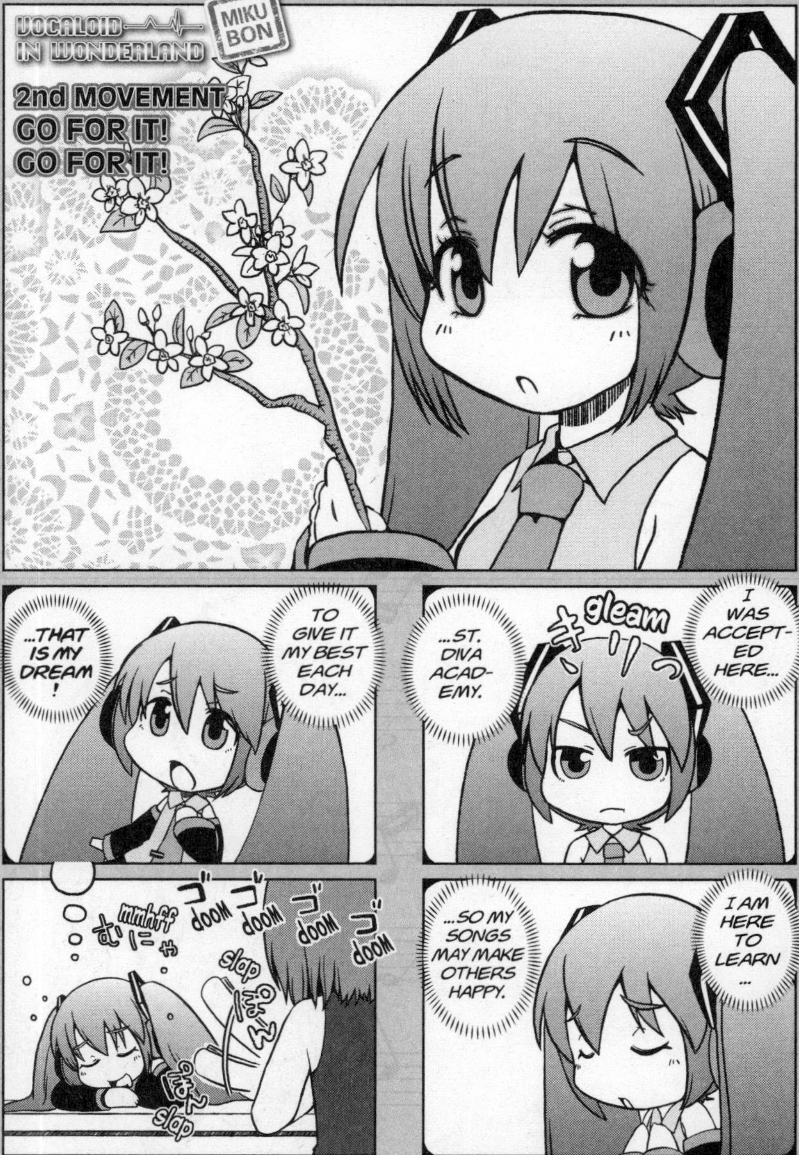
VOCALOID IN WONDERLAND
MIKU BON
2nd MOVEMENT
GO FOR IT! GO FOR IT!
I WAS ACCEPTED HERE...
gleam
...ST. DIVA ACADEMY.
TO GIVE IT MY BEST EACH DAY...
...THAT IS MY DREAM!
I AM HERE TO LEARN...
...SO MY SONGS MAY MAKE OTHERS HAPPY.
doom doom doom doom
mmhff
slap
slap

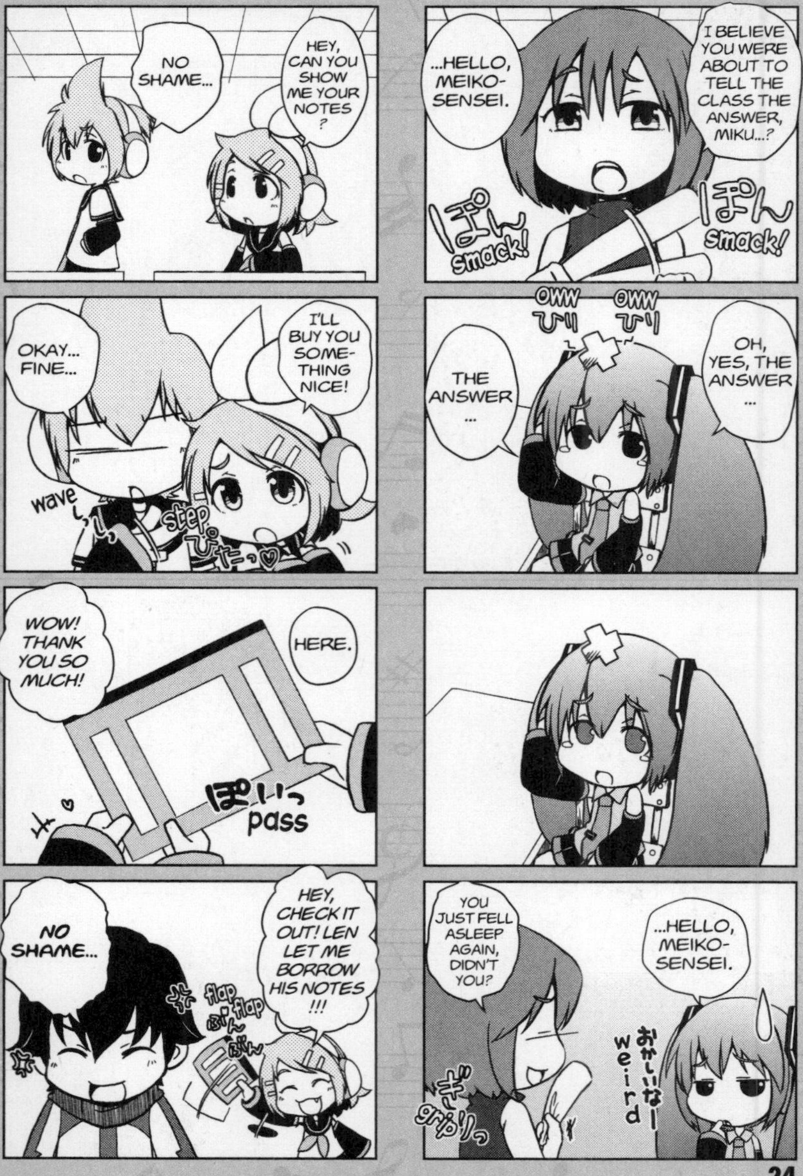
I BELIEVE YOU WERE ABOUT TO TELL THE CLASS THE ANSWER, MIKU...?
...HELLO, MEIKO-SENSEI.
ぽん smack!
ぽん smack!
OWW ひり
OWW ひり
OH, YES, THE ANSWER ...
THE ANSWER ...
...HELLO, MEIKO-SENSEI.
YOU JUST FELL ASLEEP AGAIN, DIDN'T YOU?
おかしいなー weird
ぎゅりっ grip
HEY, CAN YOU SHOW ME YOUR NOTES ?
NO SHAME...
I'LL BUY YOU SOME-THING NICE!
OKAY... FINE...
step ぴたっ
wave
HERE.
WOW! THANK YOU SO MUCH!
ぽいっ pass
HEY, CHECK IT OUT! LEN LET ME BORROW HIS NOTES !!!
NO SHAME...
flap flap ぶんぶん

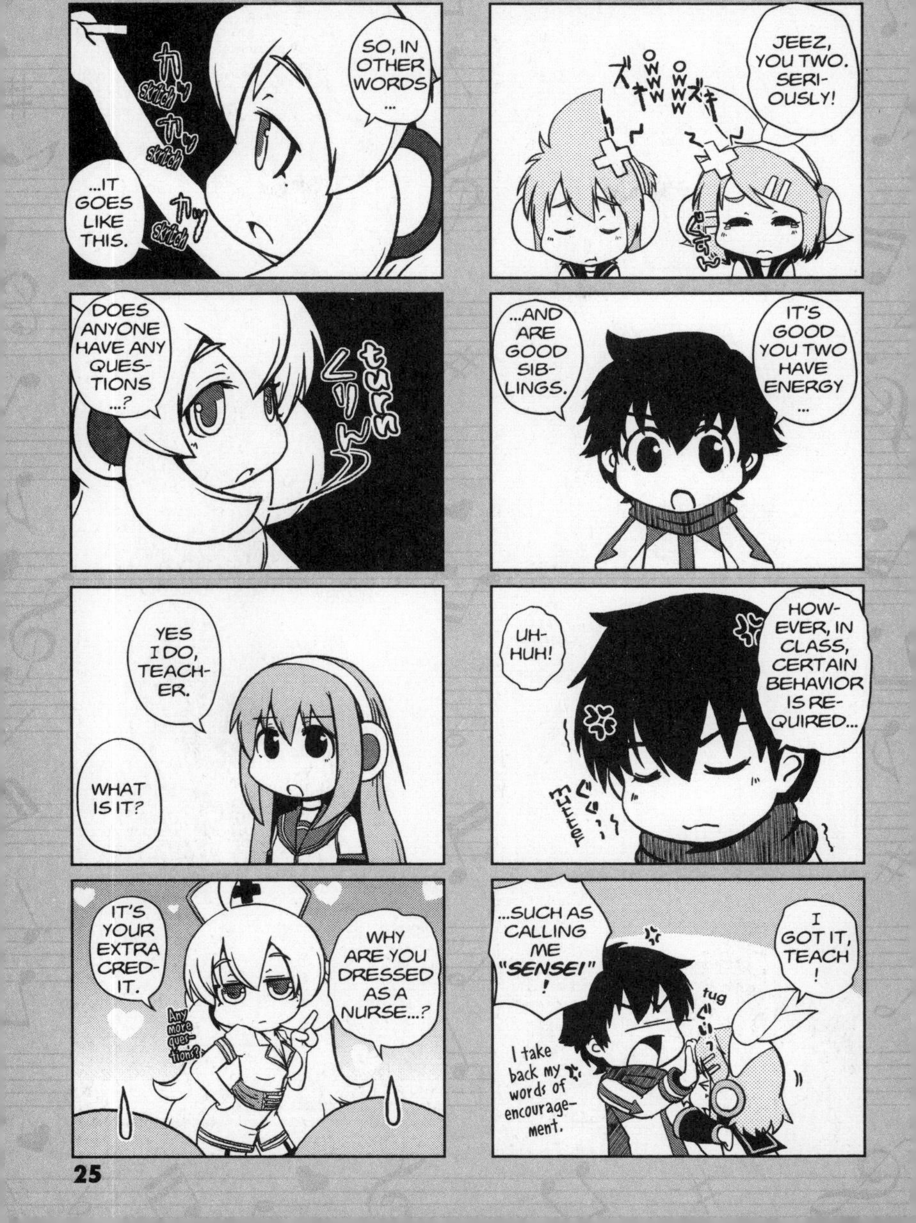
JEEZ, YOU TWO. SERIOUSLY!
OWWW
OWWWW
IT'S GOOD YOU TWO HAVE ENERGY ...
...AND ARE GOOD SIBLINGS.
HOWEVER, IN CLASS, CERTAIN BEHAVIOR IS REQUIRED...
UH-HUH!
mutter
I GOT IT, TEACH!
tug
...SUCH AS CALLING ME "SENSEI"!
I take back my words of encouragement.
SO, IN OTHER WORDS ...
skritch
skritch
skritch
...IT GOES LIKE THIS.
turn
DOES ANYONE HAVE ANY QUESTIONS ...?
YES I DO, TEACHER.
WHAT IS IT?
WHY ARE YOU DRESSED AS A NURSE...?
IT'S YOUR EXTRA CREDIT.
Any more questions?

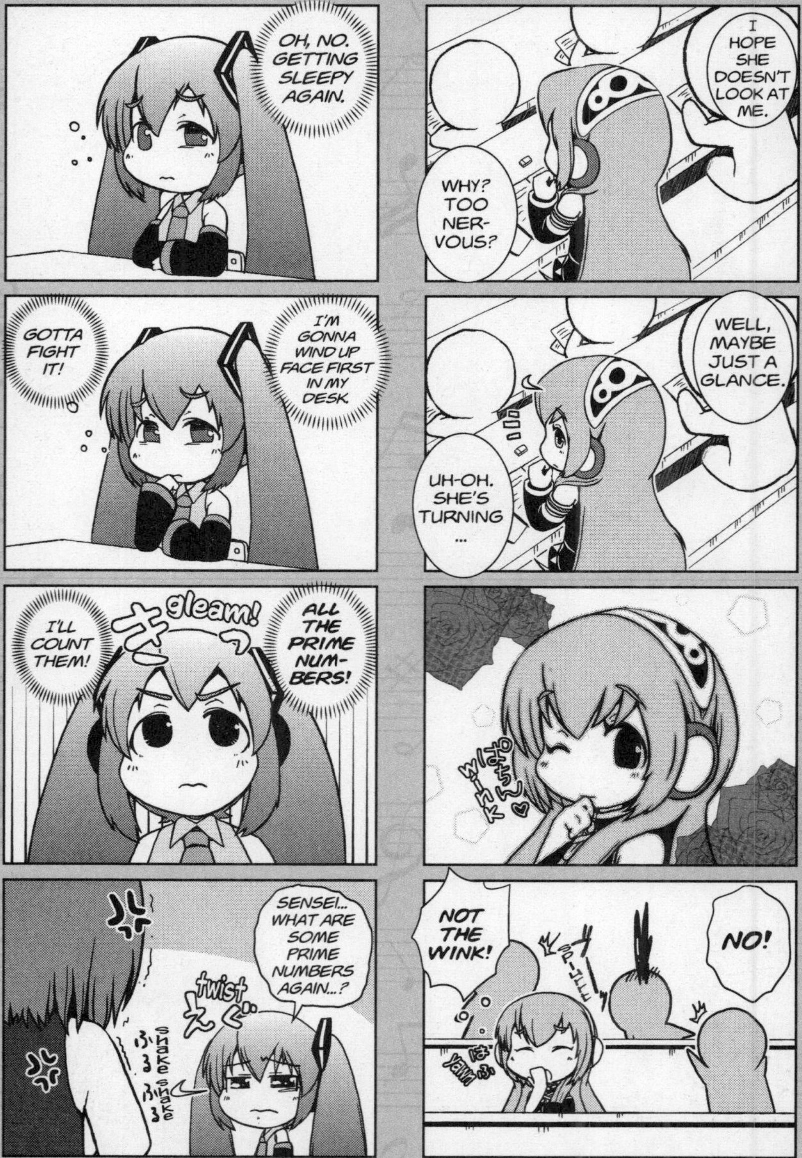
I HOPE SHE DOESN'T LOOK AT ME.
WHY? TOO NERVOUS?
WELL, MAYBE JUST A GLANCE.
UH-OH. SHE'S TURNING ...
ぱちん wink
NO!
NOT THE WINK!
はふ yawn
OH, NO. GETTING SLEEPY AGAIN.
I'M GONNA WIND UP FACE FIRST IN MY DESK.
GOTTA FIGHT IT!
ALL THE PRIME NUMBERS!
きっ gleam!
I'LL COUNT THEM!
SENSEI... WHAT ARE SOME PRIME NUMBERS AGAIN...?
えぐ twist
ふるふる shake shake

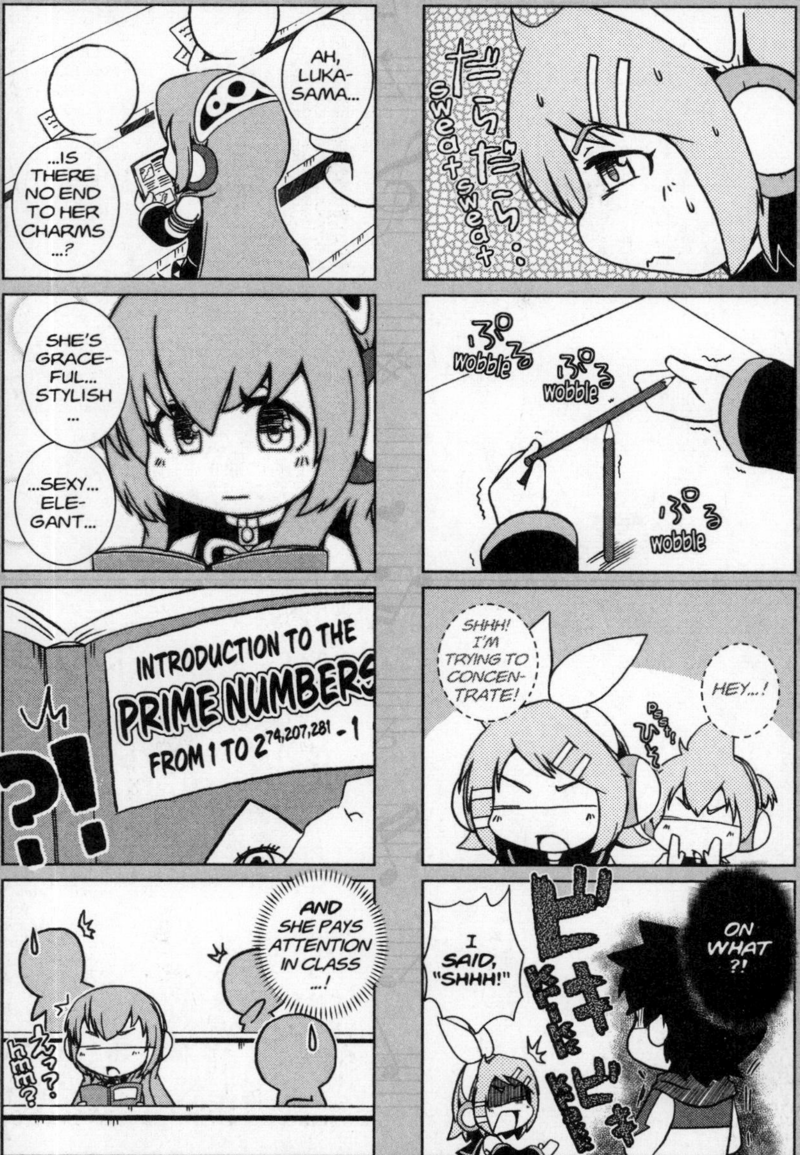

だらだら
sweat sweat
ぷる
wobble
ぷる
wobble
ぷる
wobble
HEY...!
psst
SHHH! I'M TRYING TO CONCENTRATE!
ON WHAT?!
ビキビキ
I SAID, "SHHH!"
AH, LUKA-SAMA...
...IS THERE NO END TO HER CHARMS...?
SHE'S GRACEFUL... STYLISH...
...SEXY... ELEGANT...
INTRODUCTION TO THE PRIME NUMBERS FROM 1 TO 2^74,207,281 - 1
?!
AND SHE PAYS ATTENTION IN CLASS...!
HMM?

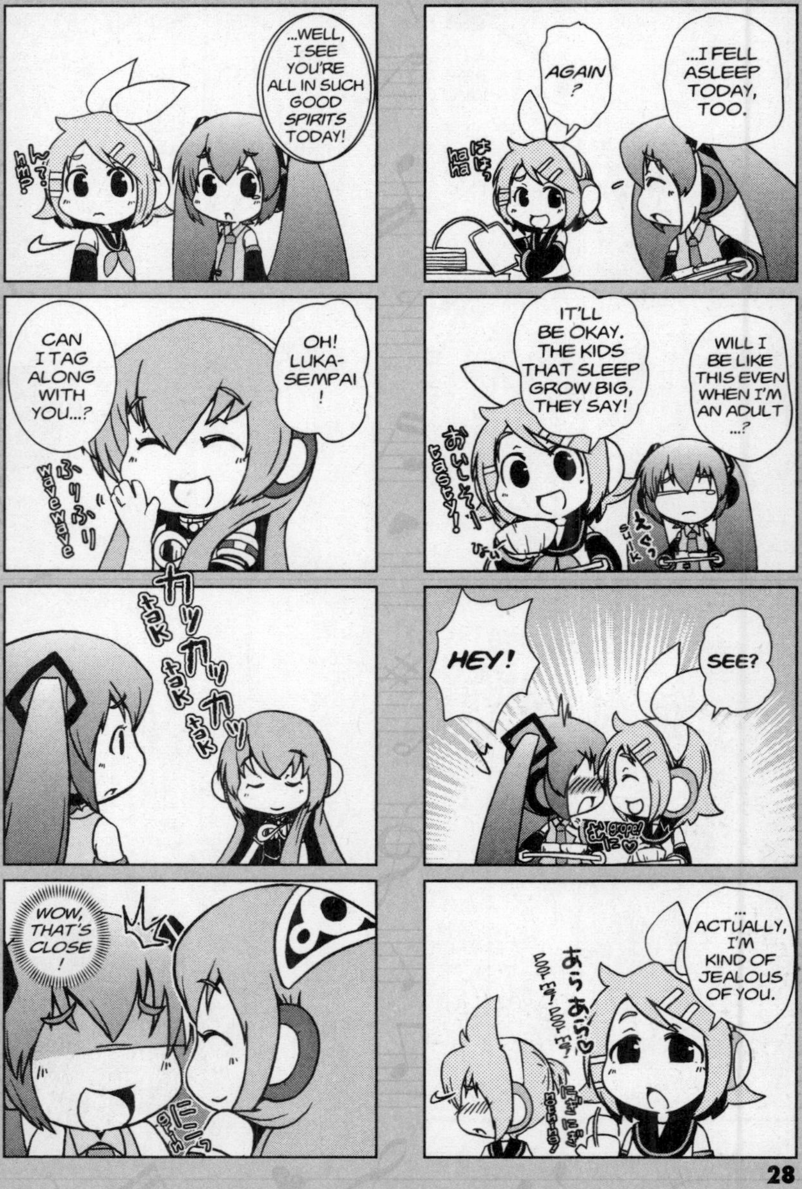

...I FELL ASLEEP TODAY, TOO.
AGAIN?
はは haha
WILL I BE LIKE THIS EVEN WHEN I'M AN ADULT...?
IT'LL BE OKAY. THE KIDS THAT SLEEP GROW BIG, THEY SAY!
SEE?
HEY!
grope!
...ACTUALLY, I'M KIND OF JEALOUS OF YOU.
あらあら♡
...WELL, I SEE YOU'RE ALL IN SUCH GOOD SPIRITS TODAY!
ん? hm?
OH! LUKA-SEMPAI!
CAN I TAG ALONG WITH YOU...?
ふりふり wave wave
カッカッカッ tak tak tak tak
WOW, THAT'S CLOSE!

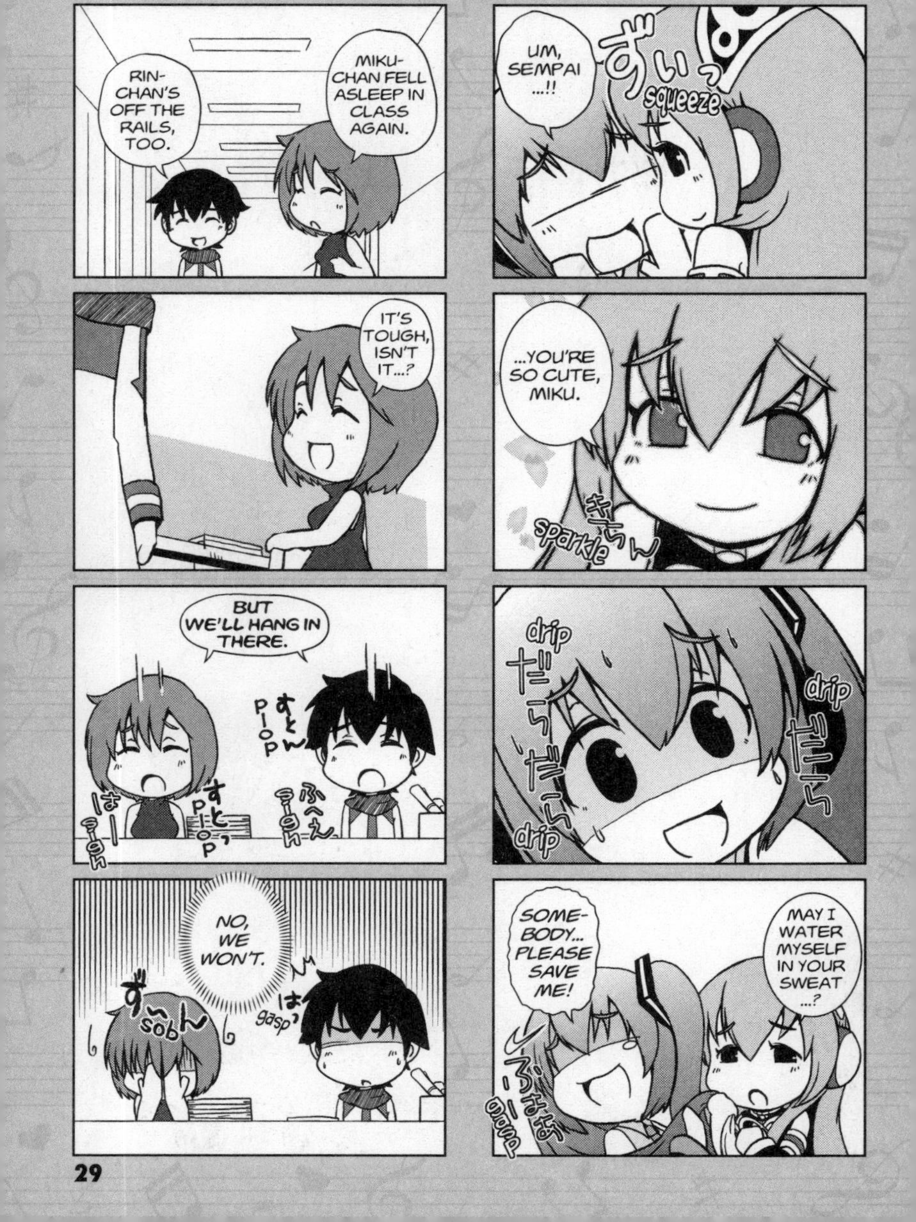
UM, SEMPAI ...!!
ずいっ
squeeze
...YOU'RE SO CUTE, MIKU.
きらん
sparkle
drip
だら
drip
だら
だら
drip
MAY I WATER MYSELF IN YOUR SWEAT ...?
SOME-BODY... PLEASE SAVE ME!
MIKU-CHAN FELL ASLEEP IN CLASS AGAIN.
RIN-CHAN'S OFF THE RAILS, TOO.
IT'S TOUGH, ISN'T IT...?
BUT WE'LL HANG IN THERE.
すとん
plop
すとっ
plop
NO, WE WON'T.
はっ
gasp
ず〜ん
sob

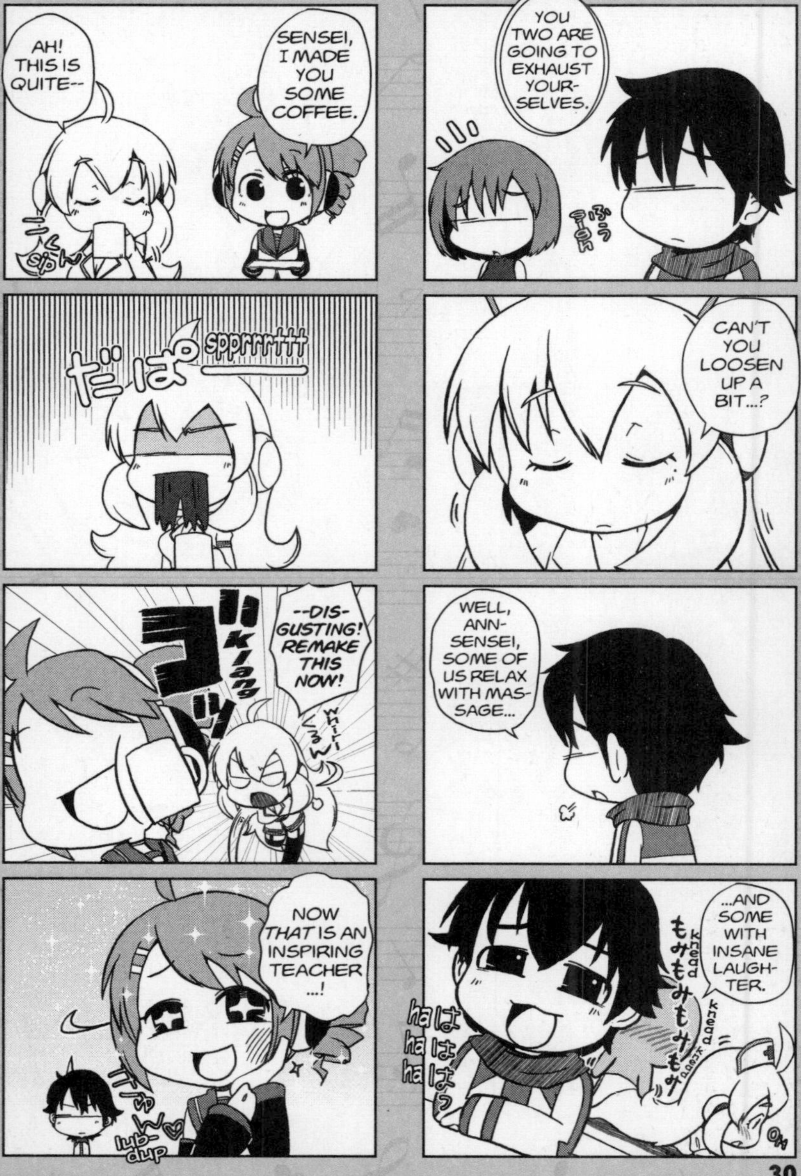
YOU TWO ARE GOING TO EXHAUST YOUR-SELVES.
CAN'T YOU LOOSEN UP A BIT...?
WELL, ANN-SENSEI, SOME OF US RELAX WITH MAS-SAGE...
...AND SOME WITH INSANE LAUGH-TER.
もみもみ knead
もみもみ knead
はははっ ha ha ha
Oh
SENSEI, I MADE YOU SOME COFFEE.
AH! THIS IS QUITE--
sip
だぱーー spprrrttt
--DIS-GUSTING! REMAKE THIS NOW!
klang
whirl
NOW THAT IS AN INSPIRING TEACHER ...!
lub-dup

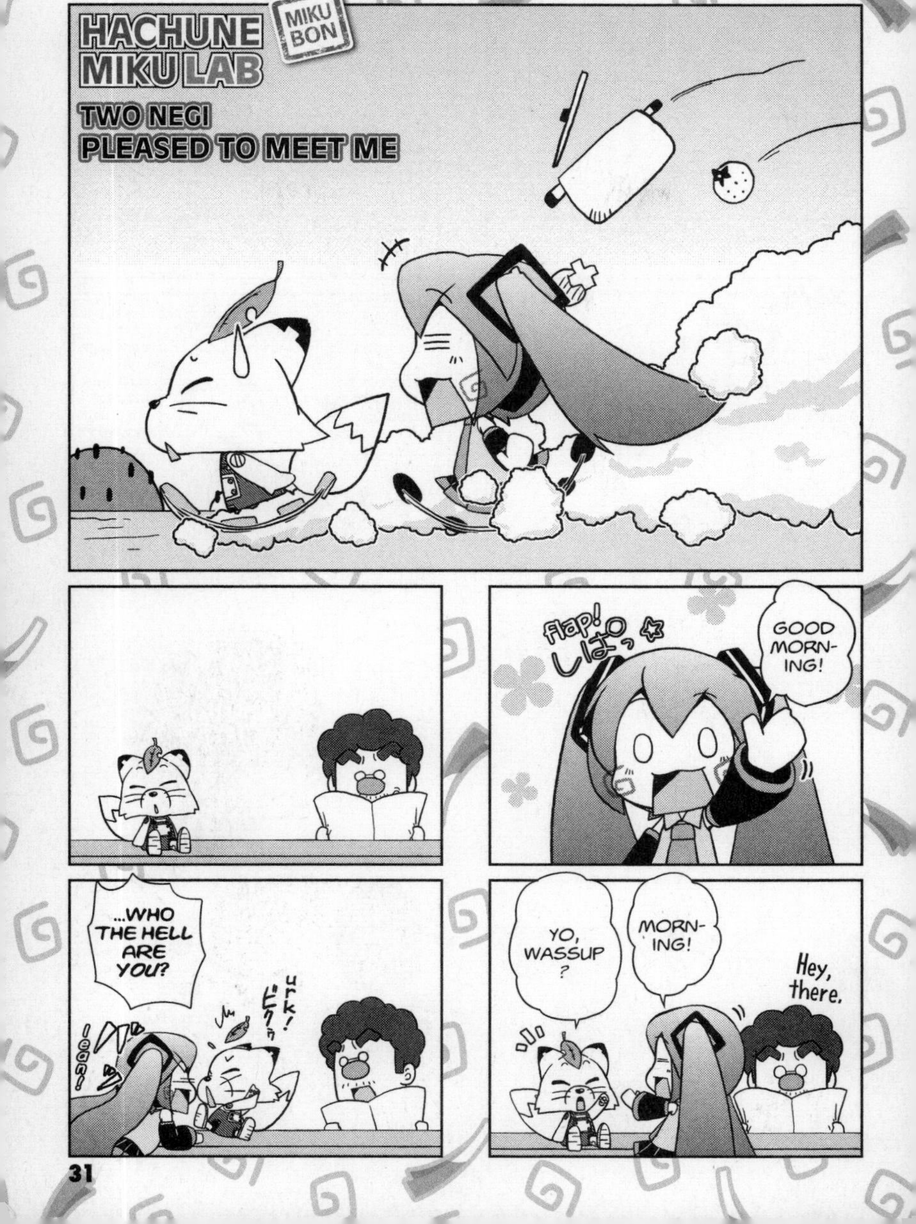
HACHUNE MIKU LAB
MIKU BON
TWO NEGI
PLEASED TO MEET ME
Flap! しぱっ
GOOD MORN-ING!
MORN-ING!
YO, WASSUP?
Hey, there.
...WHO THE HELL ARE YOU?
urk! ビクッ
lean!

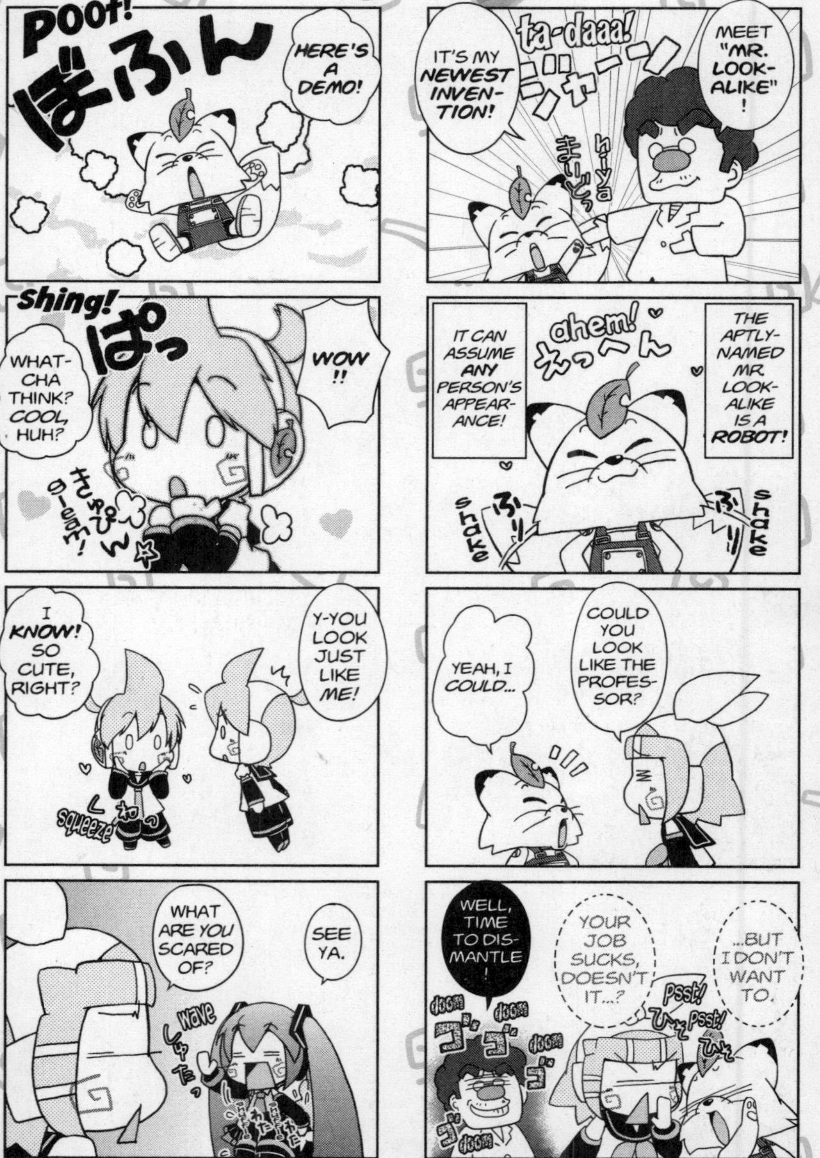
MEET "MR. LOOK-ALIKE" !
ta-daaa!
ジャーン
IT'S MY NEWEST INVENTION!
ya-ya
まいどっ
THE APTLY-NAMED MR. LOOK-ALIKE IS A ROBOT!
ahem!
えっへん
IT CAN ASSUME ANY PERSON'S APPEARANCE!
shake
ぷり
shake
ぷり
COULD YOU LOOK LIKE THE PROFESSOR?
YEAH, I COULD...
YOUR JOB SUCKS, DOESN'T IT...?
...BUT I DON'T WANT TO.
WELL, TIME TO DISMANTLE!
psst!
ひそ
psst!
ひそ
doom
ゴ
doom
ゴ
doom
ゴ
doom
ゴ
doom
HERE'S A DEMO!
POOF!
ぼふん
WOW !!
Shing!
ぱっ
WHAT-CHA THINK? COOL, HUH?
gleam!
きゅぴん
Y-YOU LOOK JUST LIKE ME!
I KNOW! SO CUTE, RIGHT?
squeeze
ぎゅっ
SEE YA.
WHAT ARE YOU SCARED OF?
wave
しゅたっ
わた
わた

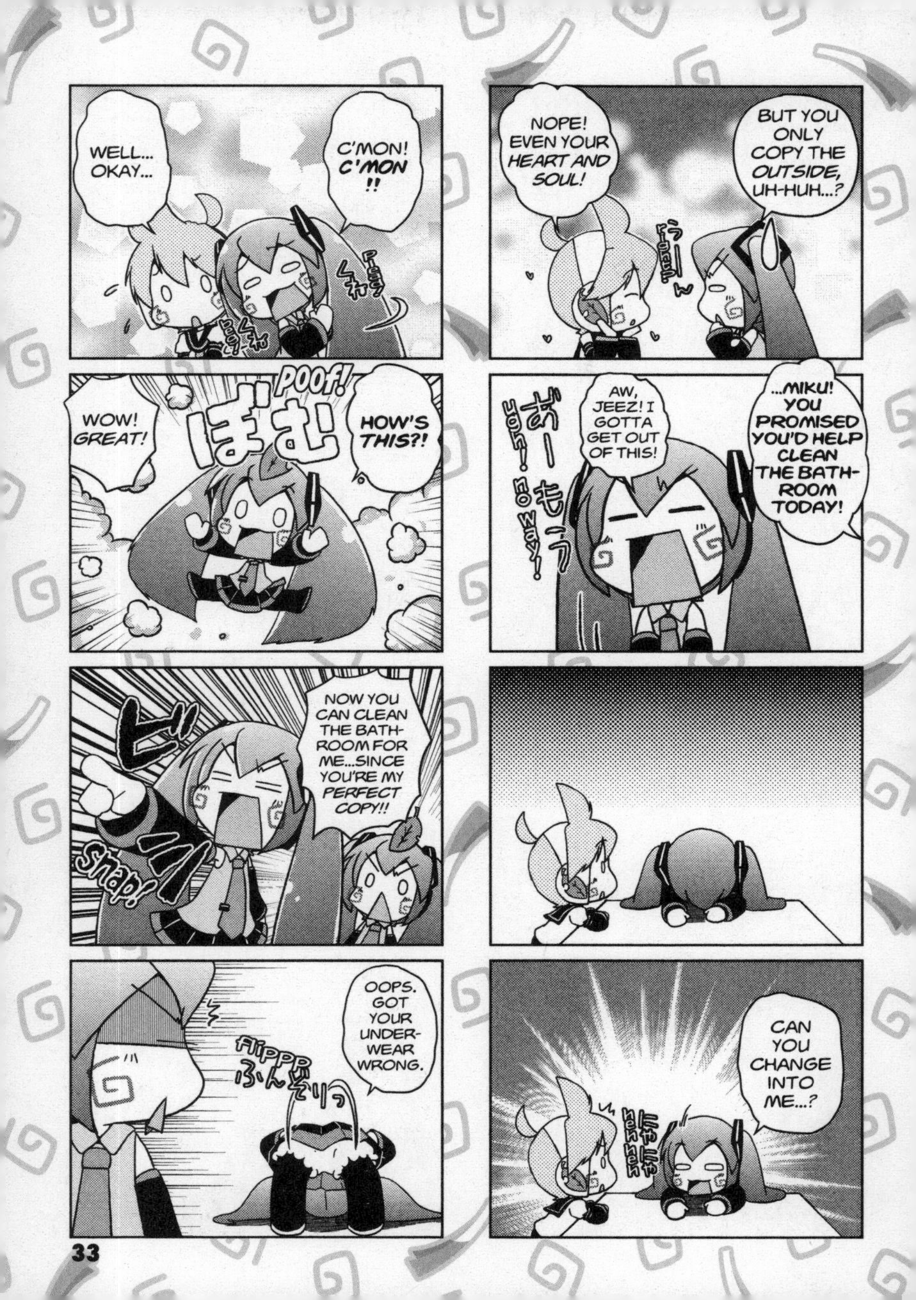
BUT YOU ONLY COPY THE OUTSIDE, UH-HUH...?
NOPE! EVEN YOUR HEART AND SOUL!
...MIKU! YOU PROMISED YOU'D HELP CLEAN THE BATH-ROOM TODAY!
AW, JEEZ! I GOTTA GET OUT OF THIS!
あーもーう
ugh! no way!
CAN YOU CHANGE INTO ME...?
にゃにゃ
heh heh
C'MON! C'MON!!
WELL... OKAY...
HOW'S THIS?!
POOF!
ぼむ
WOW! GREAT!
NOW YOU CAN CLEAN THE BATH-ROOM FOR ME...SINCE YOU'RE MY PERFECT COPY!!
snap!
OOPS. GOT YOUR UNDER-WEAR WRONG.
flippp
ふんぞりっ

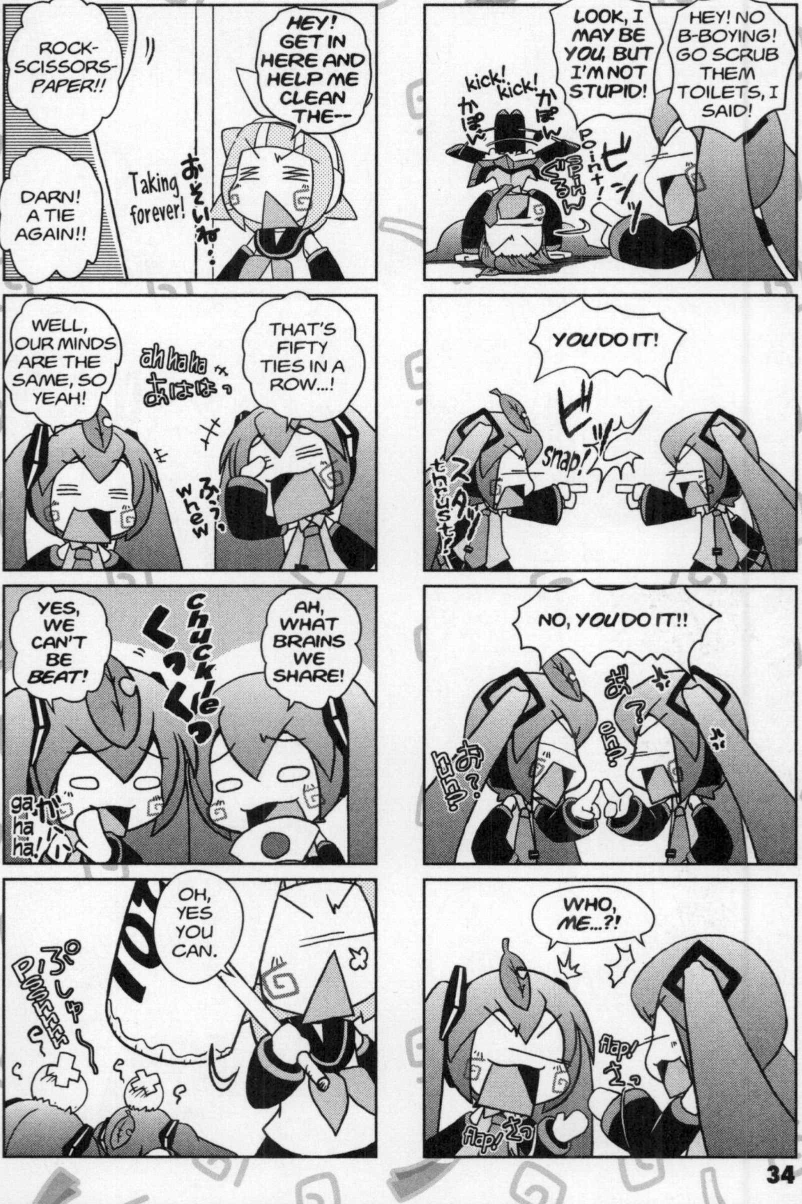
HEY! NO B-BOYING! GO SCRUB THEM TOILETS, I SAID!
LOOK, I MAY BE YOU, BUT I'M NOT STUPID!
kick! kick!
かぽん かぽん
point! ビッ
spin ぐるるん
YOU DO IT!
snap! ビッ
thrust! スタッ
NO, YOU DO IT!!
おっ? eh?
おっ? eh?
WHO, ME...?!
flap! さっ
flap! さっ
HEY! GET IN HERE AND HELP ME CLEAN THE--
ROCK-SCISSORS-PAPER!!
DARN! A TIE AGAIN!!
Taking forever! おそいね…
THAT'S FIFTY TIES IN A ROW...!
WELL, OUR MINDS ARE THE SAME, SO YEAH!
ah ha ha あははっ
whew ふぅ
AH, WHAT BRAINS WE SHARE!
YES, WE CAN'T BE BEAT!
chuckle くっくっ
ga ha ha! がはは
OH, YES YOU CAN.
P'shhhh ぷしゅ～

HATSUNE MIKU

MIKUBON

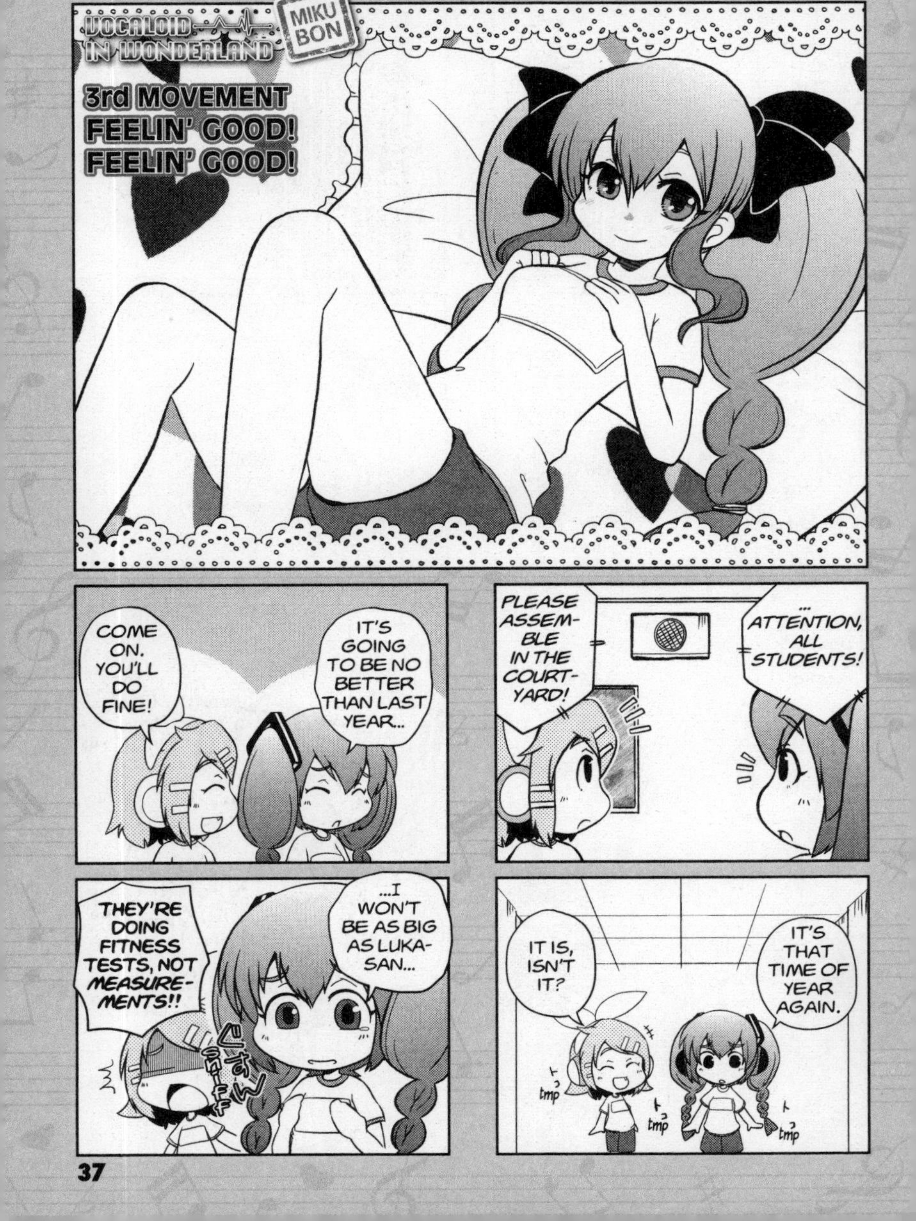
VOCALOID IN WONDERLAND
MIKU BON
3rd MOVEMENT
FEELIN' GOOD! FEELIN' GOOD!
...ATTENTION, ALL STUDENTS!
PLEASE ASSEMBLE IN THE COURTYARD!
IT'S GOING TO BE NO BETTER THAN LAST YEAR...
COME ON. YOU'LL DO FINE!
IT'S THAT TIME OF YEAR AGAIN.
IT IS, ISN'T IT?
tmp
tmp
tmp
...I WON'T BE AS BIG AS LUKA-SAN...
THEY'RE DOING FITNESS TESTS, NOT *MEASUREMENTS*!!

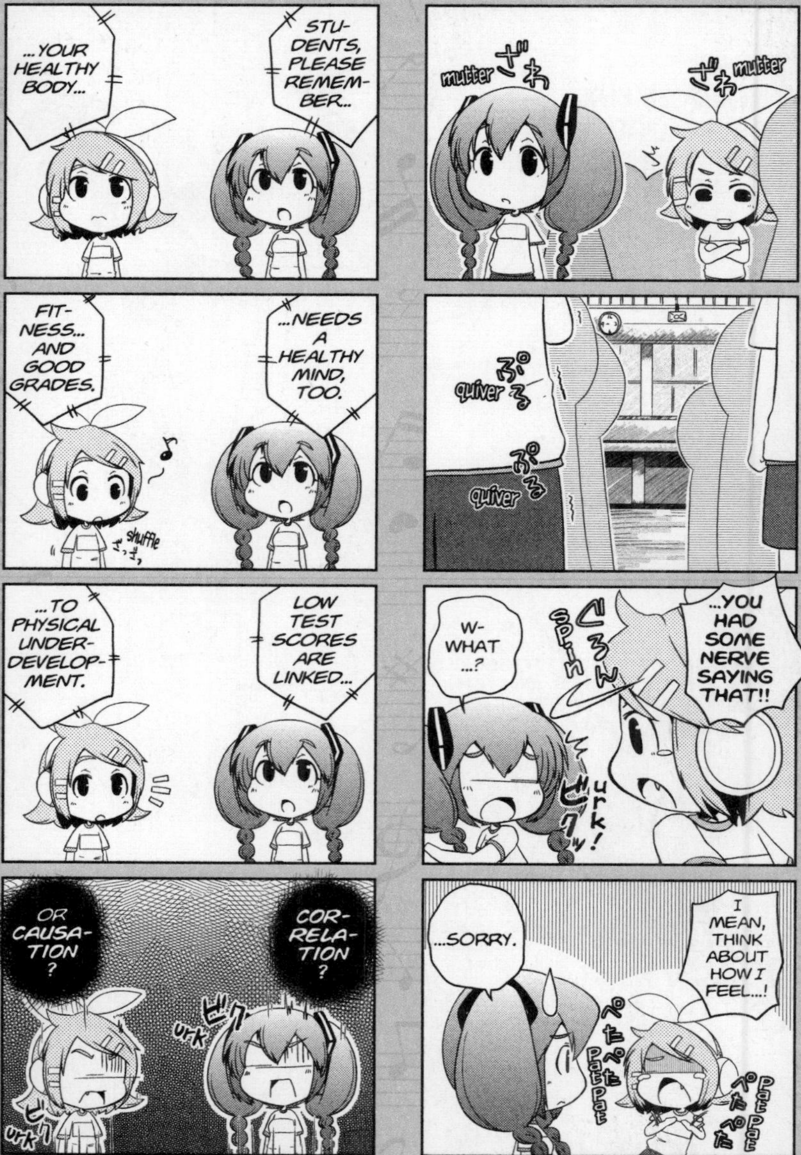
ざわ mutter
mutter ざわ
ぷる quiver
ぷる quiver
...YOU HAD SOME NERVE SAYING THAT!!
ぐるん spin
W-WHAT ...?
ビクッ urk!
I MEAN, THINK ABOUT HOW I FEEL...!
ぺたぺた patpat
ぺたぺた patpat
...SORRY.
STU-DENTS, PLEASE REMEM-BER...
...YOUR HEALTHY BODY...
...NEEDS A HEALTHY MIND, TOO.
FIT-NESS... AND GOOD GRADES.
shuffle
LOW TEST SCORES ARE LINKED...
...TO PHYSICAL UNDER-DEVELOP-MENT.
COR-RELA-TION ?
OR CAUSA-TION ?
ビク urk
ビクッ urk

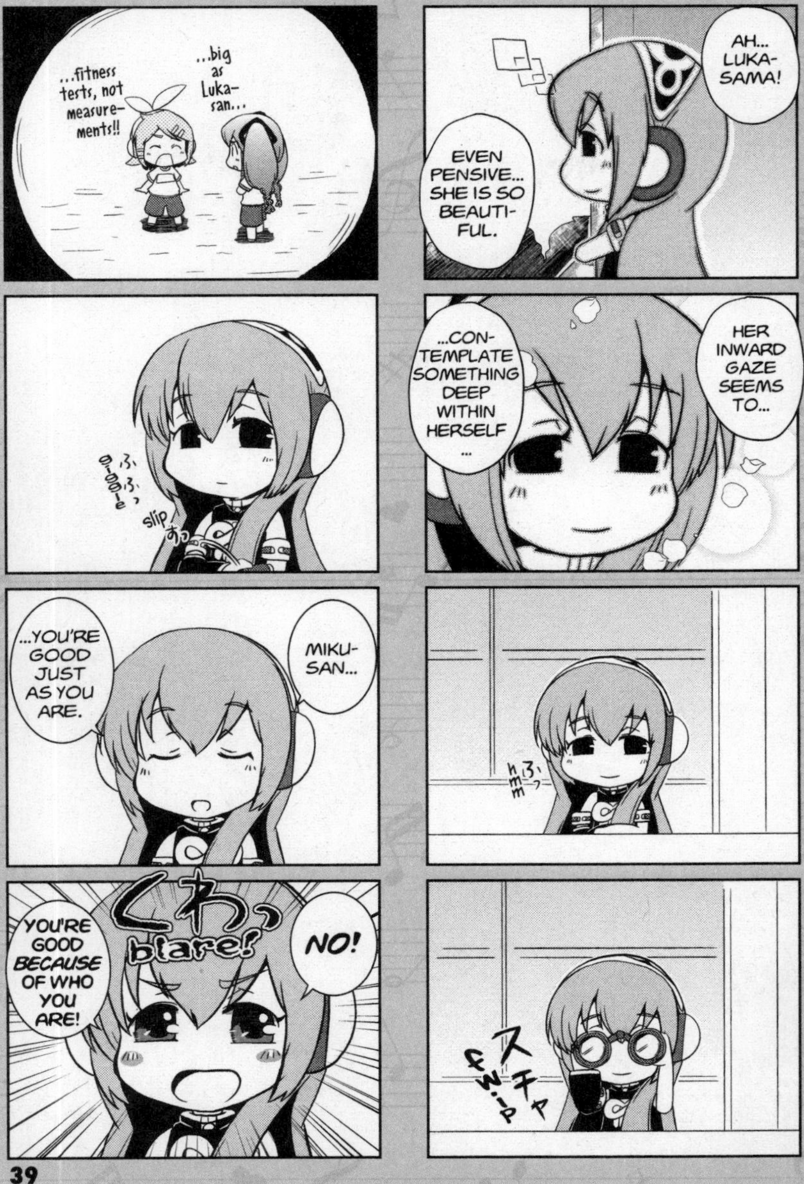
AH... LUKA-SAMA!
EVEN PENSIVE... SHE IS SO BEAUTIFUL.
...big as Luka-san...
...fitness tests, not measurements!!
HER INWARD GAZE SEEMS TO...
...CONTEMPLATE SOMETHING DEEP WITHIN HERSELF...
ふふっ
giggle
すっ
slip
ふ〜っ
hmm
MIKU-SAN...
...YOU'RE GOOD JUST AS YOU ARE.
スチャ
fwip
NO!
くわっ
blare!
YOU'RE GOOD *BECAUSE* OF WHO YOU ARE!

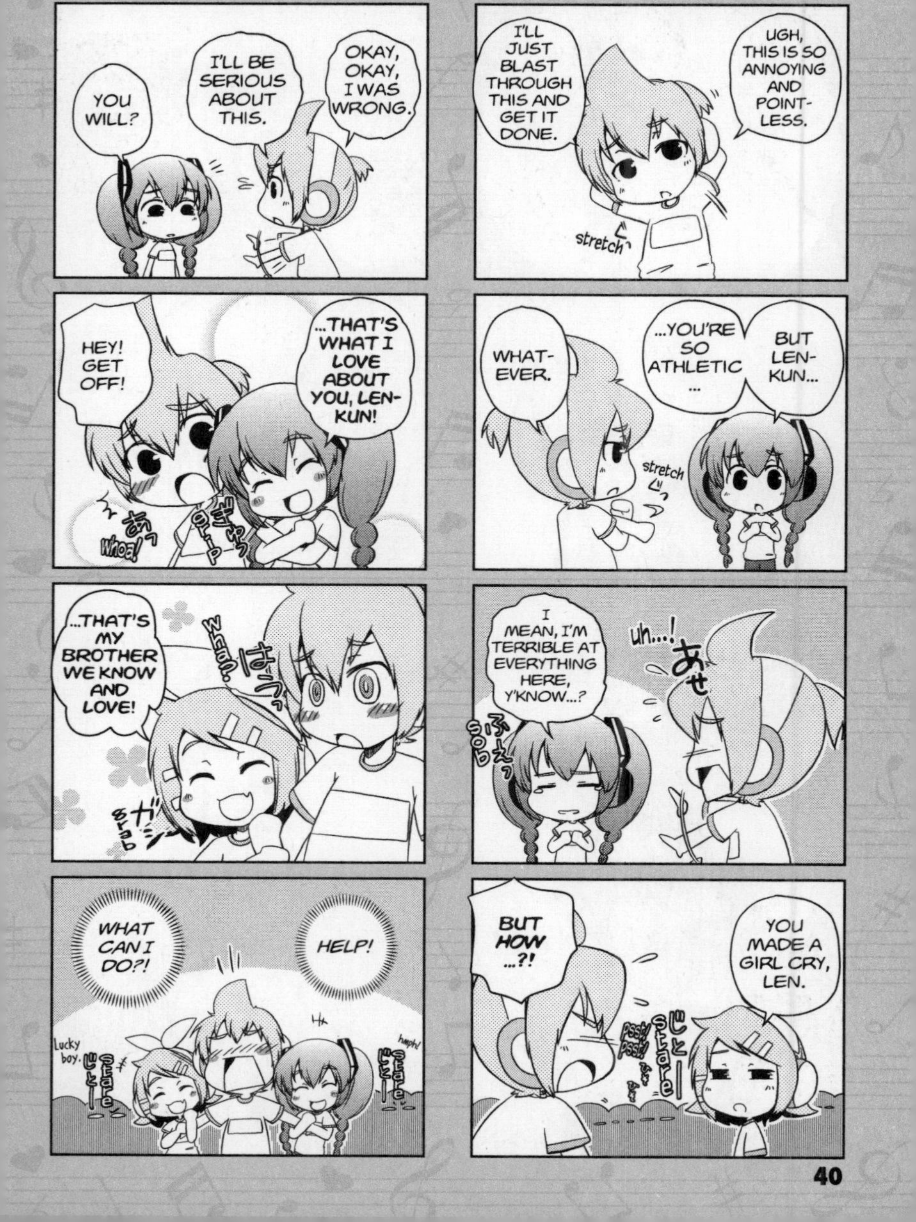

UGH, THIS IS SO ANNOYING AND POINT-LESS.
I'LL JUST BLAST THROUGH THIS AND GET IT DONE.
stretch
BUT LEN-KUN...
...YOU'RE SO ATHLETIC ...
stretch
WHAT-EVER.
uh...!
あせ
I MEAN, I'M TERRIBLE AT EVERYTHING HERE, Y'KNOW...?
ふぇっ
YOU MADE A GIRL CRY, LEN.
じとー
stare
BUT HOW ...?!
OKAY, OKAY, I WAS WRONG.
I'LL BE SERIOUS ABOUT THIS.
YOU WILL?
...THAT'S WHAT I LOVE ABOUT YOU, LEN-KUN!
HEY! GET OFF!
あっ
Whoa!
はっ
what?!
...THAT'S MY BROTHER WE KNOW AND LOVE!
grab
HELP!
WHAT CAN I DO?!
humph!
stare
じとー
stare
じとー
Lucky boy.

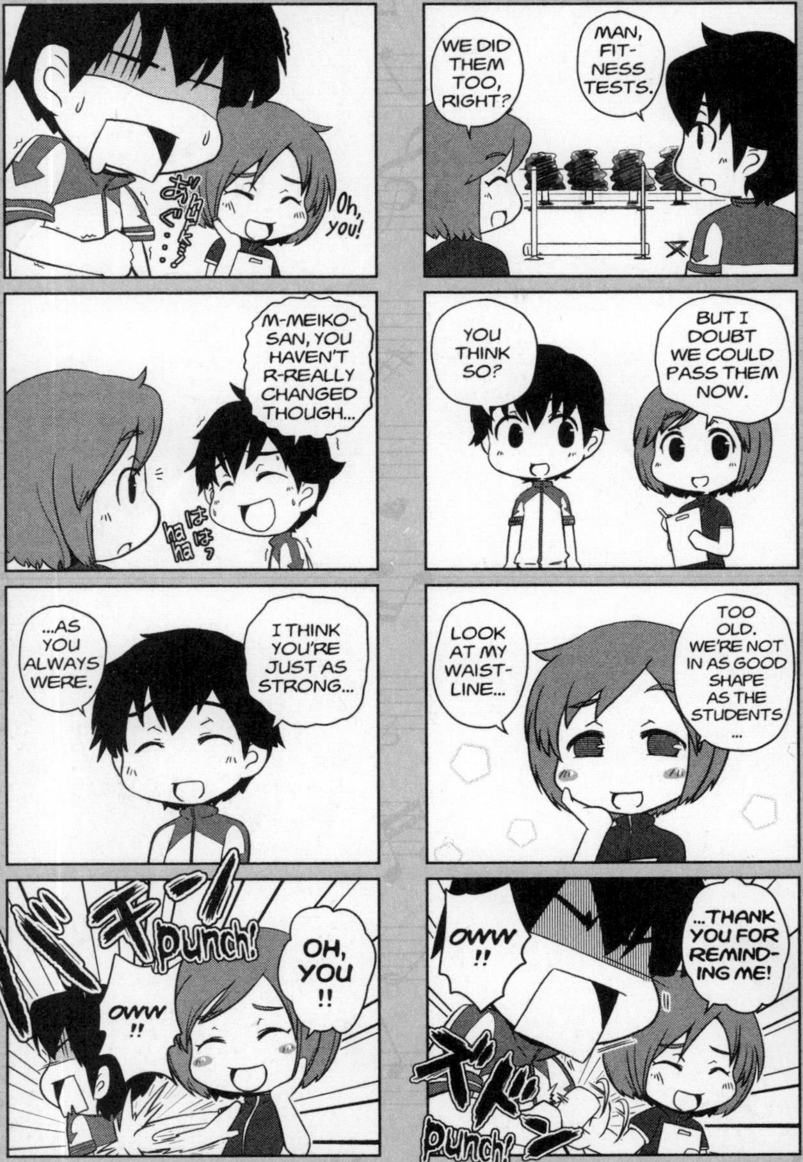
MAN, FIT-NESS TESTS.
WE DID THEM TOO, RIGHT?
Oh, you!
BUT I DOUBT WE COULD PASS THEM NOW.
YOU THINK SO?
M-MEIKO-SAN, YOU HAVEN'T R-REALLY CHANGED THOUGH...
ははっ
haha
TOO OLD. WE'RE NOT IN AS GOOD SHAPE AS THE STUDENTS ...
LOOK AT MY WAIST-LINE...
I THINK YOU'RE JUST AS STRONG...
...AS YOU ALWAYS WERE.
...THANK YOU FOR REMIND-ING ME!
OWW !!
punch!
punch!
OH, YOU !!
OWW !!

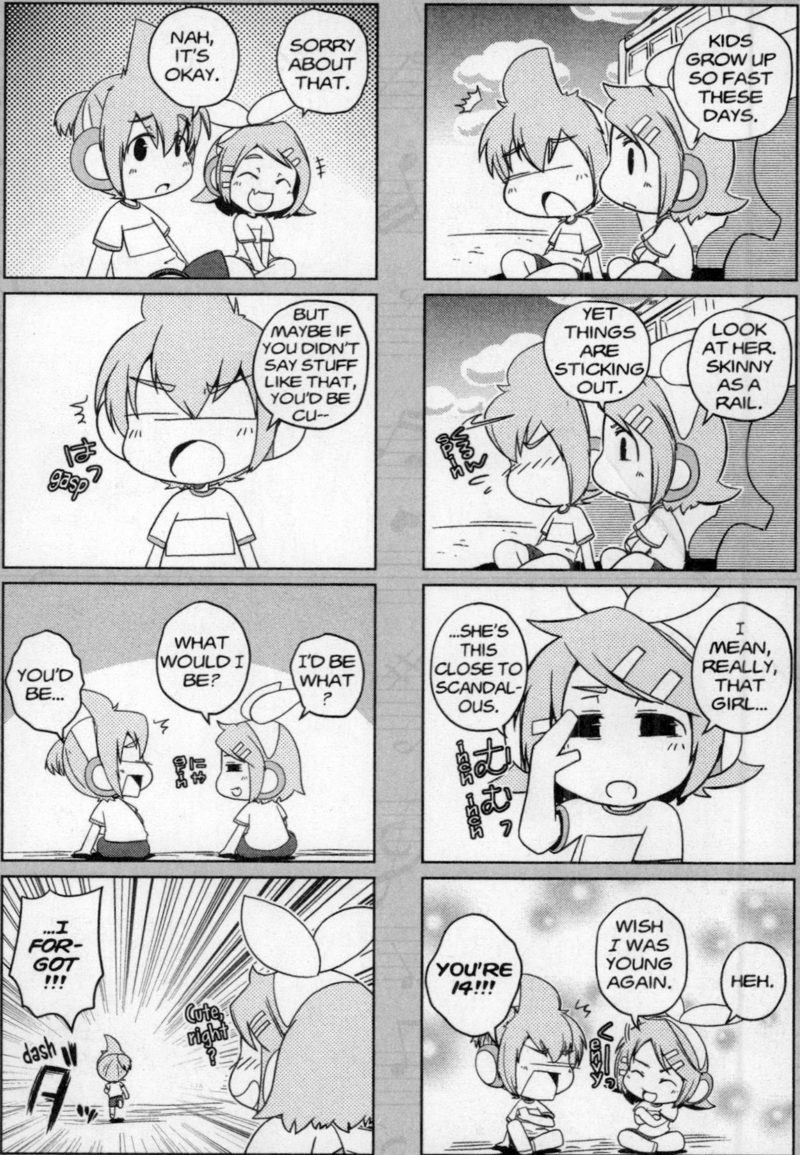
KIDS GROW UP SO FAST THESE DAYS.
LOOK AT HER. SKINNY AS A RAIL.
YET THINGS ARE STICKING OUT.
spin
I MEAN, REALLY, THAT GIRL...
...SHE'S THIS CLOSE TO SCANDAL-OUS.
むむっ
inch inch
HEH.
WISH I WAS YOUNG AGAIN.
envy
YOU'RE 14!!!
SORRY ABOUT THAT.
NAH, IT'S OKAY.
BUT MAYBE IF YOU DIDN'T SAY STUFF LIKE THAT, YOU'D BE CU--
はっ
gasp
I'D BE WHAT?
WHAT WOULD I BE?
にや
grin
YOU'D BE...
Cute, right?
...I FOR-GOT!!!
dash

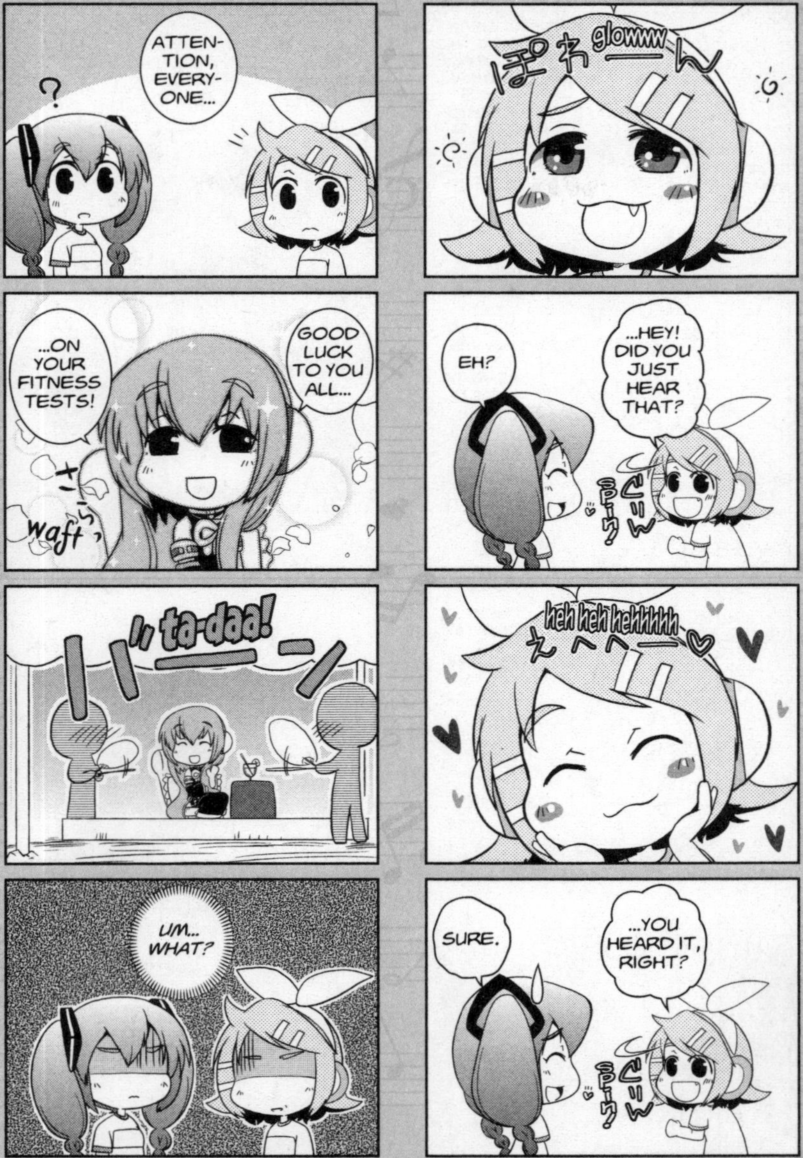
ぽわーーん
glowww
...HEY! DID YOU JUST HEAR THAT?
EH?
ぐりん
spin
えへへーー♡
heh heh hehhhhh
...YOU HEARD IT, RIGHT?
SURE.
ぐりん
spin
ATTEN-TION, EVERY-ONE...
?
GOOD LUCK TO YOU ALL...
...ON YOUR FITNESS TESTS!
さ~ら
waft
ta-daa!
UM... WHAT?

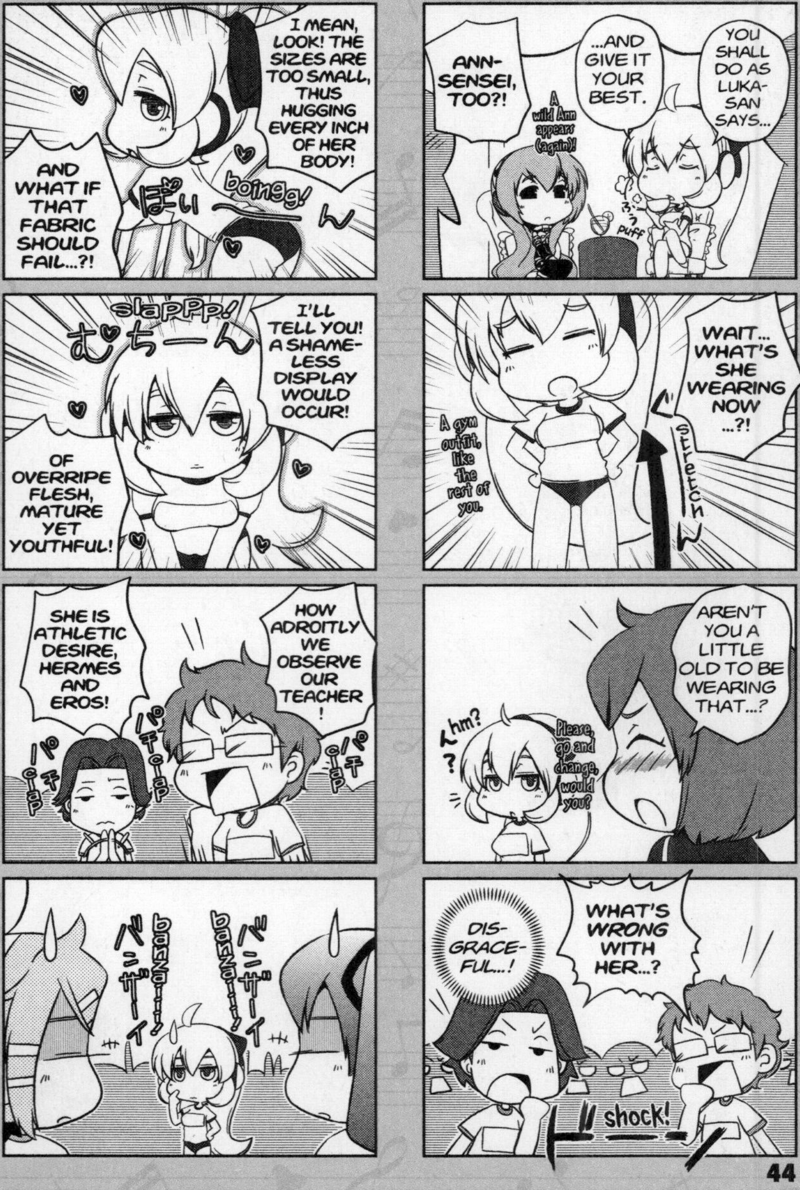
YOU SHALL DO AS LUKA-SAN SAYS...
...AND GIVE IT YOUR BEST.
ANN-SENSEI, TOO?!
A wild Ann appears (again)!
ふぅ puff
I MEAN, LOOK! THE SIZES ARE TOO SMALL, THUS HUGGING EVERY INCH OF HER BODY!
boingg!
ぼぃ〜〜〜ん
AND WHAT IF THAT FABRIC SHOULD FAIL...?!
WAIT... WHAT'S SHE WEARING NOW ...?!
ぐ stretch ん
A gym outfit, like the rest of you.
I'LL TELL YOU! A SHAMELESS DISPLAY WOULD OCCUR!
slapPp!
むちーん
OF OVERRIPE FLESH, MATURE YET YOUTHFUL!
AREN'T YOU A LITTLE OLD TO BE WEARING THAT...?
Please, go and change, would you?
hm? ん?
HOW ADROITLY WE OBSERVE OUR TEACHER!
パチ clap
SHE IS ATHLETIC DESIRE, HERMES AND EROS!
パチ clap
パチ clap
WHAT'S WRONG WITH HER...?
DIS-GRACE-FUL...!
shock!
ドー
バンザーイ banzai!
バンザーイ banzai!

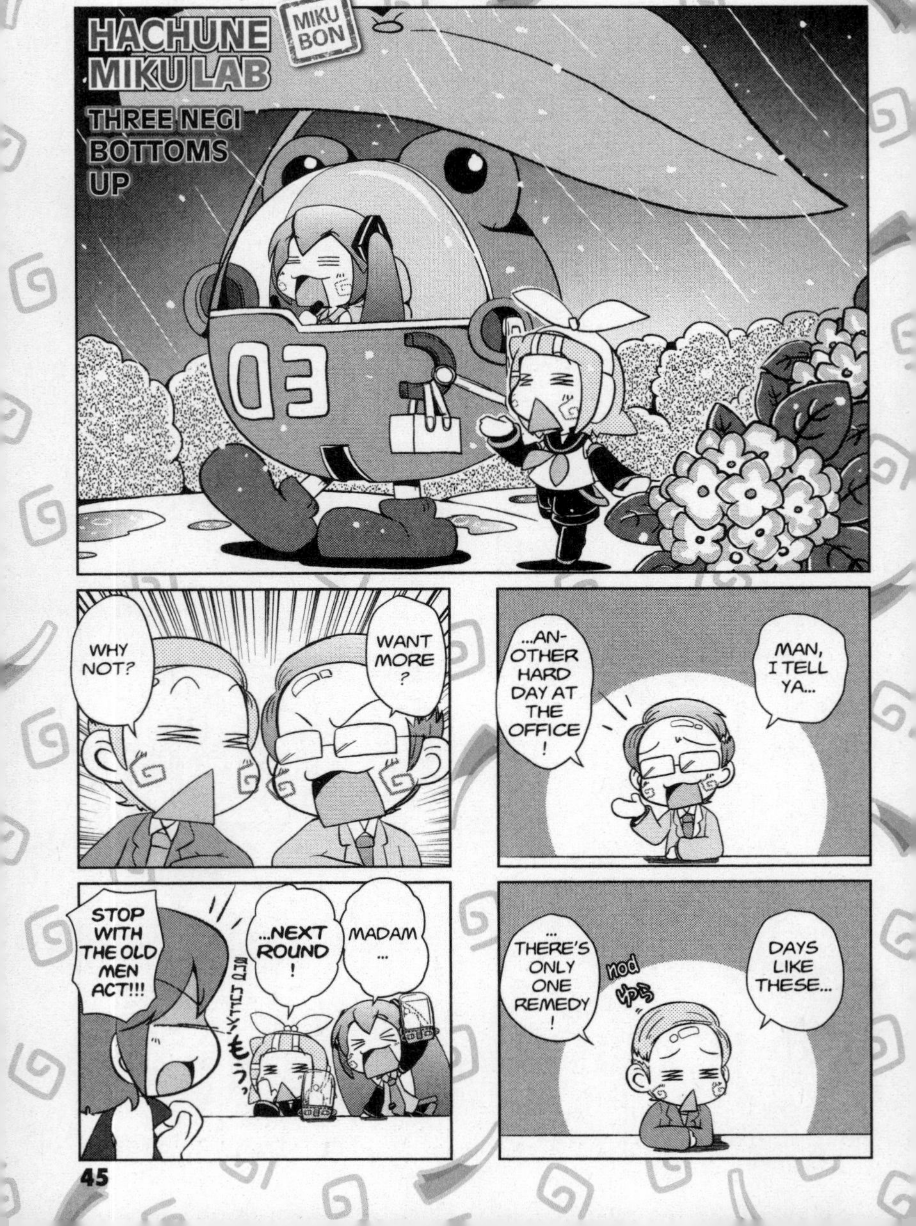
HACHUNE MIKU LAB
MIKU BON
THREE NEGI BOTTOMS UP
MAN, I TELL YA...
...AN-OTHER HARD DAY AT THE OFFICE!
WANT MORE?
WHY NOT?
DAYS LIKE THESE...
nod
ゆら
...THERE'S ONLY ONE REMEDY!
MADAM...
...NEXT ROUND!
STOP WITH THE OLD MEN ACT!!!

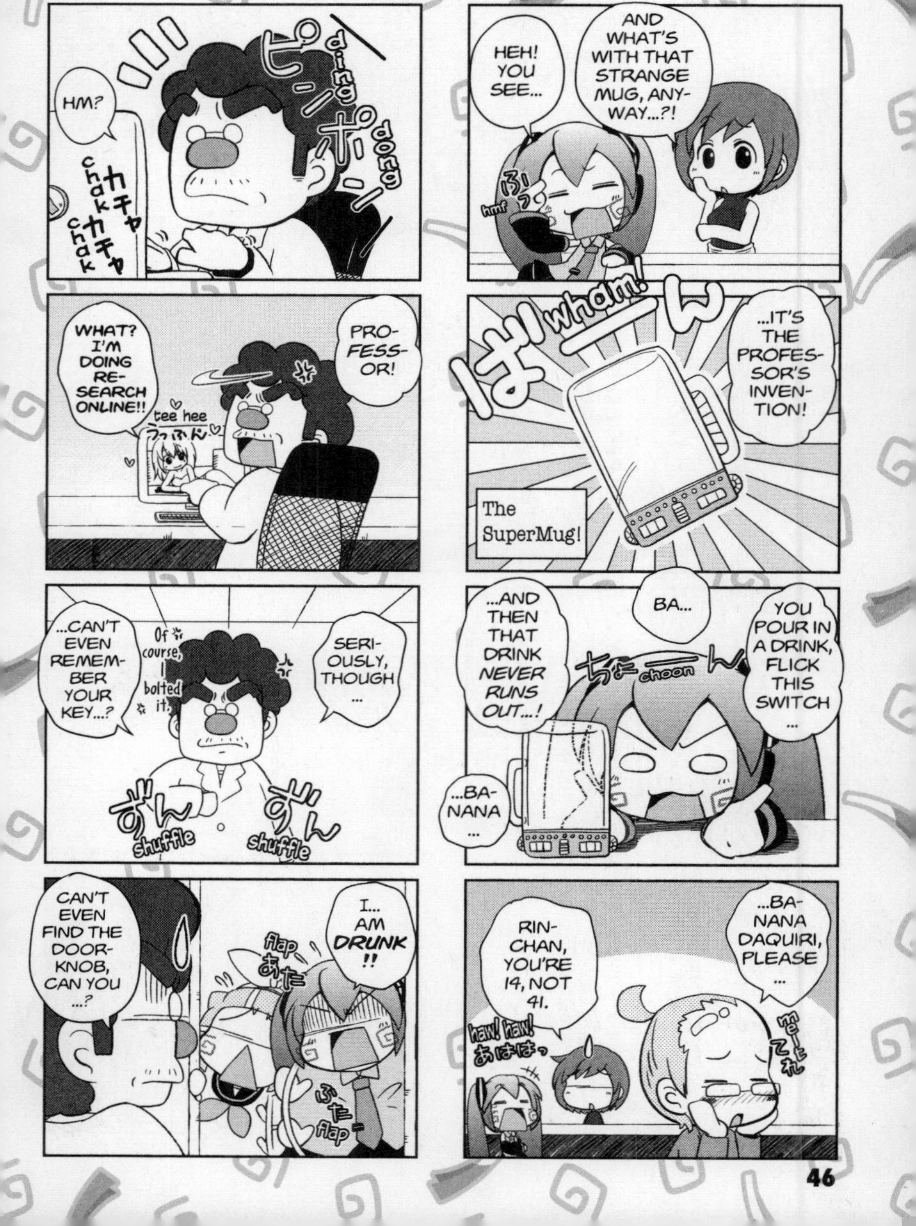
AND WHAT'S WITH THAT STRANGE MUG, ANY-WAY...?!
HEH! YOU SEE...
ふっ hmf
...IT'S THE PROFES-SOR'S INVEN-TION!
ぱーん wham!
The SuperMug!
YOU POUR IN A DRINK, FLICK THIS SWITCH ...
BA...
ちょーん choon
...AND THEN THAT DRINK NEVER RUNS OUT...!
...BA-NANA ...
...BA-NANA DAQUIRI, PLEASE ...
RIN-CHAN, YOU'RE 14, NOT 41.
haw! haw! あははっ
ピーンポーン ding dong
HM?
カチャカチャ chak chak
PRO-FESS-OR!
WHAT? I'M DOING RE-SEARCH ONLINE!!
うっふん tee hee
SERI-OUSLY, THOUGH ...
Of course, I bolted it.
...CAN'T EVEN REMEM-BER YOUR KEY...?
ずん shuffle
ずん shuffle
I... AM DRUNK!!
あた flap
ふた flap
CAN'T EVEN FIND THE DOOR-KNOB, CAN YOU ...?

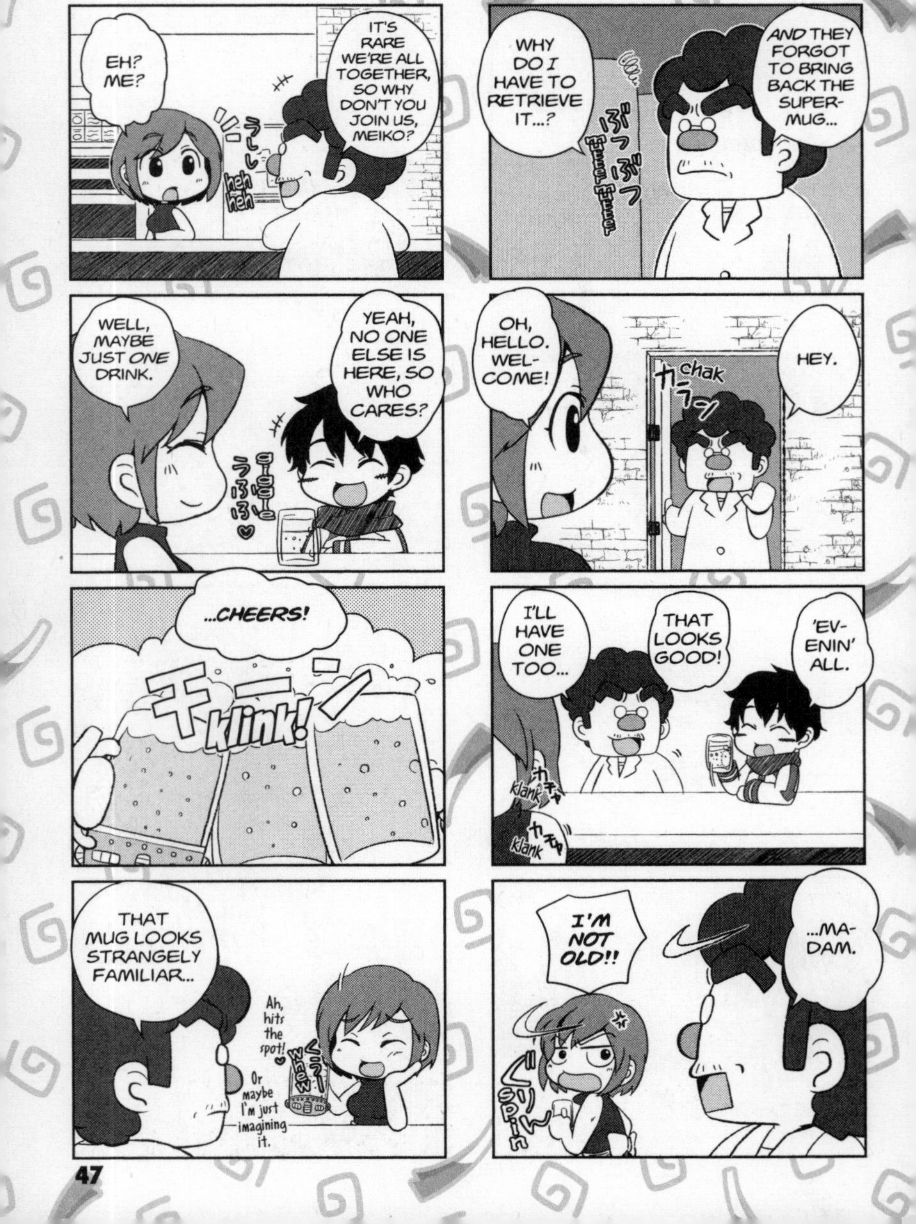
AND THEY FORGOT TO BRING BACK THE SUPER-MUG...
WHY DO I HAVE TO RETRIEVE IT...?
ぶつぶつ
HEY.
カラーン
chak
OH, HELLO. WEL-COME!
'EV-ENIN' ALL.
THAT LOOKS GOOD!
I'LL HAVE ONE TOO...
カチャ
klank
カチャ
klank
...MA-DAM.
I'M NOT OLD!!
ぐりん
spin
IT'S RARE WE'RE ALL TOGETHER, SO WHY DON'T YOU JOIN US, MEIKO?
うしし
heh heh
EH? ME?
YEAH, NO ONE ELSE IS HERE, SO WHO CARES?
うふふ
giggle
WELL, MAYBE JUST ONE DRINK.
...CHEERS!
チーン
klink!
THAT MUG LOOKS STRANGELY FAMILIAR...
Ah, hits the spot!
くぅー
Or maybe I'm just imagining it.

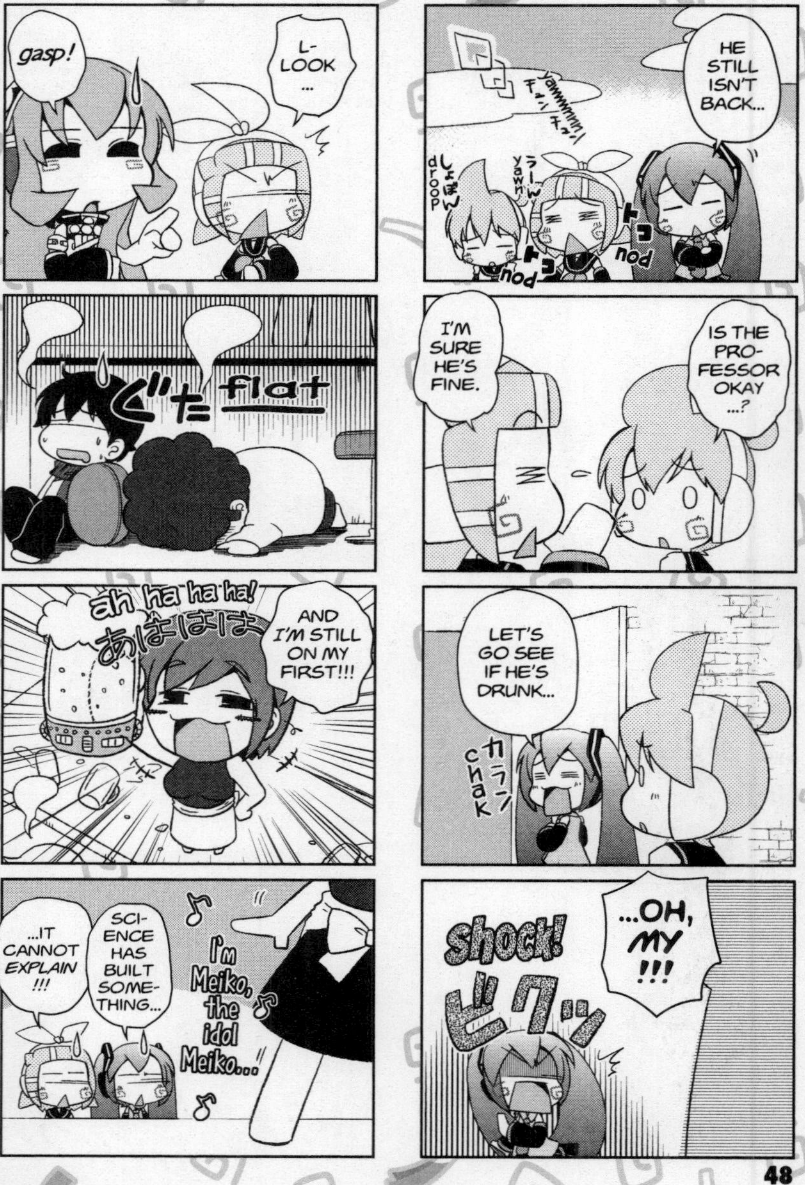
HE STILL ISN'T BACK...
yawwwwwn
チュンチュン
ラ～ yawn
しょぼん droop
トコ nod
トコ nod
IS THE PRO-FESSOR OKAY ...?
I'M SURE HE'S FINE.
LET'S GO SEE IF HE'S DRUNK...
カラン chak
...OH, MY !!!
Shock!
ビクッ
L-LOOK ...
gasp!
ぐでた flat
AND I'M STILL ON MY FIRST!!!
ah ha ha ha!
あははは
I'm Meiko, the idol Meiko...
SCI-ENCE HAS BUILT SOME-THING...
...IT CANNOT EXPLAIN !!!

HATSUNE MIKU MIKUBON

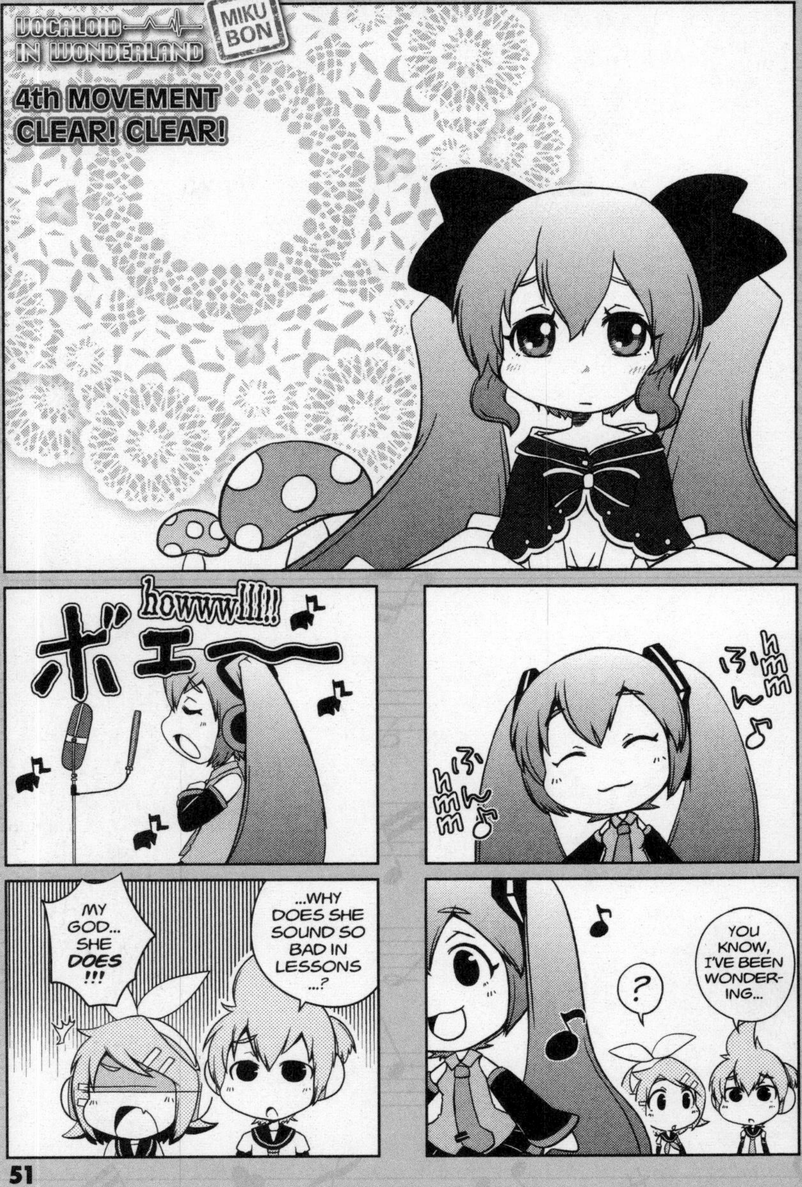
VOCALOID IN WONDERLAND
MIKU BON
4th MOVEMENT
CLEAR! CLEAR!
ふんふん
hmmm
ふんふん
hmmm
ボエ〜
howwwl!!!
YOU KNOW, I'VE BEEN WONDER-ING...
?
...WHY DOES SHE SOUND SO BAD IN LESSONS ...?
MY GOD... SHE *DOES* !!!

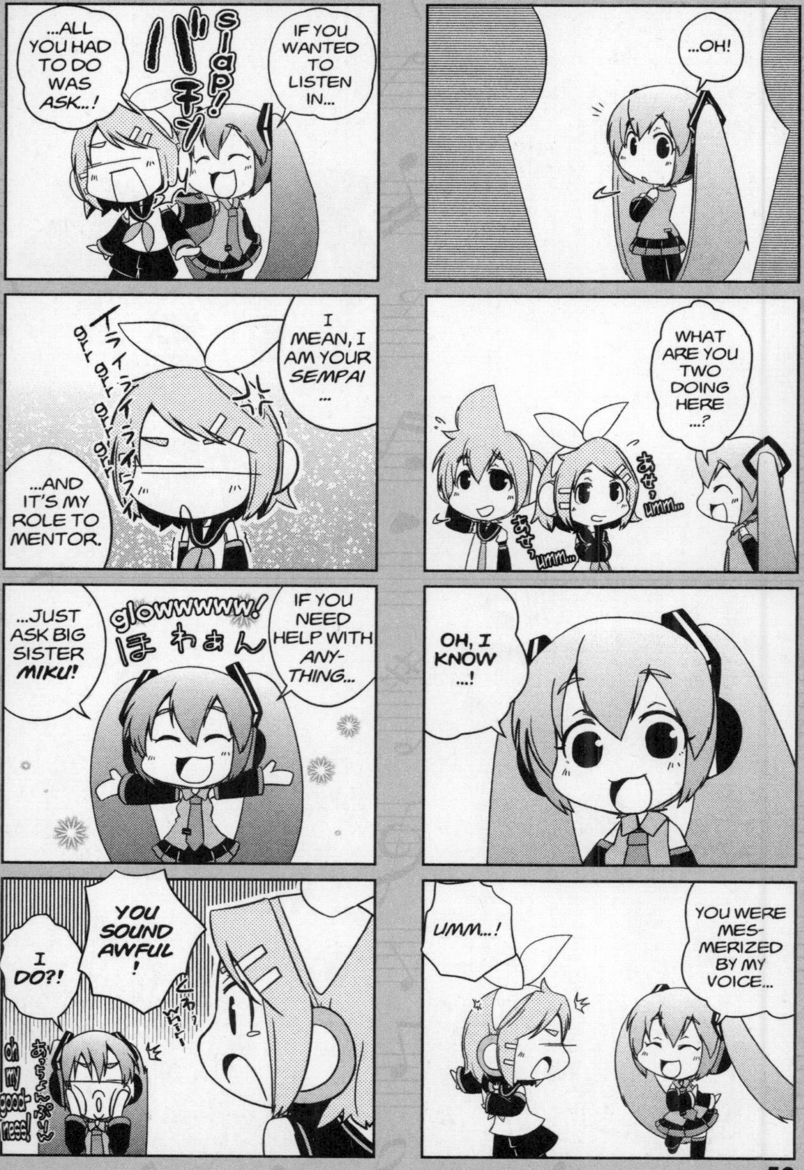
...OH!
WHAT ARE YOU TWO DOING HERE ...?
あせっ umm...
あせっ umm...
OH, I KNOW ...!
YOU WERE MES-MERIZED BY MY VOICE...
UMM...!
slap! バチン
IF YOU WANTED TO LISTEN IN...
...ALL YOU HAD TO DO WAS ASK...!
I MEAN, I AM YOUR SEMPAI ...
イライライライラ
grr grr grr grr
...AND IT'S MY ROLE TO MENTOR.
IF YOU NEED HELP WITH ANY-THING...
glowwwww! ほわぁん
...JUST ASK BIG SISTER MIKU!
YOU SOUND AWFUL!
I DO?!
oh my goodness!

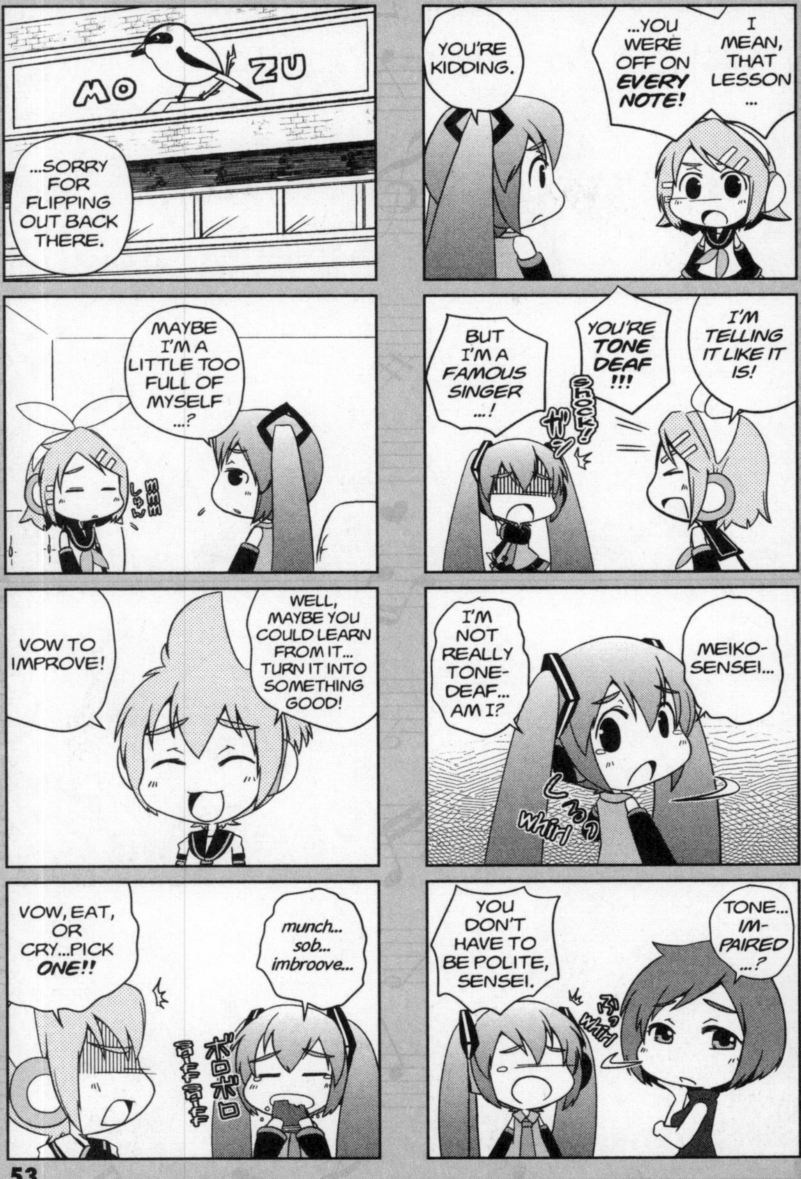
I MEAN, THAT LESSON ...
...YOU WERE OFF ON EVERY NOTE!
YOU'RE KIDDING.
I'M TELLING IT LIKE IT IS!
YOU'RE TONE DEAF!!!
SHOCK!
BUT I'M A FAMOUS SINGER ...!
MEIKO-SENSEI...
I'M NOT REALLY TONE-DEAF... AM I?
whirl
TONE... IM-PAIRED ...?
whirl
YOU DON'T HAVE TO BE POLITE, SENSEI.
MO ZU
...SORRY FOR FLIPPING OUT BACK THERE.
MAYBE I'M A LITTLE TOO FULL OF MYSELF ...?
mmm
WELL, MAYBE YOU COULD LEARN FROM IT... TURN IT INTO SOMETHING GOOD!
VOW TO IMPROVE!
munch... sob... imbroove...
sniff sniff
VOW, EAT, OR CRY...PICK ONE!!

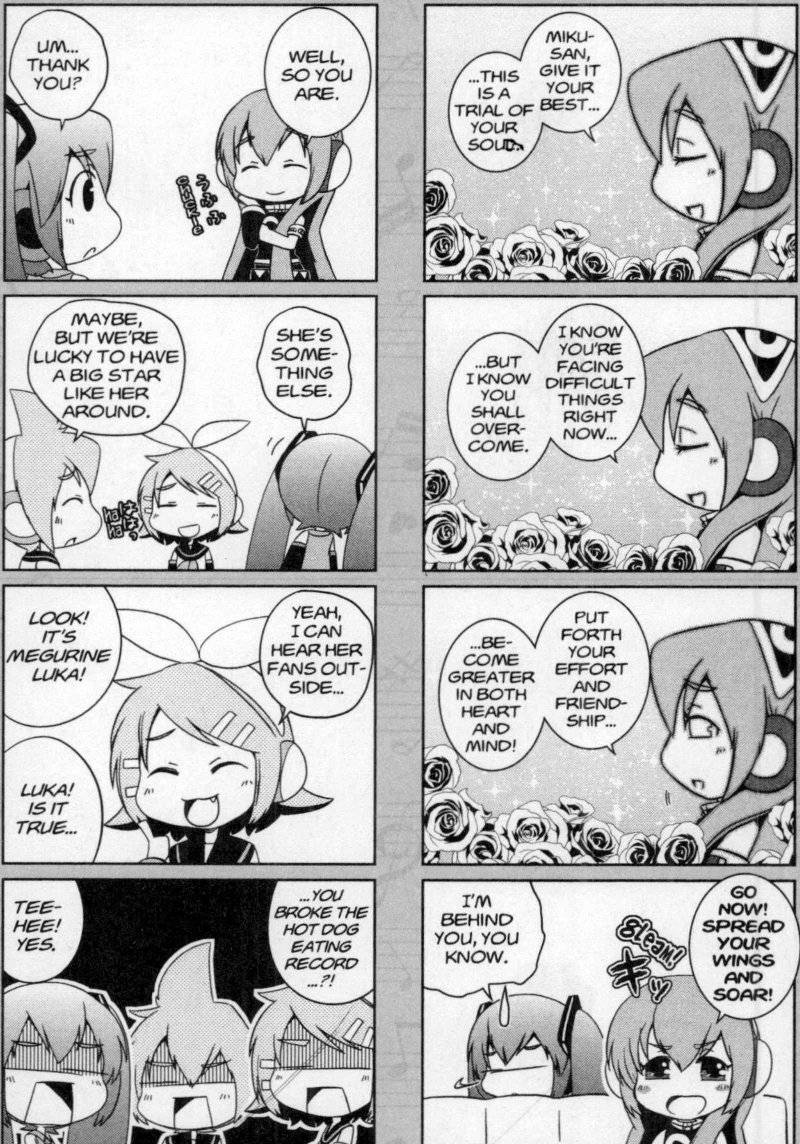
MIKU-SAN, GIVE IT YOUR BEST...
...THIS IS A TRIAL OF YOUR SOUL...
I KNOW YOU'RE FACING DIFFICULT THINGS RIGHT NOW...
...BUT I KNOW YOU SHALL OVERCOME.
PUT FORTH YOUR EFFORT AND FRIENDSHIP...
...BE-COME GREATER IN BOTH HEART AND MIND!
GO NOW! SPREAD YOUR WINGS AND SOAR!
Gleam! キッ
I'M BEHIND YOU, YOU KNOW.
WELL, SO YOU ARE.
うふふ Chuckle
UM... THANK YOU?
SHE'S SOME-THING ELSE.
MAYBE, BUT WE'RE LUCKY TO HAVE A BIG STAR LIKE HER AROUND.
はは ha ha
YEAH, I CAN HEAR HER FANS OUT-SIDE...
LOOK! IT'S MEGURINE LUKA!
LUKA! IS IT TRUE...
...YOU BROKE THE HOT DOG EATING RECORD ...?!
TEE-HEE! YES.

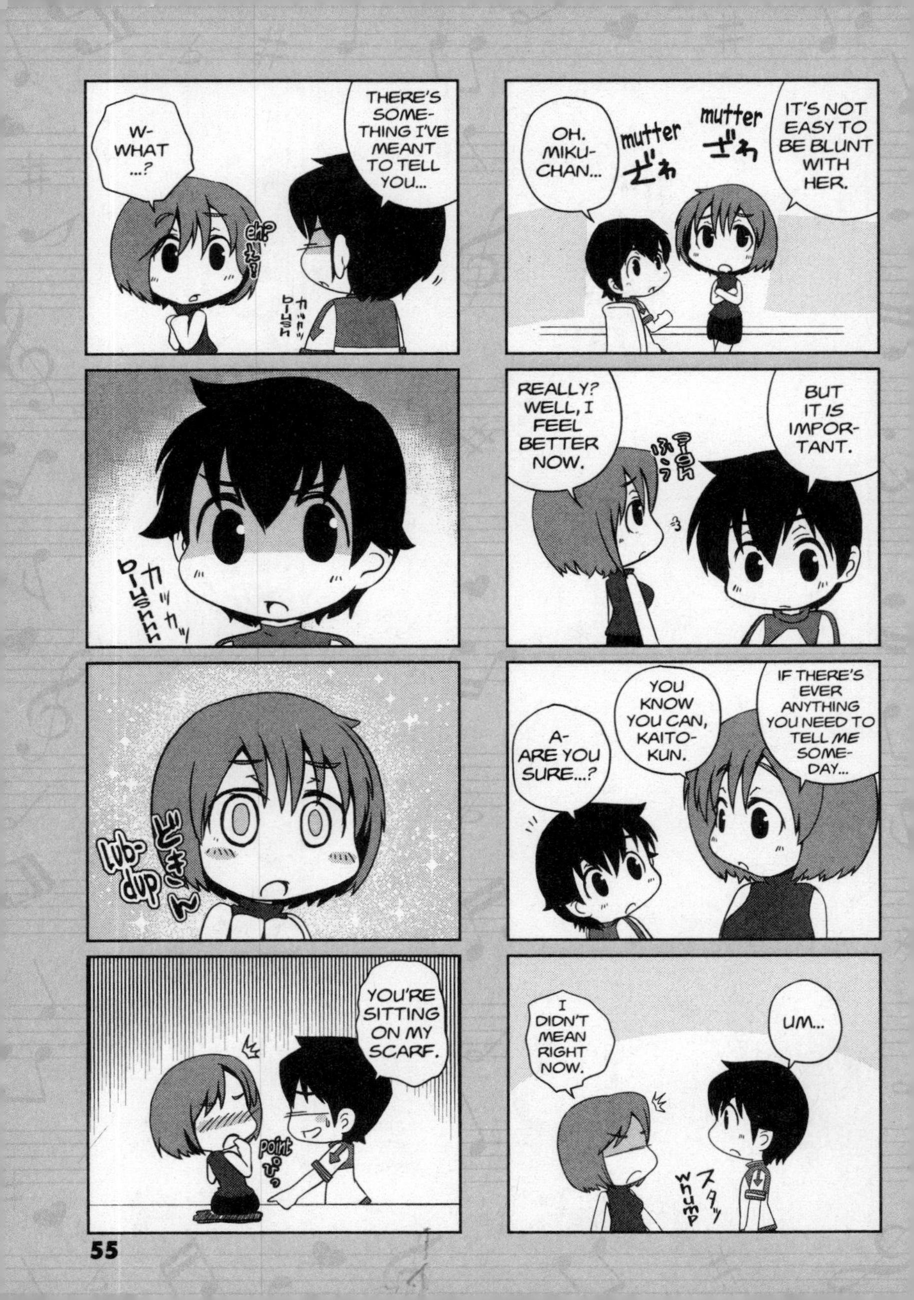
mutter ざわ
mutter ざわ
IT'S NOT EASY TO BE BLUNT WITH HER.
OH. MIKU-CHAN...
BUT IT IS IMPORTANT.
ふう
REALLY? WELL, I FEEL BETTER NOW.
IF THERE'S EVER ANYTHING YOU NEED TO TELL ME SOMEDAY...
YOU KNOW YOU CAN, KAITO-KUN.
A- ARE YOU SURE...?
UM...
I DIDN'T MEAN RIGHT NOW.
スタッ whump
THERE'S SOMETHING I'VE MEANT TO TELL YOU...
W-WHAT ...?
eh? え?
blush
カッカッ blushhh
どきん lub-dup
YOU'RE SITTING ON MY SCARF.
point ぴっ

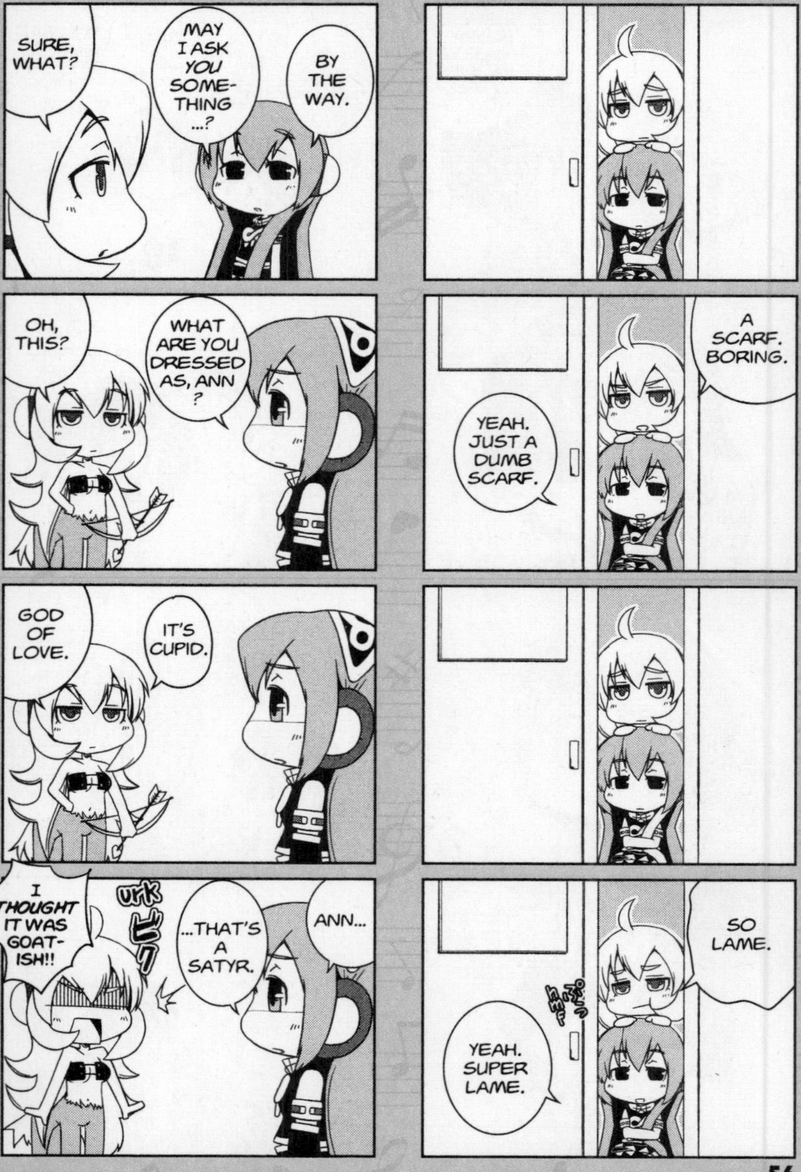
A SCARF. BORING.
YEAH. JUST A DUMB SCARF.
SO LAME.
YEAH. SUPER LAME.
BY THE WAY.
MAY I ASK *YOU* SOMETHING...?
SURE, WHAT?
WHAT ARE YOU DRESSED AS, ANN?
OH, THIS?
IT'S CUPID.
GOD OF LOVE.
ANN...
...THAT'S A SATYR.
urk
I *THOUGHT* IT WAS GOAT-ISH!!

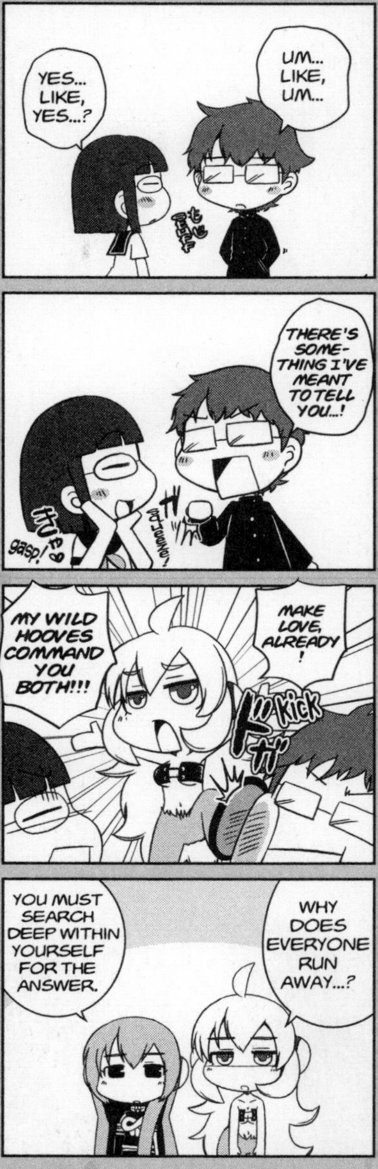
UM... LIKE, UM...
YES... LIKE, YES...?
もじ
FIDGET
THERE'S SOMETHING I'VE MEANT TO TELL YOU...!
ガッ
SQUEEZE!
きゃ♥
gasp!
MAKE LOVE, ALREADY!
MY WILD HOOVES COMMAND YOU BOTH!!!
ド kick
ガッ
WHY DOES EVERYONE RUN AWAY...?
YOU MUST SEARCH DEEP WITHIN YOURSELF FOR THE ANSWER.

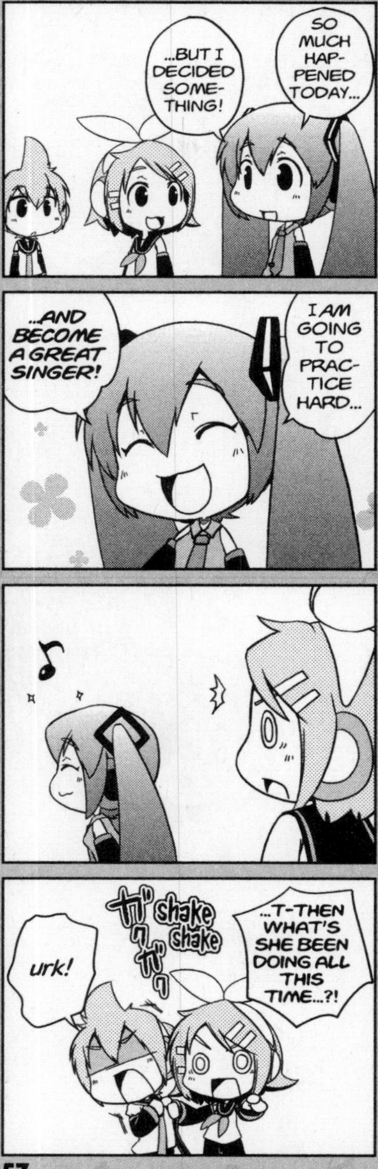
SO MUCH HAP-PENED TODAY...
...BUT I DECIDED SOME-THING!
I AM GOING TO PRAC-TICE HARD...
...AND BECOME A GREAT SINGER!
...T-THEN WHAT'S SHE BEEN DOING ALL THIS TIME...?!
ガクガク shake shake
urk!

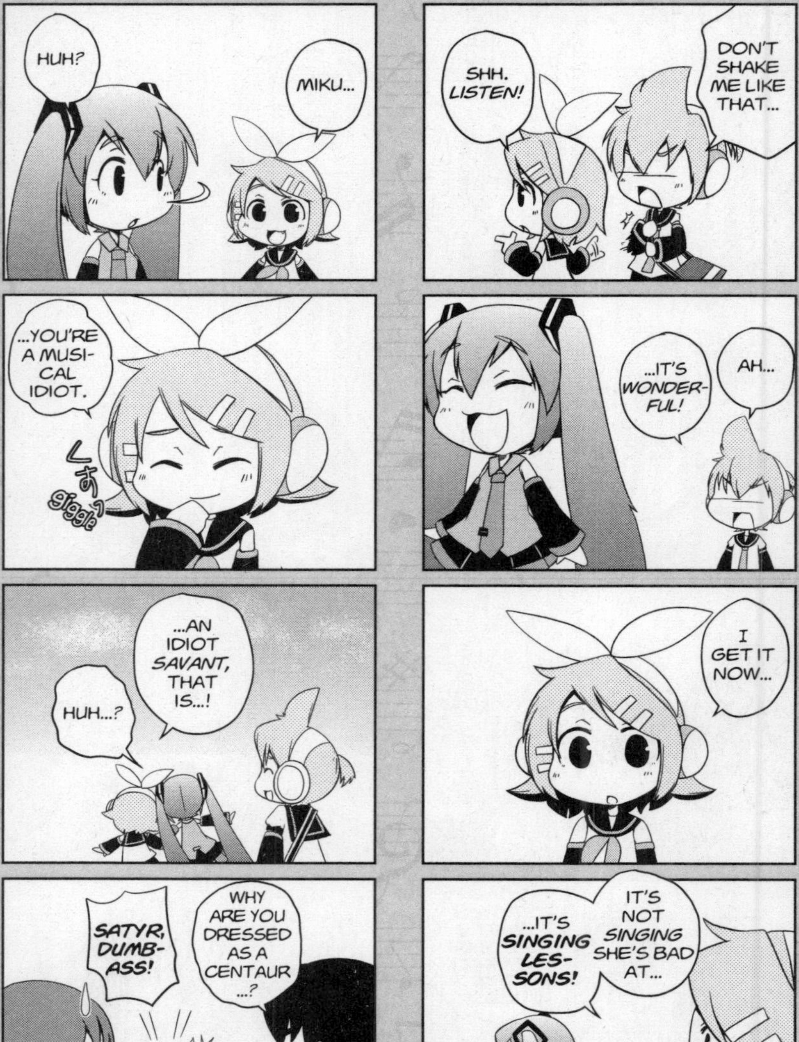
DON'T SHAKE ME LIKE THAT...
SHH. LISTEN!
MIKU...
HUH?
AH...
...IT'S WONDERFUL!
...YOU'RE A MUSICAL IDIOT.
giggle
I GET IT NOW...
...AN IDIOT SAVANT, THAT IS...!
HUH...?
IT'S NOT SINGING SHE'S BAD AT...
...IT'S SINGING LESSONS!
WHY ARE YOU DRESSED AS A CENTAUR ...?
SATYR, DUMBASS!

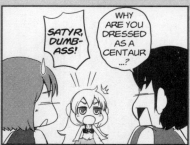

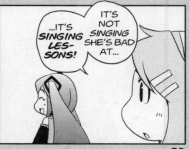

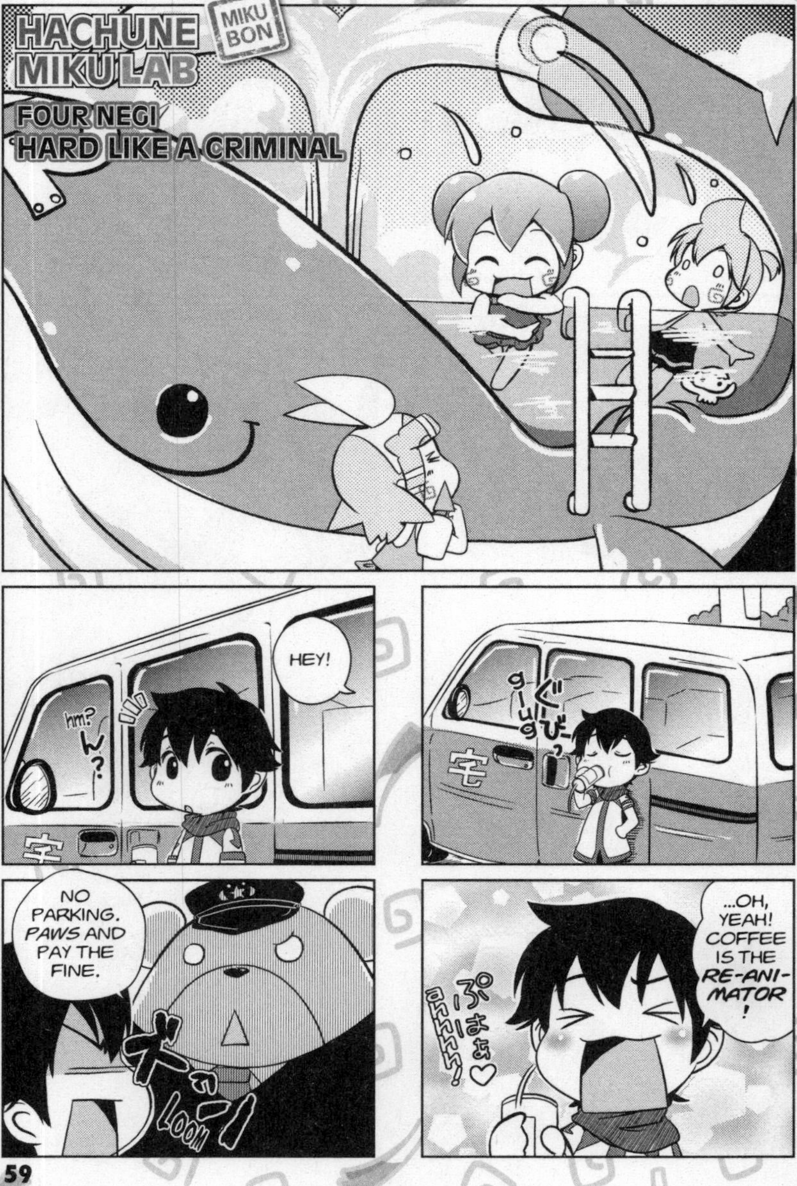
HACHUNE MIKU LAB
MIKU BON
FOUR NEGI
HARD LIKE A CRIMINAL
ぐびっ
g-ug
HEY!
hm?
ん?
...OH, YEAH! COFFEE IS THE RE-ANIMATOR!
ぷはぁ～♡
NO PARKING. PAWS AND PAY THE FINE.
ギャー!
LOOM

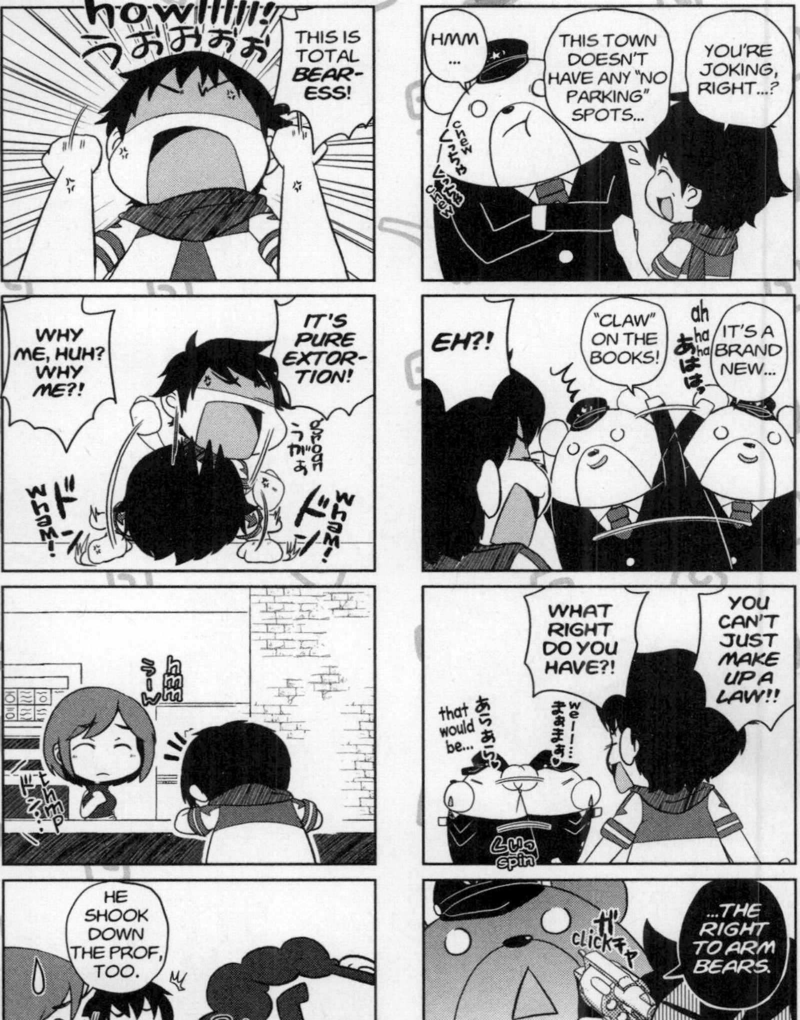
YOU'RE JOKING, RIGHT...?
THIS TOWN DOESN'T HAVE ANY "NO PARKING" SPOTS...
HMM ...
chew くっちゃ
chew くっちゃ
IT'S A BRAND NEW...
ah ha ha あははっ
"CLAW" ON THE BOOKS!
EH?!
YOU CAN'T JUST MAKE UP A LAW!!
WHAT RIGHT DO YOU HAVE?!
well... まぁまぁ
that would be... あらあら
くるっ spin
...THE RIGHT TO ARM BEARS.
click ガチャ
shiver ぶるぶる
THIS IS TOTAL BEAR-ESS!
howl!!!!! うおおおぉ
IT'S PURE EXTORTION!
WHY ME, HUH? WHY ME?!
groan うがぁ
wham! ドン
wham! ドン
hmm う〜ん
hmp ドン
HE SHOOK DOWN THE PROF, TOO.
eh? はっ
sobb しくしく
sobb しくしく

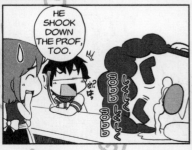

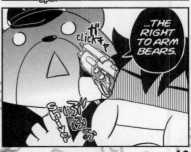

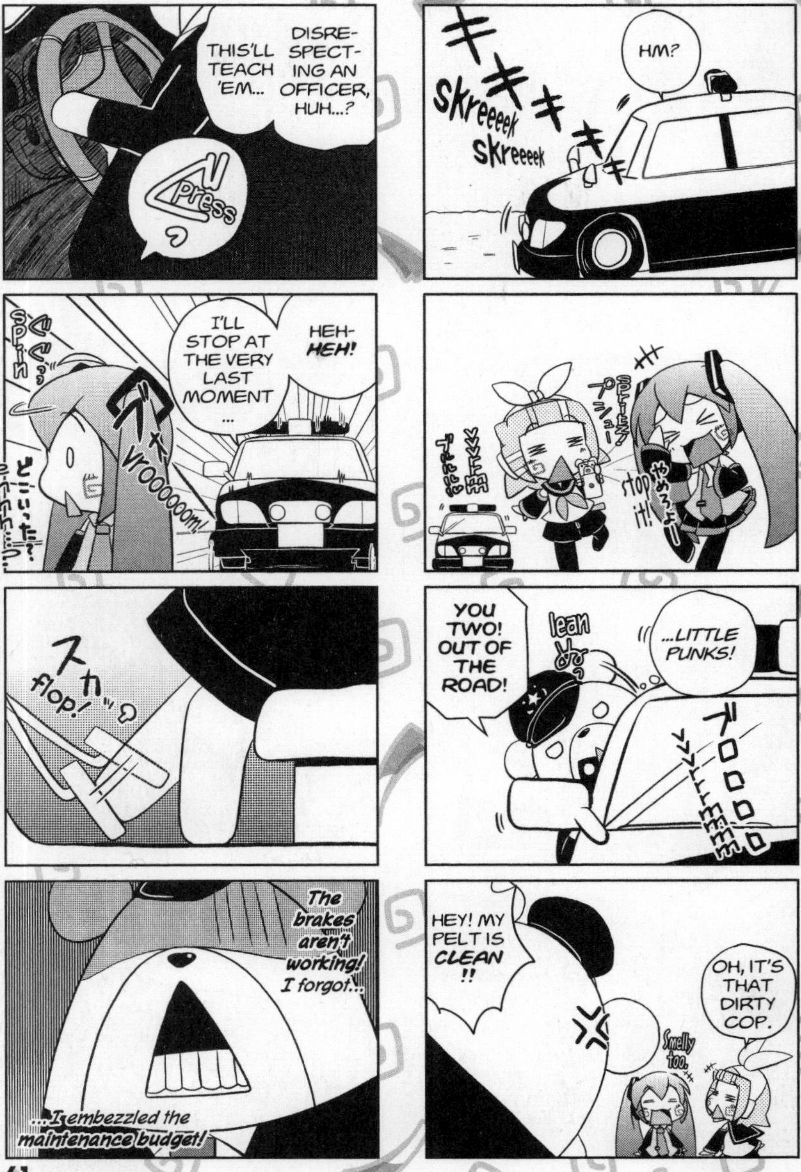
HM?
キキキキ
skreeeek skreeeek
DISRE-SPECTING AN OFFICER, HUH...?
THIS'LL TEACH 'EM...
press
spritz! プシュー
stop it! やめろよー
HEH-HEH!
I'LL STOP AT THE VERY LAST MOMENT ...
vroooooom!
spin
ehhhh...? どこいった?
...LITTLE PUNKS!
lean
YOU TWO! OUT OF THE ROAD!
vrrrmmmm
flop!
OH, IT'S THAT DIRTY COP.
Smelly too.
HEY! MY PELT IS CLEAN !!
The brakes aren't working! I forgot...
...I embezzled the maintenance budget!

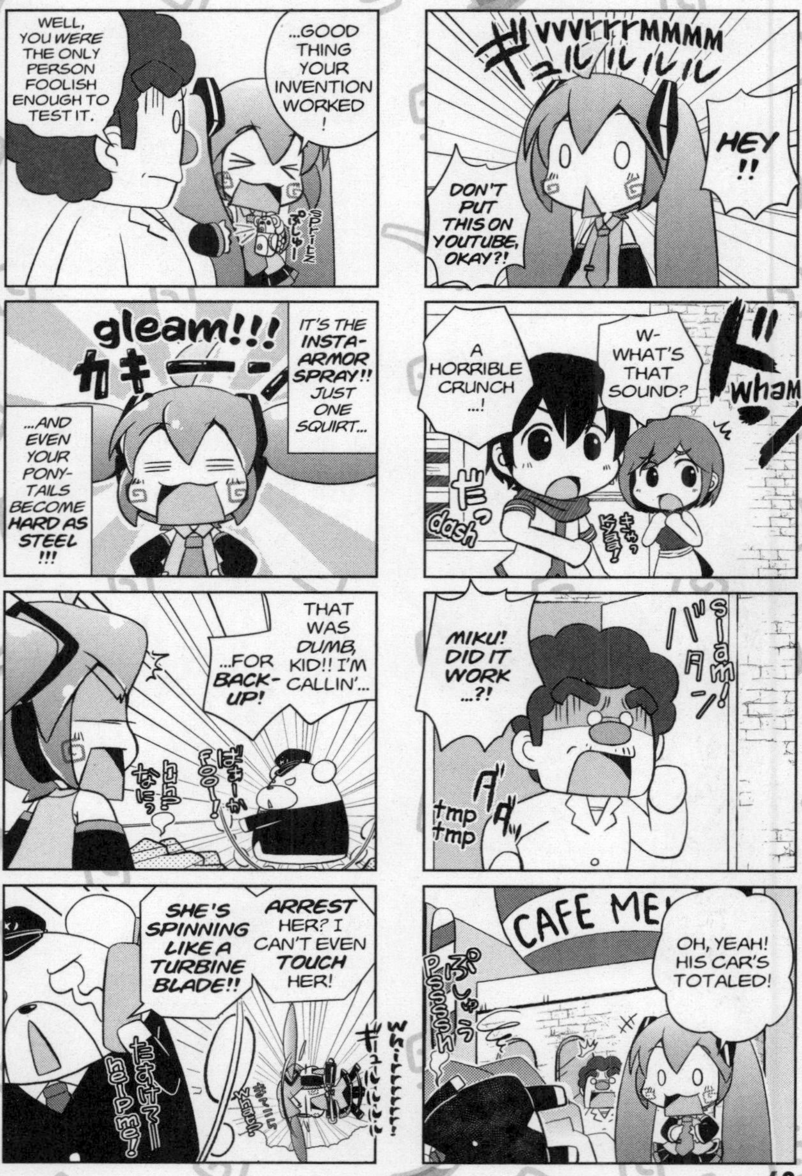
vvvvrrrMMMM
ギュルルルルル
HEY !!
DON'T PUT THIS ON YOUTUBE, OKAY?!
...GOOD THING YOUR INVENTION WORKED !
WELL, YOU WERE THE ONLY PERSON FOOLISH ENOUGH TO TEST IT.
ぷしゅー
spritz
W- WHAT'S THAT SOUND?
A HORRIBLE CRUNCH ...!
ド
wham!
ダッ
dash
IT'S THE INSTA-ARMOR SPRAY!! JUST ONE SQUIRT...
...AND EVEN YOUR PONY-TAILS BECOME HARD AS STEEL !!!
gleam!!!
カキーーン
MIKU! DID IT WORK ...?!
バターン
slam!
ダダッ
tmp tmp
THAT WAS DUMB, KID!! I'M CALLIN'...
...FOR BACK-UP!
ばーか
fool!
なにっ
huh?
CAFE ME
OH, YEAH! HIS CAR'S TOTALED!
ぷしゅう
Psssshh
ARREST HER? I CAN'T EVEN TOUCH HER!
SHE'S SPINNING LIKE A TURBINE BLADE!!
ギュルルルル
whirrrrrr!
たすけて
help me!

HATSUNE MIKU

MIKUBON

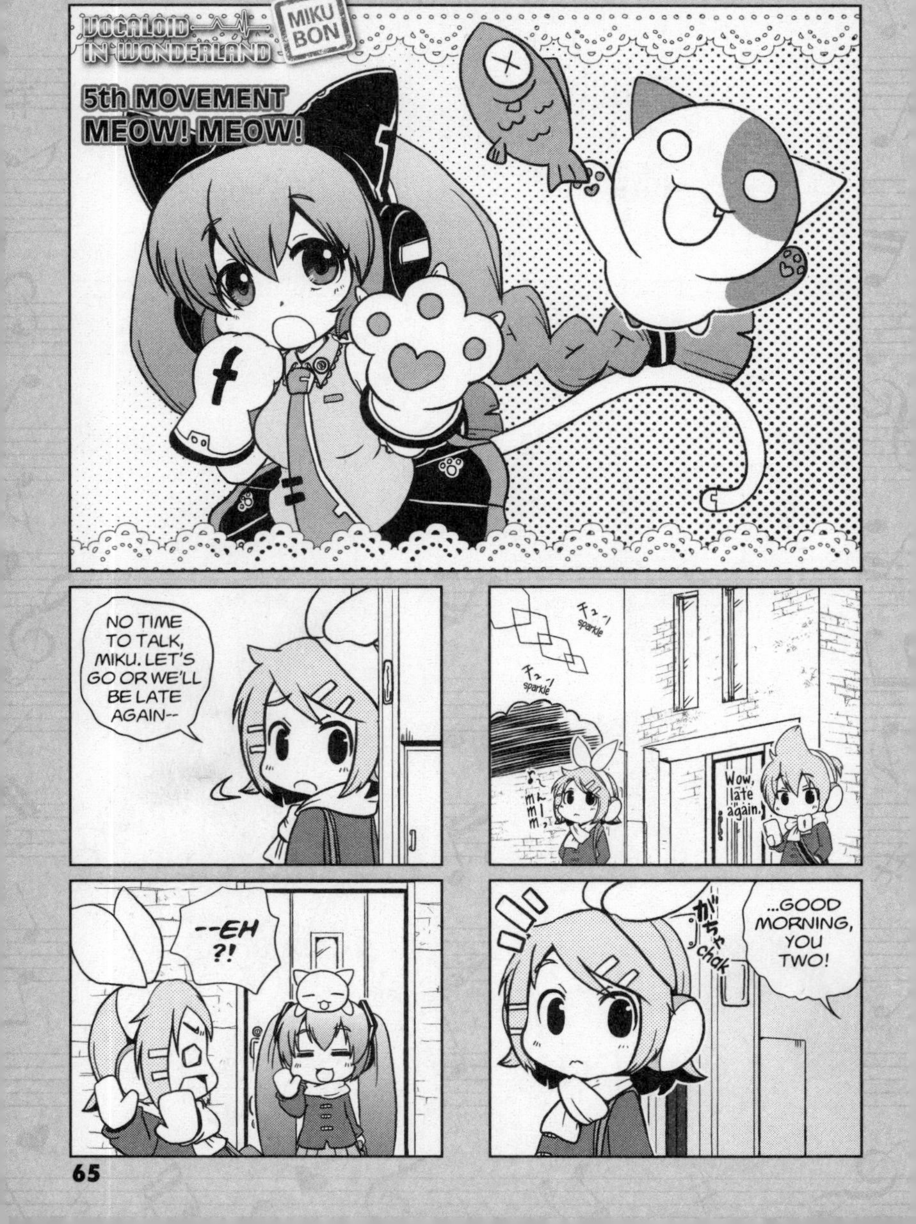
VOCALOID IN WONDERLAND
MIKU BON
5th MOVEMENT
MEOW! MEOW!
チュン sparkle
チュン sparkle
♪~ m~ m, m,
Wow, late again,
NO TIME TO TALK, MIKU. LET'S GO OR WE'LL BE LATE AGAIN--
ガチャ chak
...GOOD MORNING, YOU TWO!
--EH ?!

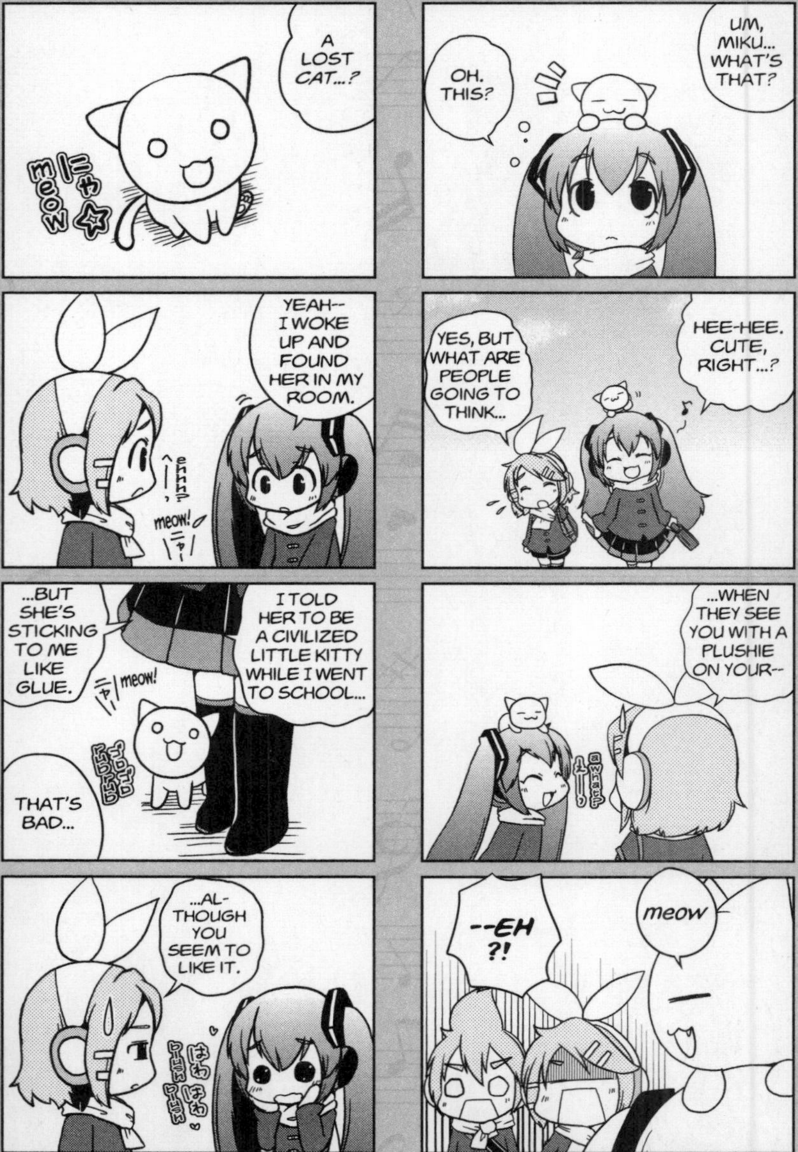
UM, MIKU... WHAT'S THAT?
OH. THIS?
HEE-HEE. CUTE, RIGHT...?
YES, BUT WHAT ARE PEOPLE GOING TO THINK...
...WHEN THEY SEE YOU WITH A PLUSHIE ON YOUR--
meow
--EH ?!
A LOST CAT...?
にゃ☆
meow
YEAH-- I WOKE UP AND FOUND HER IN MY ROOM.
ehhh?
meow!
I TOLD HER TO BE A CIVILIZED LITTLE KITTY WHILE I WENT TO SCHOOL...
...BUT SHE'S STICKING TO ME LIKE GLUE.
meow!
THAT'S BAD...
...AL- THOUGH YOU SEEM TO LIKE IT.
はわ はわ

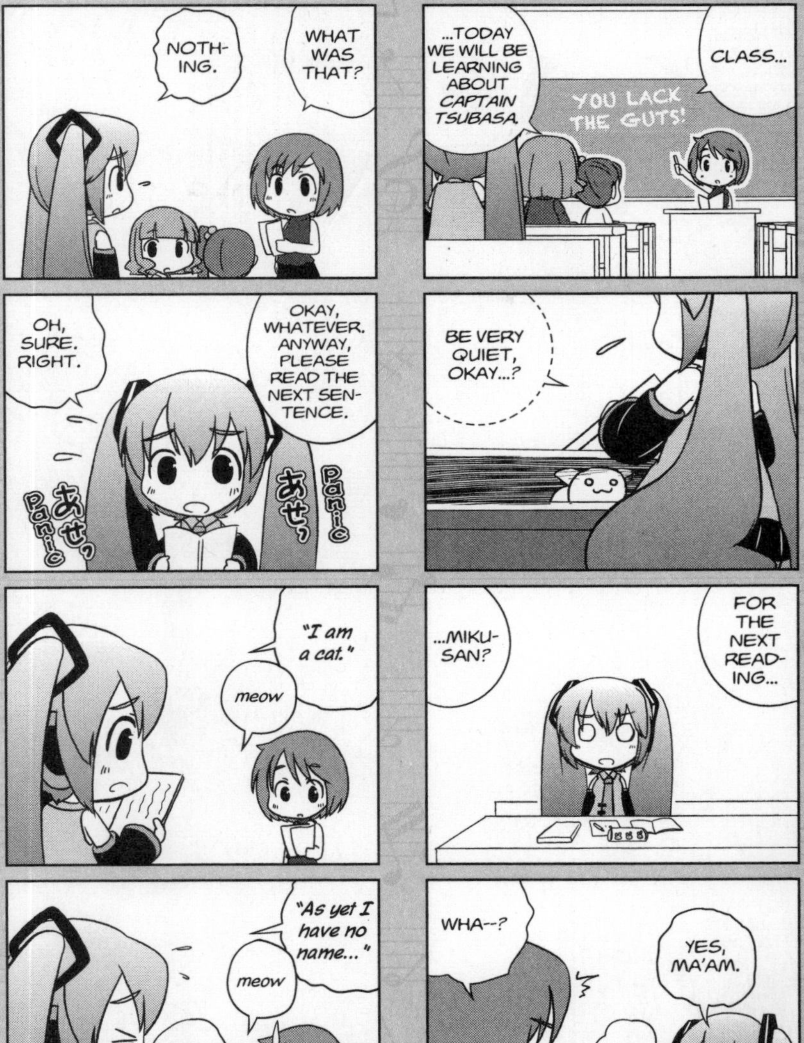
CLASS...
...TODAY WE WILL BE LEARNING ABOUT CAPTAIN TSUBASA.
YOU LACK THE GUTS!
WHAT WAS THAT?
NOTHING.
BE VERY QUIET, OKAY...?
OKAY, WHATEVER. ANYWAY, PLEASE READ THE NEXT SENTENCE.
OH, SURE. RIGHT.
Panic あせっ
Panic あせっ
FOR THE NEXT READING...
...MIKU-SAN?
"I am a cat."
meow
YES, MA'AM.
WHA--?
meow
"As yet I have no name..."
meow
IS THIS HOW KIDS TALK NOW...?

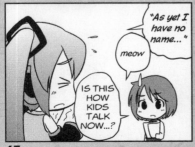

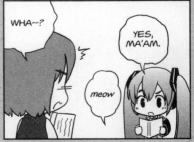

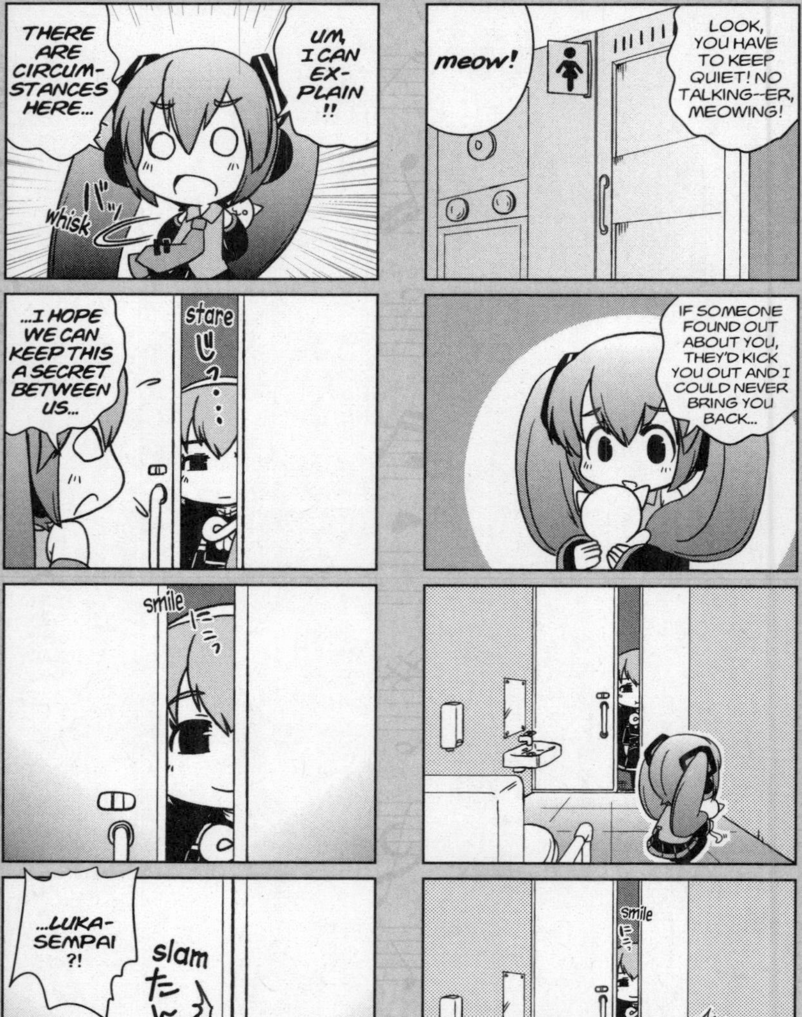
meow!
LOOK, YOU HAVE TO KEEP QUIET! NO TALKING--ER, MEOWING!
IF SOMEONE FOUND OUT ABOUT YOU, THEY'D KICK YOU OUT AND I COULD NEVER BRING YOU BACK...
smile
urk!
UM, I CAN EXPLAIN!!
THERE ARE CIRCUMSTANCES HERE...
whisk
stare
...I HOPE WE CAN KEEP THIS A SECRET BETWEEN US...
smile
slam
...LUKA-SEMPAI?!

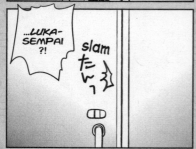

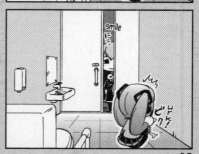

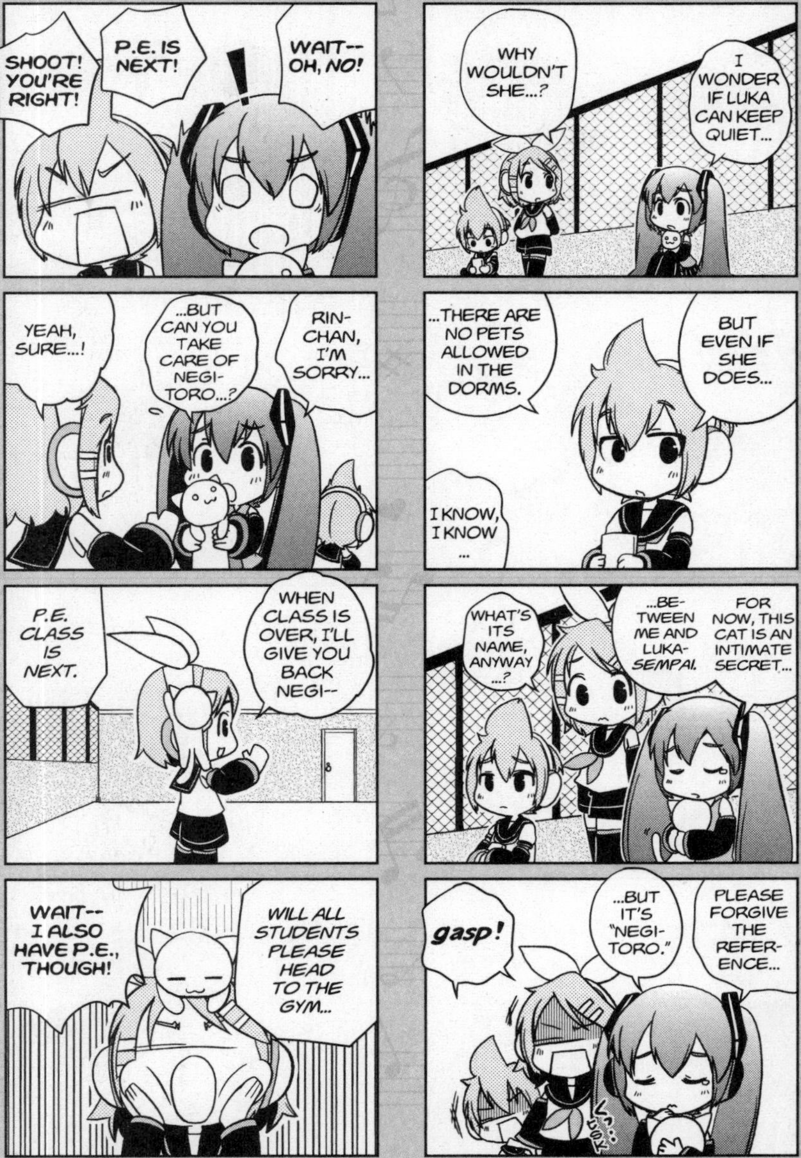
I WONDER IF LUKA CAN KEEP QUIET...
WHY WOULDN'T SHE...?
WAIT-- OH, NO!
!
P.E. IS NEXT!
SHOOT! YOU'RE RIGHT!
BUT EVEN IF SHE DOES...
...THERE ARE NO PETS ALLOWED IN THE DORMS.
I KNOW, I KNOW ...
RIN-CHAN, I'M SORRY...
...BUT CAN YOU TAKE CARE OF NEGI-TORO...?
YEAH, SURE...!
FOR NOW, THIS CAT IS AN INTIMATE SECRET...
...BE-TWEEN ME AND LUKA-SEMPAI.
WHAT'S ITS NAME, ANYWAY ...?
WHEN CLASS IS OVER, I'LL GIVE YOU BACK NEGI--
P.E. CLASS IS NEXT.
PLEASE FORGIVE THE REFER-ENCE...
...BUT IT'S "NEGI-TORO."
gasp!
WILL ALL STUDENTS PLEASE HEAD TO THE GYM...
WAIT-- I ALSO HAVE P.E., THOUGH!

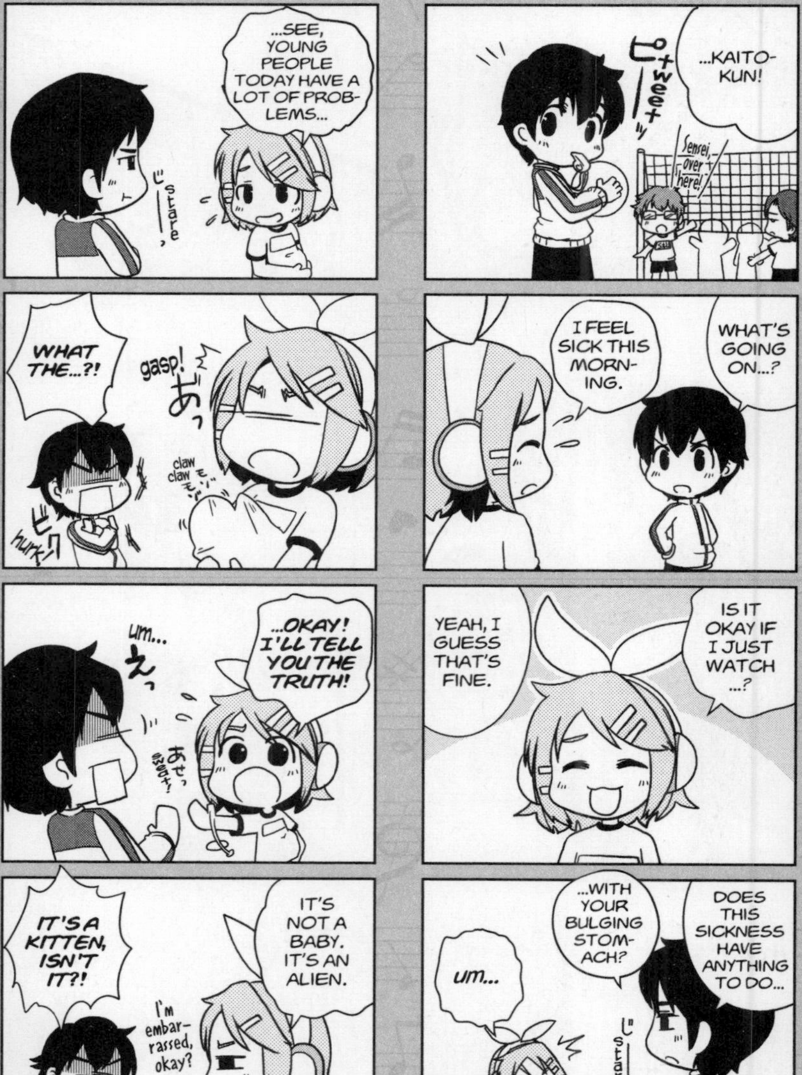
...KAITO-KUN!
ピーッ
tweet
Sensei, over here!
WHAT'S GOING ON...?
I FEEL SICK THIS MORNING.
IS IT OKAY IF I JUST WATCH ...?
YEAH, I GUESS THAT'S FINE.
DOES THIS SICKNESS HAVE ANYTHING TO DO...
...WITH YOUR BULGING STOMACH?
UM...
じー
stare
ビクッ
urk!
...SEE, YOUNG PEOPLE TODAY HAVE A LOT OF PROBLEMS...
じー
stare
WHAT THE...?!
gasp!
あっ
claw claw
モゾモゾ
ビクッ
hurk!
...OKAY! I'LL TELL YOU THE TRUTH!
um...
えっ
あせっ
sweat!
IT'S NOT A BABY. IT'S AN ALIEN.
IT'S A KITTEN, ISN'T IT?!
I'm embarrassed, okay?

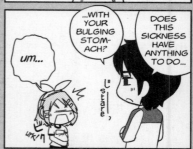

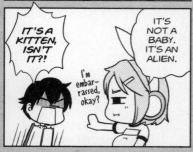

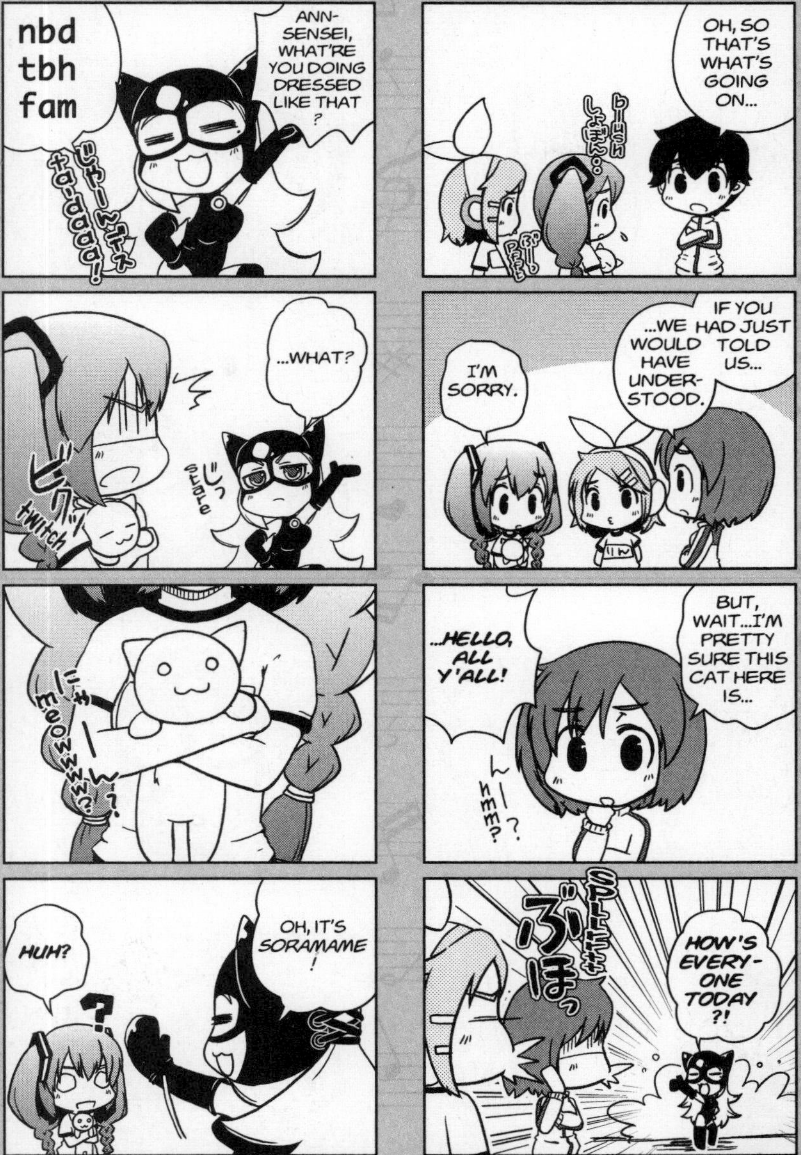
OH, SO THAT'S WHAT'S GOING ON...
しょぼん。。 blush
ぶー pfft
IF YOU HAD JUST TOLD US...
...WE WOULD HAVE UNDERSTOOD.
I'M SORRY.
BUT, WAIT...I'M PRETTY SURE THIS CAT HERE IS...
...HELLO, ALL Y'ALL!
ん–? hmm?
ぶほっ
HOW'S EVERY-ONE TODAY?!
ANN-SENSEI, WHAT'RE YOU DOING DRESSED LIKE THAT?
nbd tbh fam
じゃーん デス ta-daaaa!
...WHAT?
ビクッ twitch
じっ stare
にゃ~ん? meowwww?
OH, IT'S SORAMAME!
HUH?
?

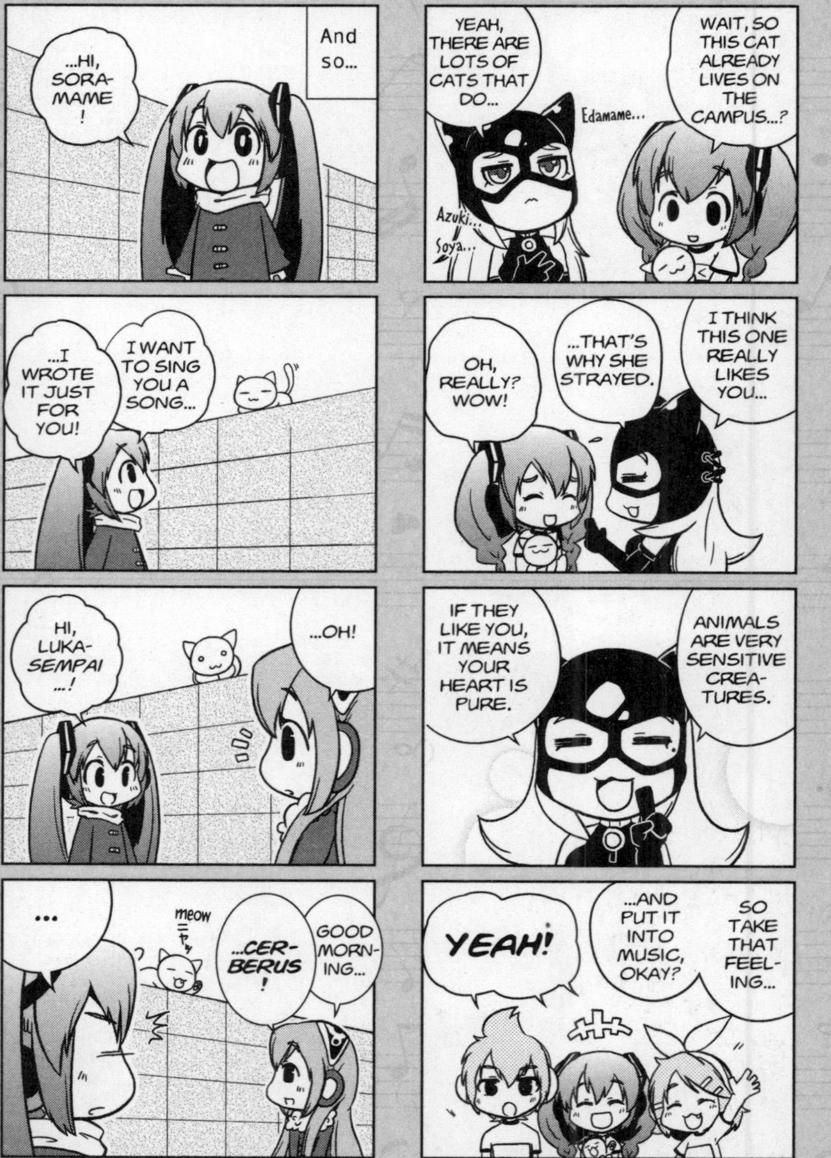
WAIT, SO THIS CAT ALREADY LIVES ON THE CAMPUS...?
YEAH, THERE ARE LOTS OF CATS THAT DO...
Edamame...
Azuki...
Soya...
I THINK THIS ONE REALLY LIKES YOU...
...THAT'S WHY SHE STRAYED.
OH, REALLY? WOW!
ANIMALS ARE VERY SENSITIVE CREA-TURES.
IF THEY LIKE YOU, IT MEANS YOUR HEART IS PURE.
SO TAKE THAT FEEL-ING...
...AND PUT IT INTO MUSIC, OKAY?
YEAH!
And so...
...HI, SORA-MAME!
I WANT TO SING YOU A SONG...
...I WROTE IT JUST FOR YOU!
...OH!
HI, LUKA-SEMPAI...!
GOOD MORN-ING...
...CER-BERUS!
meow
...

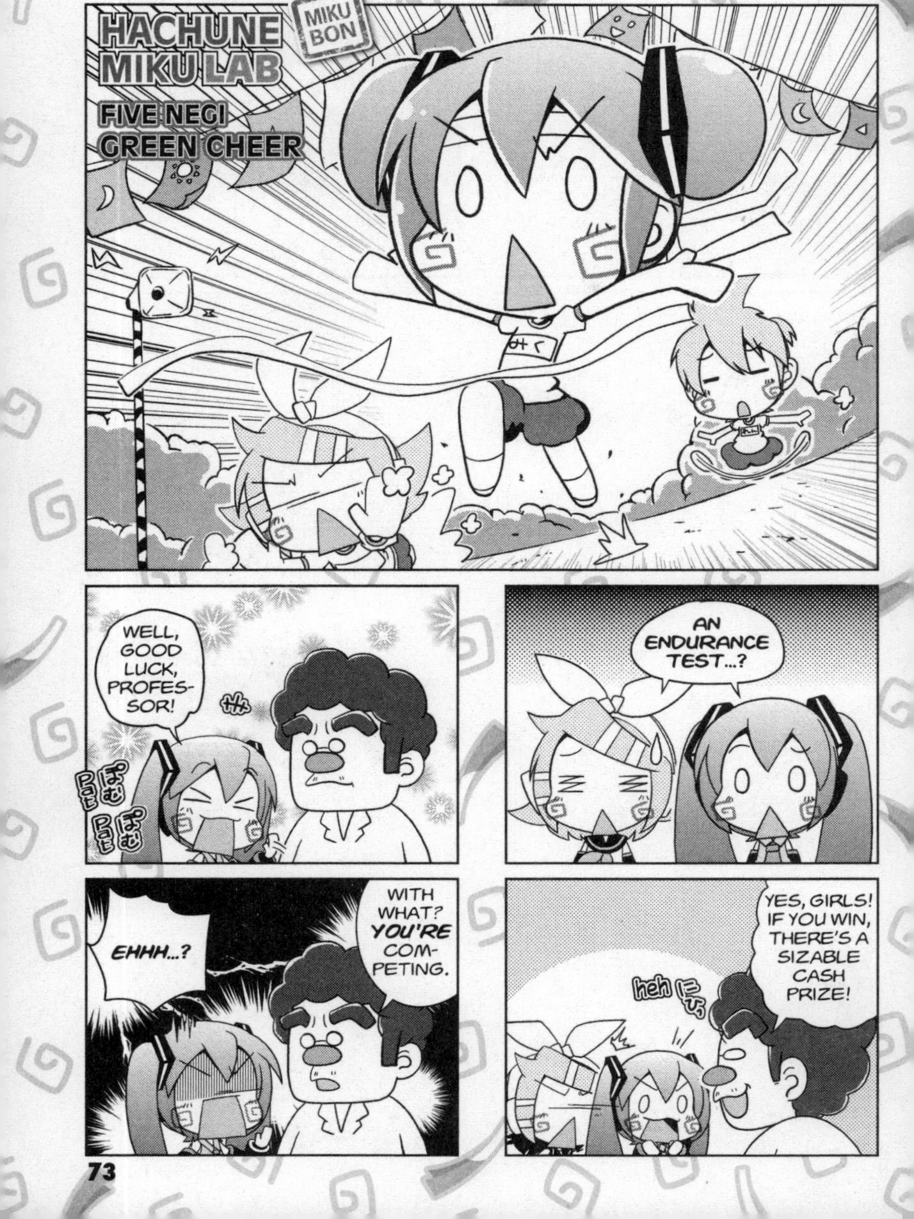
HACHUNE MIKU LAB
MIKU BON
FIVE NEGI GREEN CHEER
AN ENDURANCE TEST...?
WELL, GOOD LUCK, PROFES-SOR!
Pat ぽむ
Pat ぽむ
YES, GIRLS! IF YOU WIN, THERE'S A SIZABLE CASH PRIZE!
heh にっ
WITH WHAT? ***YOU'RE*** COM-PETING.
EHHH...?

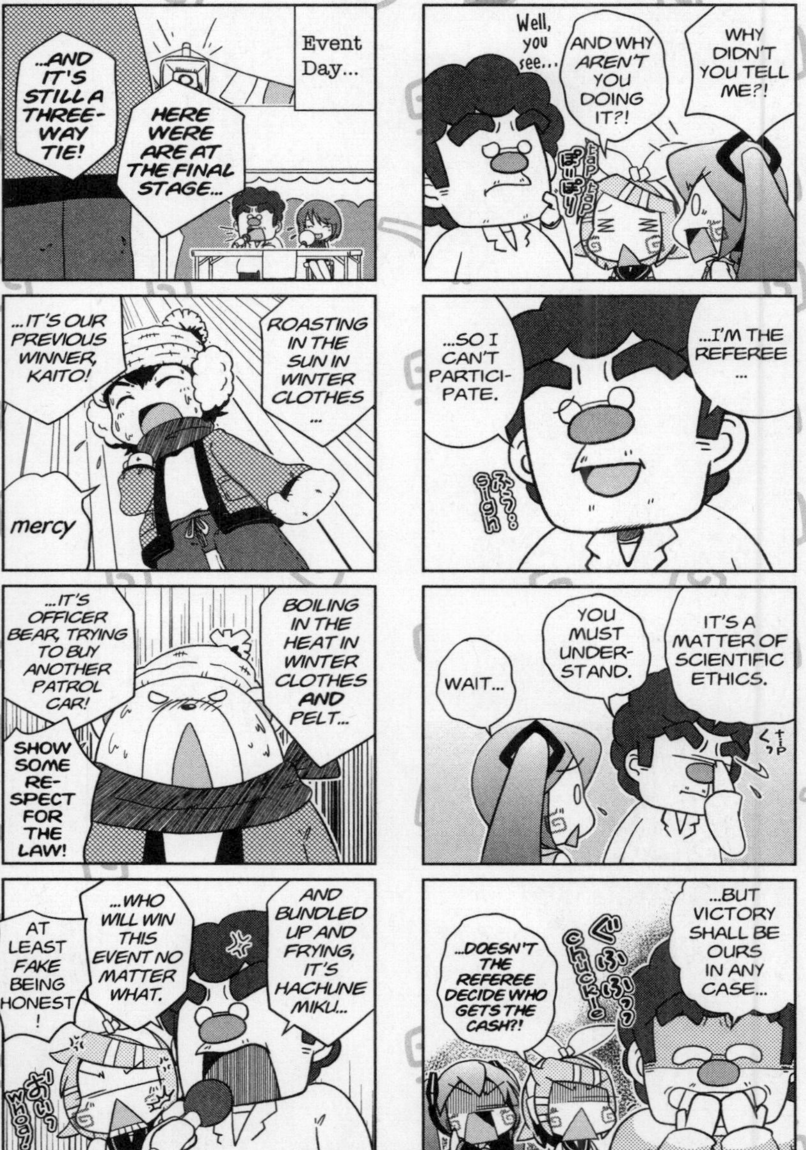
WHY DIDN'T YOU TELL ME?!
AND WHY AREN'T YOU DOING IT?!
Well, you see...
tap tap
...I'M THE REFEREE ...
...SO I CAN'T PARTICIPATE.
sigh
IT'S A MATTER OF SCIENTIFIC ETHICS.
YOU MUST UNDERSTAND.
WAIT...
tip
...BUT VICTORY SHALL BE OURS IN ANY CASE...
chuckle
...DOESN'T THE REFEREE DECIDE WHO GETS THE CASH?!
Event Day...
HERE WERE ARE AT THE FINAL STAGE...
...AND IT'S STILL A THREE-WAY TIE!
ROASTING IN THE SUN IN WINTER CLOTHES ...
...IT'S OUR PREVIOUS WINNER, KAITO!
mercy
BOILING IN THE HEAT IN WINTER CLOTHES AND PELT...
...IT'S OFFICER BEAR, TRYING TO BUY ANOTHER PATROL CAR!
SHOW SOME RESPECT FOR THE LAW!
AND BUNDLED UP AND FRYING, IT'S HACHUNE MIKU...
...WHO WILL WIN THIS EVENT NO MATTER WHAT.
AT LEAST FAKE BEING HONEST!
whoa!

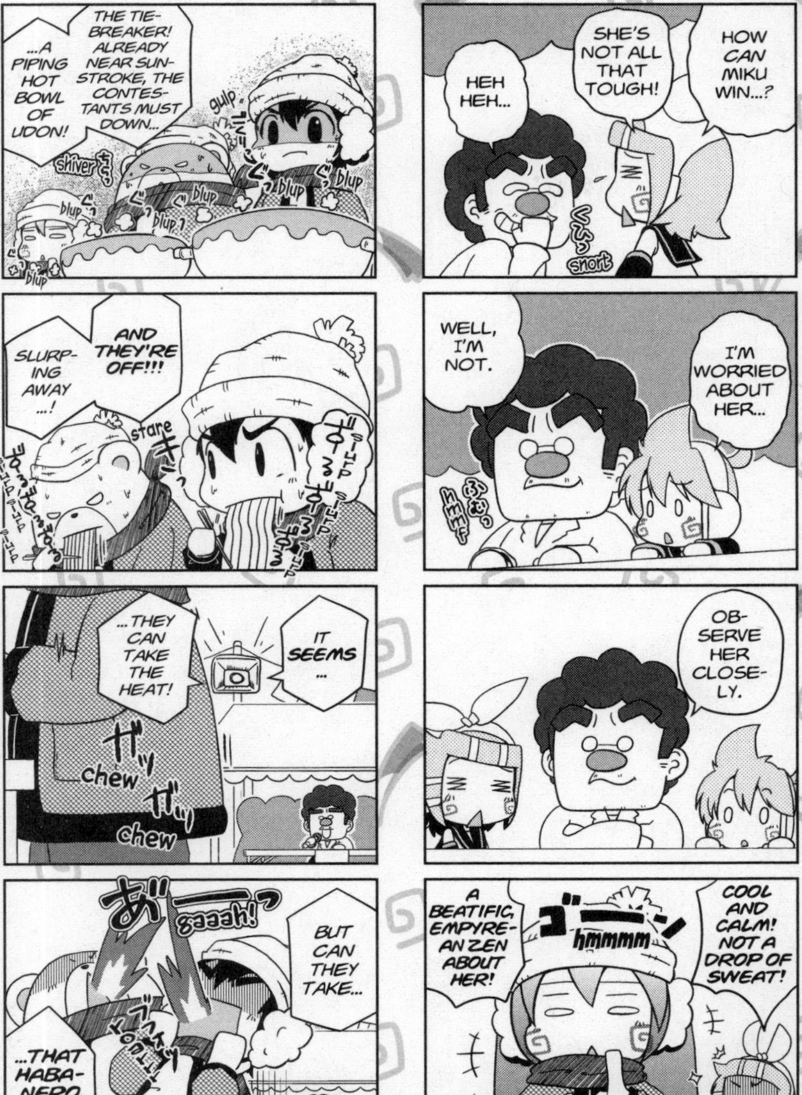
HOW CAN MIKU WIN...?
SHE'S NOT ALL THAT TOUGH!
HEH HEH...
snort
I'M WORRIED ABOUT HER...
WELL, I'M NOT.
hmmf
OB-SERVE HER CLOSE-LY.
COOL AND CALM! NOT A DROP OF SWEAT!
hmmmm
A BEATIFIC, EMPYRE-AN ZEN ABOUT HER!
THE TIE-BREAKER! ALREADY NEAR SUN-STROKE, THE CONTES-TANTS MUST DOWN...
...A PIPING HOT BOWL OF UDON!
gulp
shiver
blup
blup
blup
blup
blup
blup
AND THEY'RE OFF!!!
SLURP-ING AWAY ...!
stare
slurp
slurp
slurp
slurp
IT SEEMS ...
...THEY CAN TAKE THE HEAT!
chew
chew
aaaah!
BUT CAN THEY TAKE...
...THAT HABA-NERO BROTH ...?

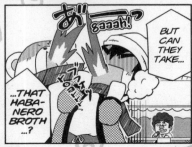

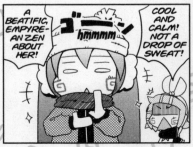

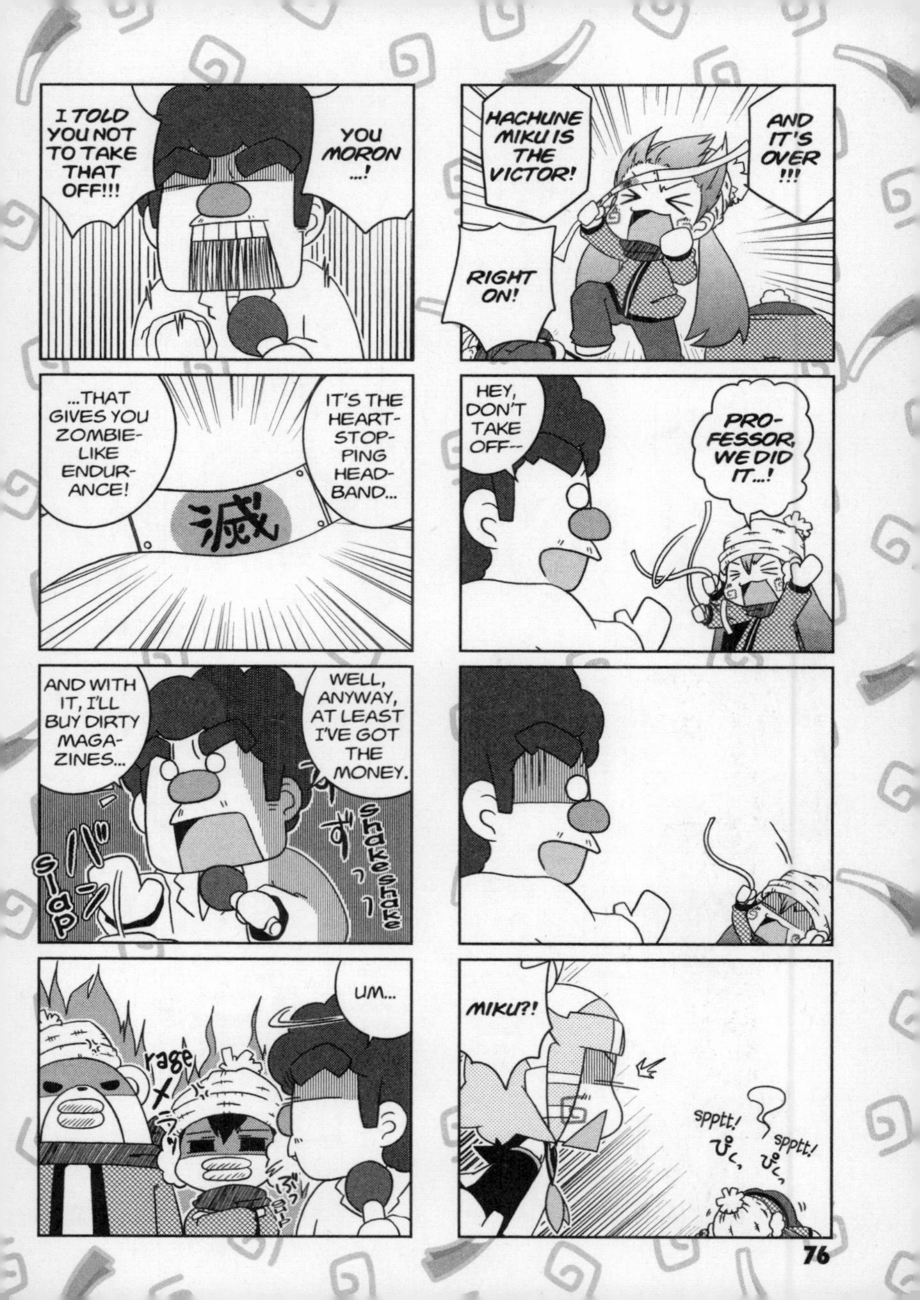
AND IT'S OVER!!!
HACHUNE MIKU IS THE VICTOR!
RIGHT ON!
YOU MORON...!
I TOLD YOU NOT TO TAKE THAT OFF!!!
PRO-FESSOR, WE DID IT...!
HEY, DON'T TAKE OFF--
IT'S THE HEART-STOPPING HEAD-BAND...
...THAT GIVES YOU ZOMBIE-LIKE ENDUR-ANCE!
滅
WELL, ANYWAY, AT LEAST I'VE GOT THE MONEY.
shake shake
AND WITH IT, I'LL BUY DIRTY MAGA-ZINES...
slap
MIKU?!
spptt!
ぴく
spptt!
ぴく
UM...
rage

HATSUNE MIKU

MIKUBON

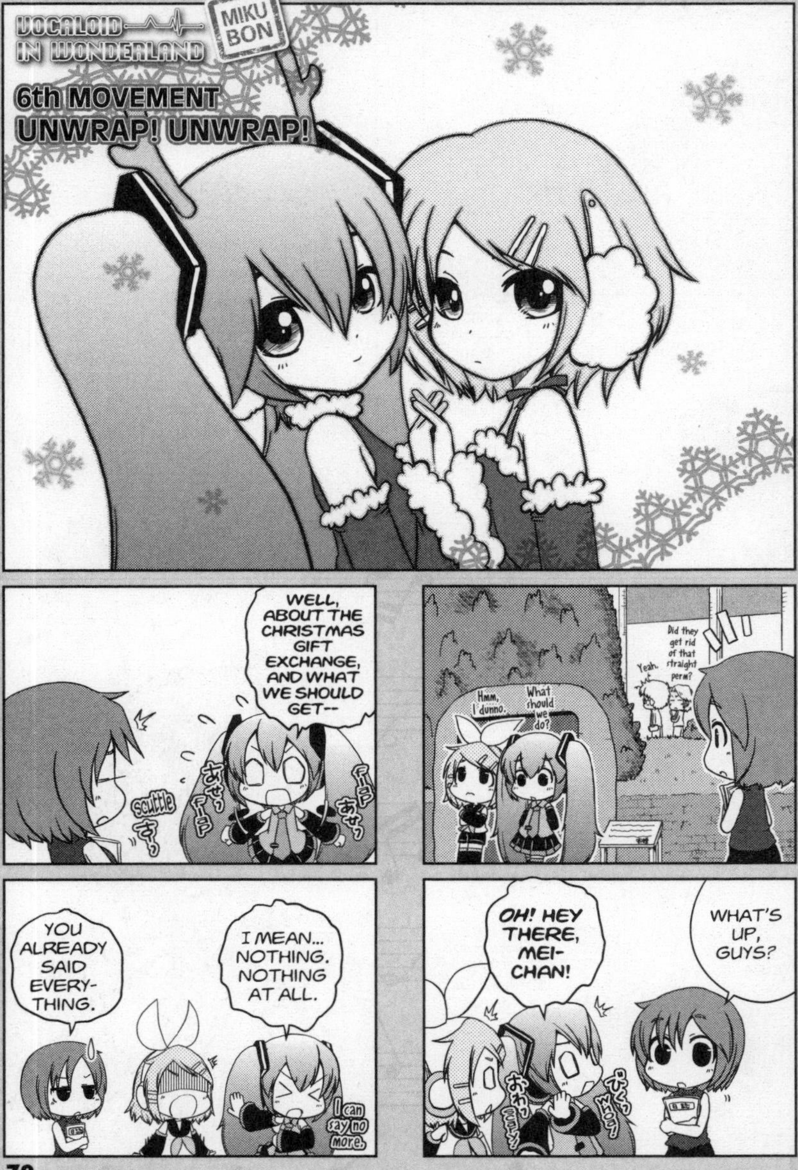
VOCALOID IN WONDERLAND
MIKU BON
6th MOVEMENT
UNWRAP! UNWRAP!
Did they get rid of that straight perm?
Yeah.
What should we do?
Hmm, I dunno.
WELL, ABOUT THE CHRISTMAS GIFT EXCHANGE, AND WHAT WE SHOULD GET--
scuttle
WHAT'S UP, GUYS?
OH! HEY THERE, MEI-CHAN!
I MEAN... NOTHING. NOTHING AT ALL.
I can say no more.
YOU ALREADY SAID EVERY-THING.

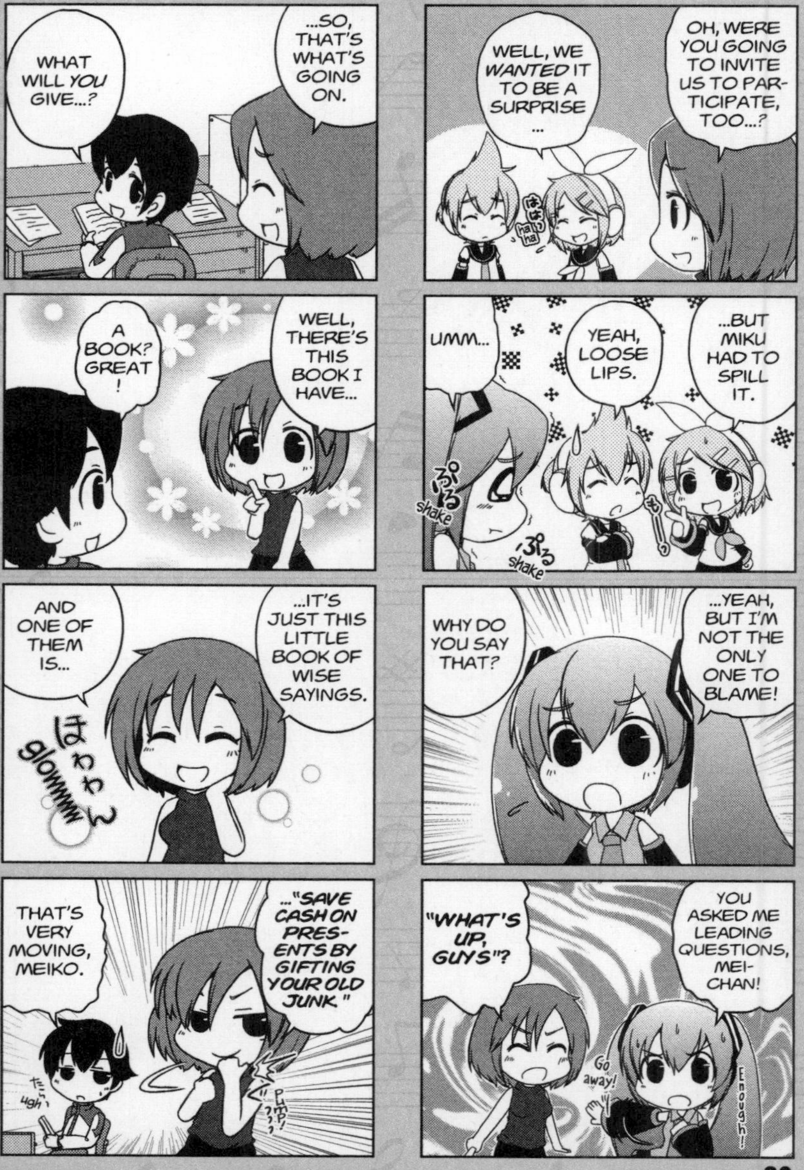
OH, WERE YOU GOING TO INVITE US TO PARTICIPATE, TOO...?
WELL, WE *WANTED* IT TO BE A SURPRISE ...
ははっ haha
...BUT MIKU HAD TO SPILL IT.
YEAH, LOOSE LIPS.
UMM...
ぷる shake
ぷる shake
...YEAH, BUT I'M NOT THE ONLY ONE TO BLAME!
WHY DO YOU SAY THAT?
YOU ASKED ME LEADING QUESTIONS, MEI-CHAN!
Enough!
Go away!
"WHAT'S UP, GUYS"?
...SO, THAT'S WHAT'S GOING ON.
WHAT WILL *YOU* GIVE...?
WELL, THERE'S THIS BOOK I HAVE...
A BOOK? GREAT!
...IT'S JUST THIS LITTLE BOOK OF WISE SAYINGS.
AND ONE OF THEM IS...
ほわわん glowwww
..."SAVE CASH ON PRESENTS BY GIFTING YOUR OLD JUNK."
THAT'S VERY MOVING, MEIKO.
PUMP!?

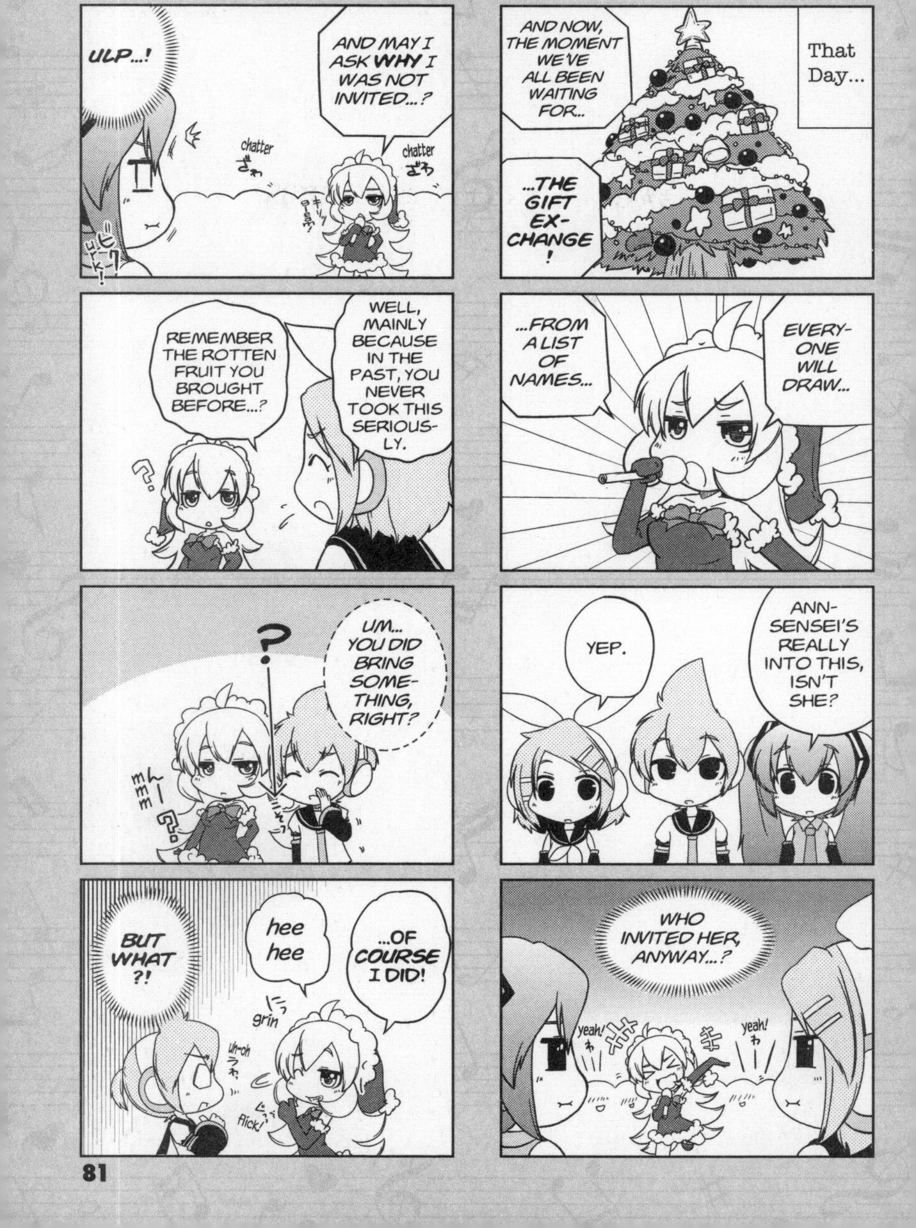
That Day...
AND NOW, THE MOMENT WE'VE ALL BEEN WAITING FOR...
...THE GIFT EX-CHANGE!
EVERY-ONE WILL DRAW...
...FROM A LIST OF NAMES...
ANN-SENSEI'S REALLY INTO THIS, ISN'T SHE?
YEP.
WHO INVITED HER, ANYWAY...?
yeah!
yeah!
AND MAY I ASK WHY I WAS NOT INVITED...?
chatter
chatter
ULP...!
URK-!
WELL, MAINLY BECAUSE IN THE PAST, YOU NEVER TOOK THIS SERIOUS-LY.
REMEMBER THE ROTTEN FRUIT YOU BROUGHT BEFORE...?
UM... YOU DID BRING SOME-THING, RIGHT?
mmm
...OF COURSE I DID!
hee hee
BUT WHAT?!
grin
uh-oh
flick!

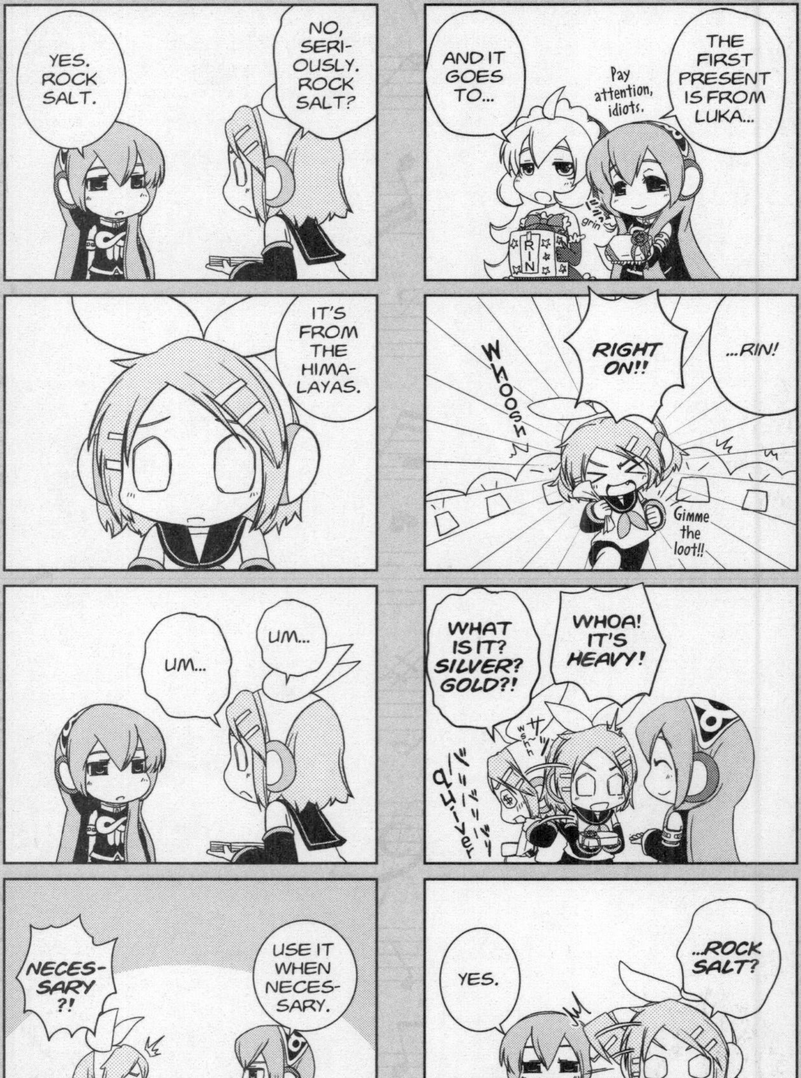
THE FIRST PRESENT IS FROM LUKA...
Pay attention, idiots.
AND IT GOES TO...
grin
...RIN!
RIGHT ON!!
WHOOSH
Gimme the loot!!
WHOA! IT'S HEAVY!
WHAT IS IT? SILVER? GOLD?!
wsh
quiver
...ROCK SALT?
YES.
psst
NO, SERI-OUSLY. ROCK SALT?
YES. ROCK SALT.
IT'S FROM THE HIMA-LAYAS.
UM...
UM...
USE IT WHEN NECES-SARY.
NECES-SARY?!

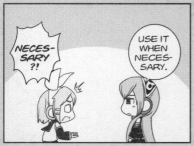

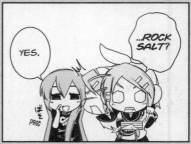

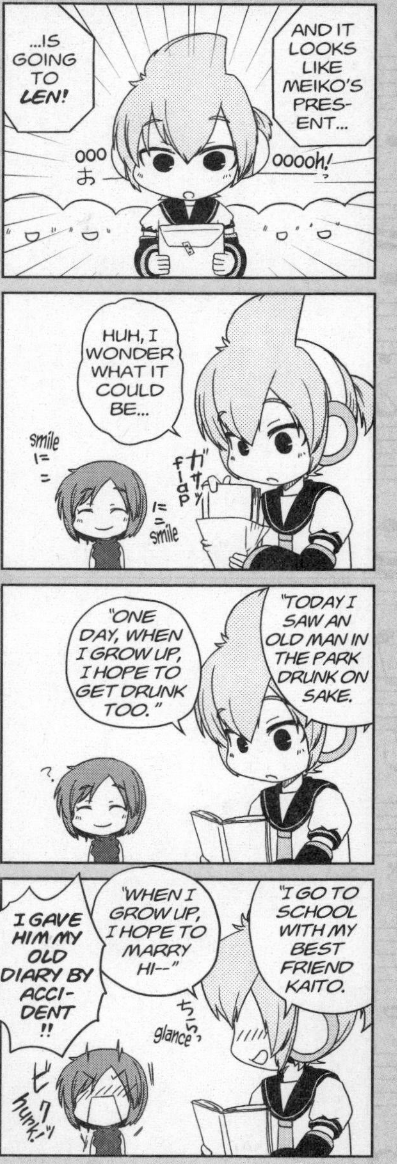
AND IT LOOKS LIKE MEIKO'S PRESENT...
...IS GOING TO LEN!
ooo
お—
ooooh!
HUH, I WONDER WHAT IT COULD BE...
smile
にこ
ガサッ
flap
にこ
smile
"TODAY I SAW AN OLD MAN IN THE PARK DRUNK ON SAKE.
"ONE DAY, WHEN I GROW UP, I HOPE TO GET DRUNK TOO."
?
"I GO TO SCHOOL WITH MY BEST FRIEND KAITO.
"WHEN I GROW UP, I HOPE TO MARRY HI--"
ちらっ
glance
I GAVE HIM MY OLD DIARY BY ACCIDENT!!
ビクッ
hunk!

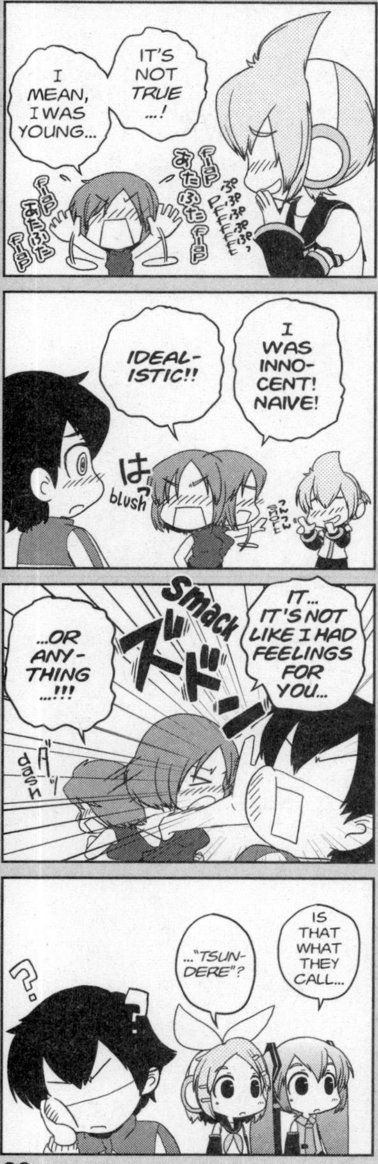
IT'S NOT TRUE...!
I MEAN, I WAS YOUNG...
ぷぷぷぷ
PFFFFFF
あたふた
flap
あたふた
flap
I WAS INNOCENT! NAIVE!
IDEALISTIC!!
はっ
blush
smile
IT... IT'S NOT LIKE I HAD FEELINGS FOR YOU...
...OR ANYTHING...!!!
smack
ズドーン
ダッ
dash
IS THAT WHAT THEY CALL...
..."TSUNDERE"?
?
?

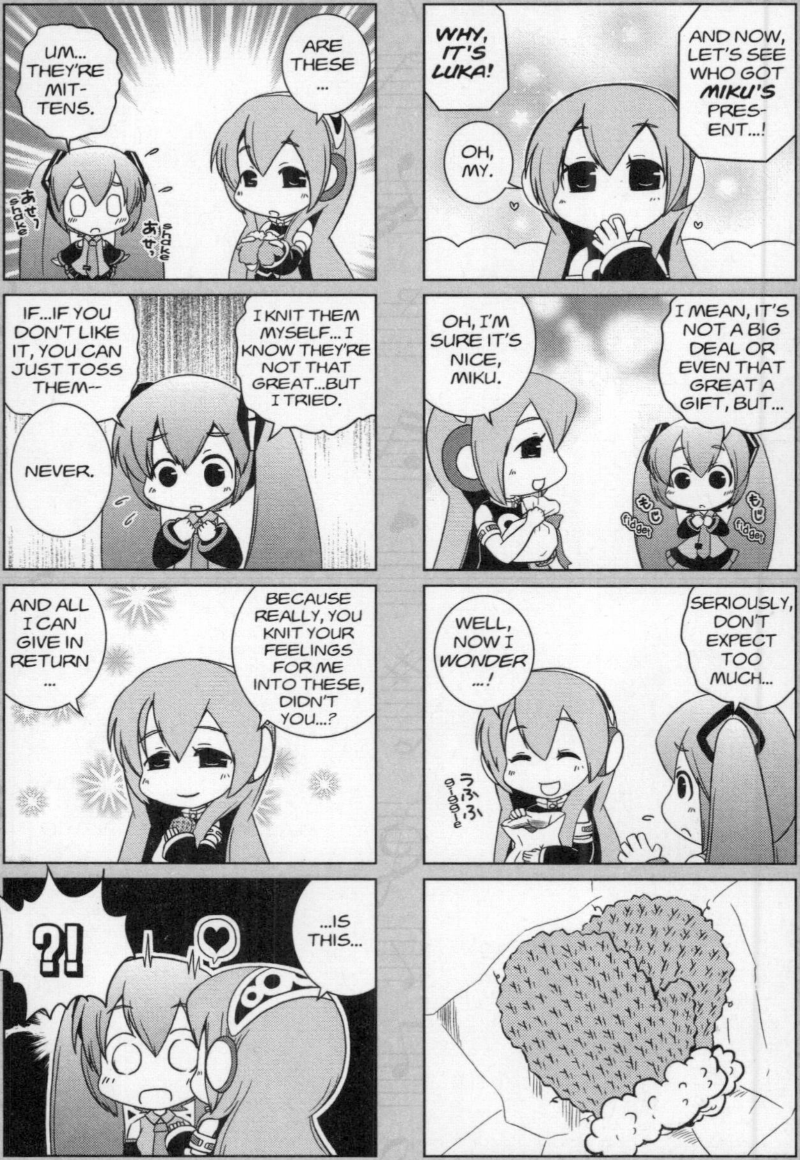
AND NOW, LET'S SEE WHO GOT **MIKU'S** PRESENT...!
WHY, IT'S LUKA!
OH, MY.
ARE THESE ...
UM... THEY'RE MIT-TENS.
あせっ shake
あせ, shake
I MEAN, IT'S NOT A BIG DEAL OR EVEN THAT GREAT A GIFT, BUT...
OH, I'M SURE IT'S NICE, MIKU.
もじ fidget
もじ fidget
I KNIT THEM MYSELF... I KNOW THEY'RE NOT THAT GREAT...BUT I TRIED.
IF...IF YOU DON'T LIKE IT, YOU CAN JUST TOSS THEM--
NEVER.
SERIOUSLY, DON'T EXPECT TOO MUCH...
WELL, NOW I *WONDER* ...!
うふふ giggle
BECAUSE REALLY, YOU KNIT YOUR FEELINGS FOR ME INTO THESE, DIDN'T YOU...?
AND ALL I CAN GIVE IN RETURN ...
...IS THIS...
?!

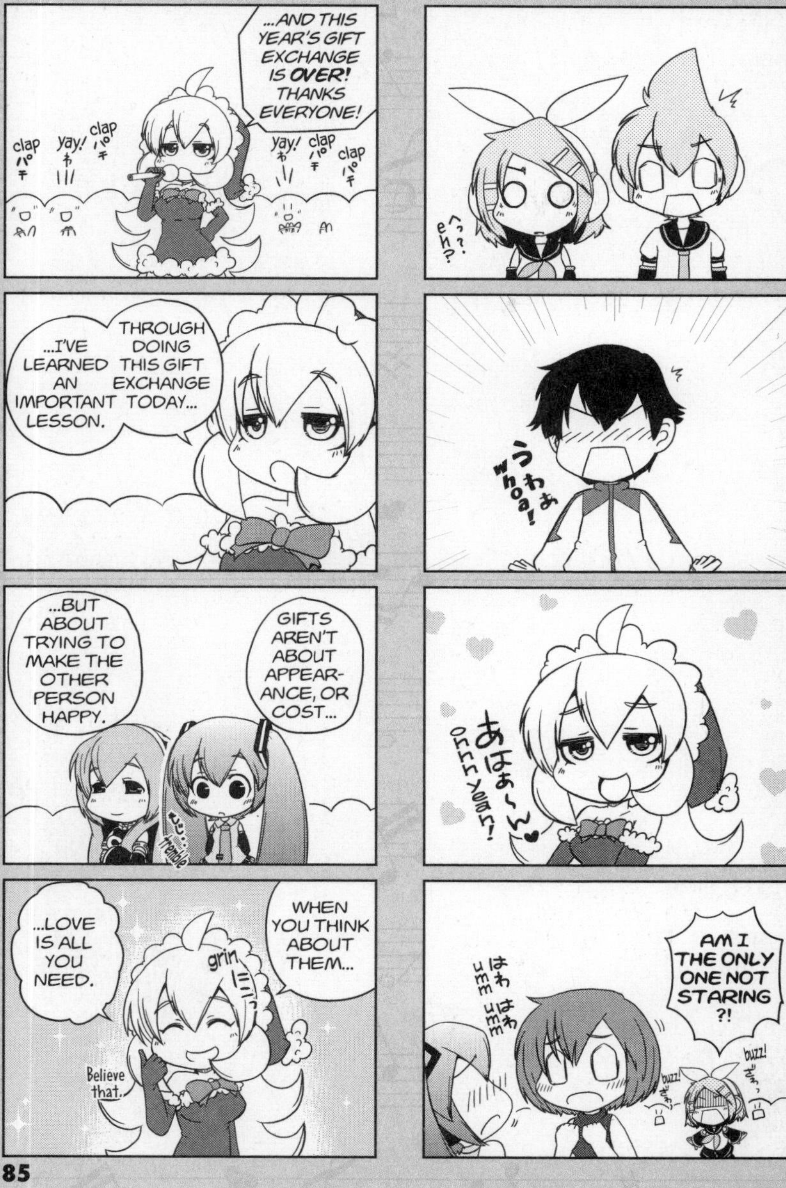

へっ？ eh?
うわぁ whoa!
あはぁ～ん Ohhhh yeah!
はわ umm はわ umm
AM I THE ONLY ONE NOT STARING?!
ざわっ buzz!
ざわっ buzz!
...AND THIS YEAR'S GIFT EXCHANGE IS OVER! THANKS EVERYONE!
clap パチ
yay! わ
clap パチ
yay! わ
clap パチ
clap パチ
THROUGH DOING THIS GIFT EXCHANGE TODAY...
...I'VE LEARNED AN IMPORTANT LESSON.
GIFTS AREN'T ABOUT APPEARANCE, OR COST...
...BUT ABOUT TRYING TO MAKE THE OTHER PERSON HAPPY.
tremble
WHEN YOU THINK ABOUT THEM...
...LOVE IS ALL YOU NEED.
grin ニコッ
Believe that.

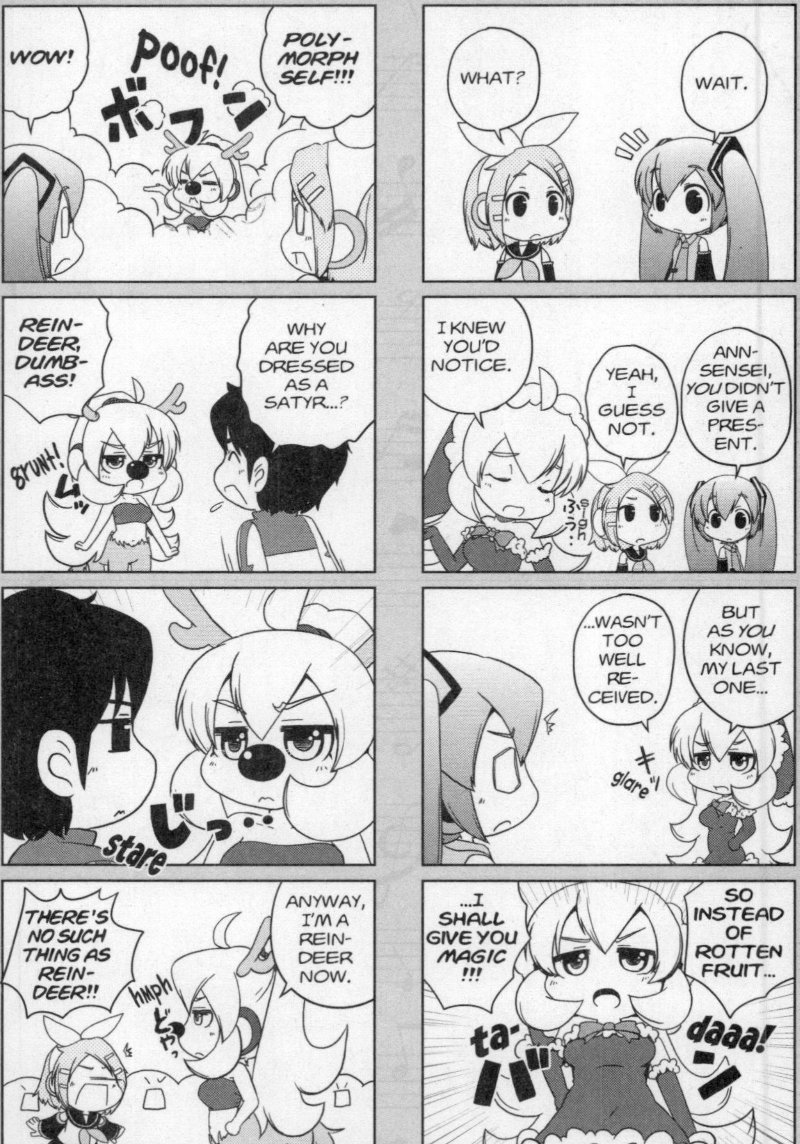
WAIT.
WHAT?
ANN-SENSEI, YOU DIDN'T GIVE A PRES-ENT.
YEAH, I GUESS NOT.
sigh
I KNEW YOU'D NOTICE.
BUT AS YOU KNOW, MY LAST ONE...
...WASN'T TOO WELL RE-CEIVED.
glare
SO INSTEAD OF ROTTEN FRUIT...
...I SHALL GIVE YOU MAGIC!!!
ta-daaa!
POLY-MORPH SELF!!!
Poof!
ボフン
WOW!
WHY ARE YOU DRESSED AS A SATYR...?
REIN-DEER, DUMB-ASS!
grunt!
ムッ
stare
じっ
ANYWAY, I'M A REIN-DEER NOW.
hmph
どやっ
THERE'S NO SUCH THING AS REIN-DEER!!

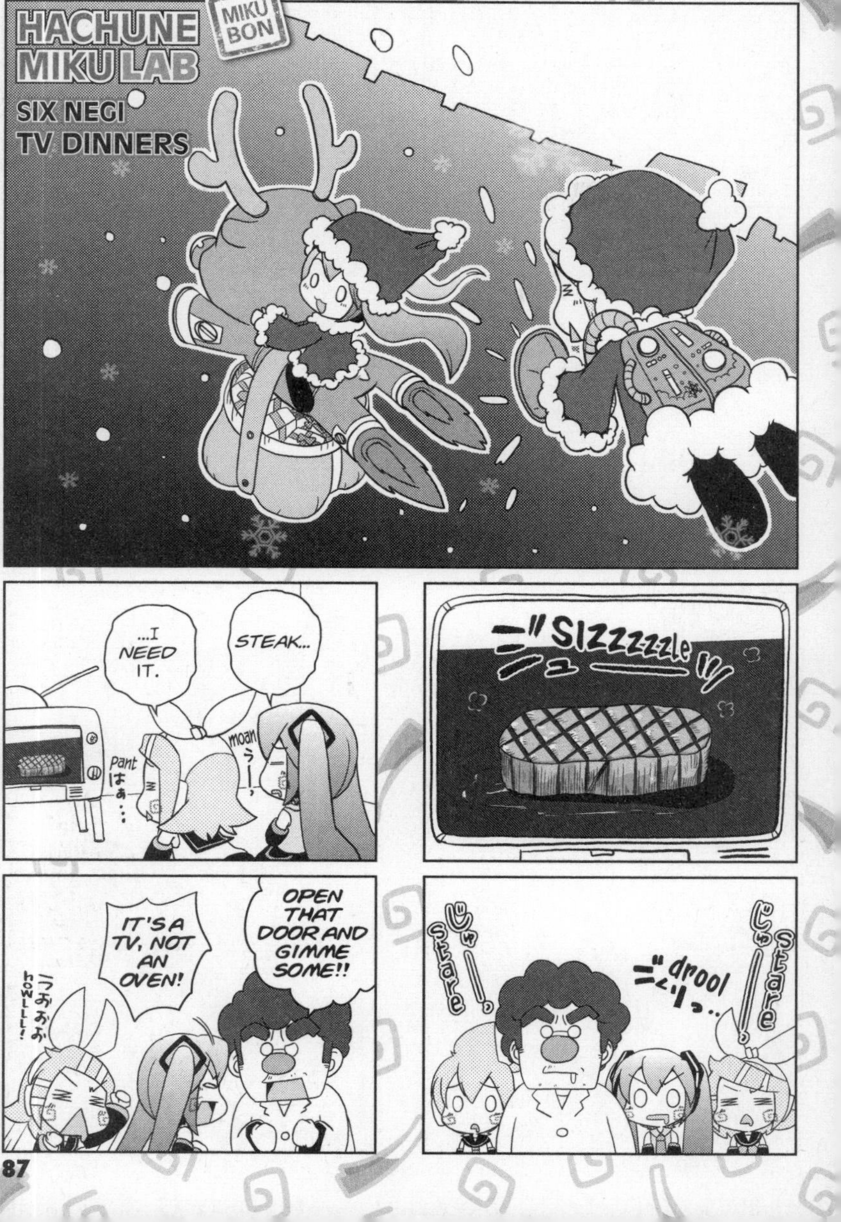
HACHUNE MIKU LAB
MIKU BON
SIX NEGI TV DINNERS
ジュー SIZZZzzzle
STEAK...
...I NEED IT.
moan う—,
pant はぁ...
じゅー stare
ゴクリっ... drool
じゅー stare
OPEN THAT DOOR AND GIMME SOME!!
IT'S A TV, NOT AN OVEN!
うおおお HOWLLL!

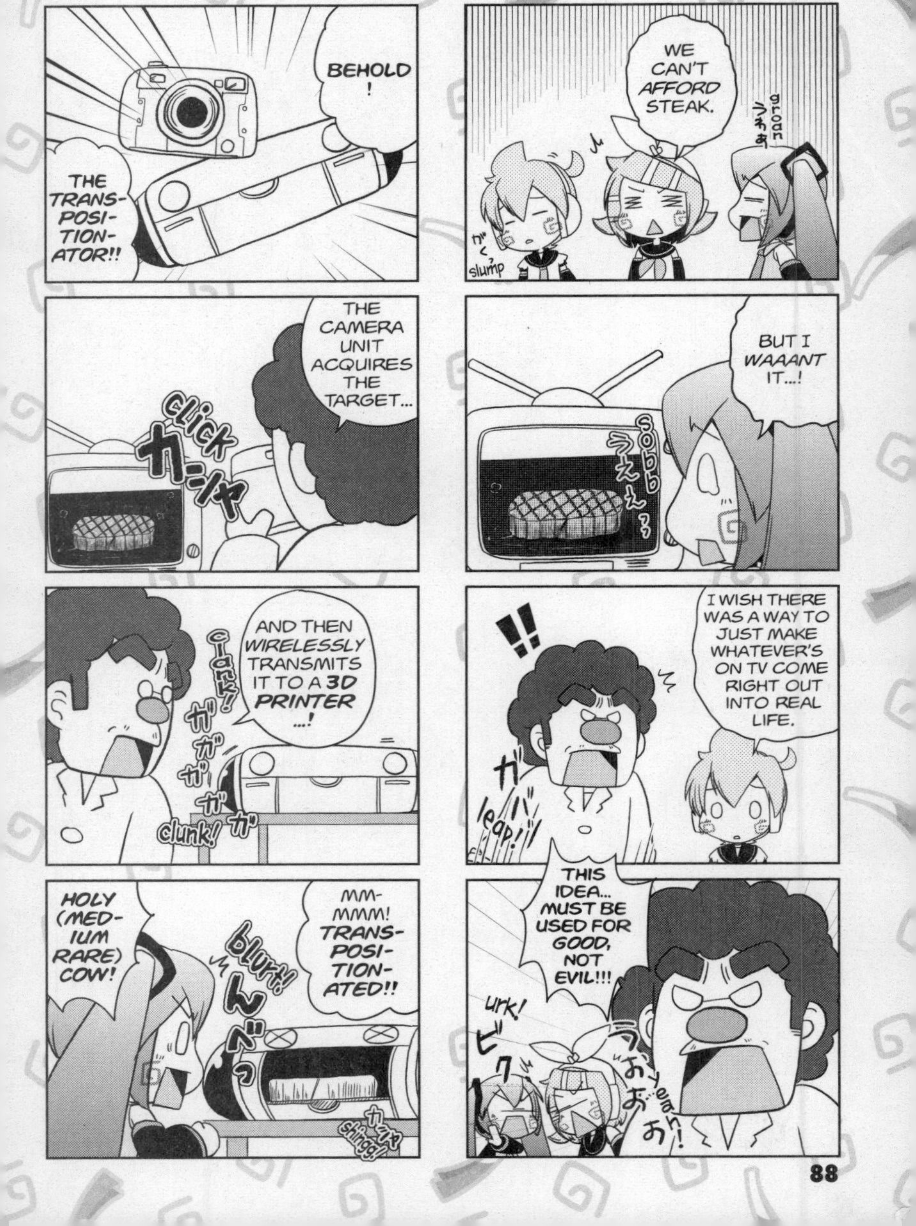

WE CAN'T AFFORD STEAK.
groan
うわあ
がくっ
slump
BUT I WAAANT IT...!
sobb
うえぇ〜
I WISH THERE WAS A WAY TO JUST MAKE WHATEVER'S ON TV COME RIGHT OUT INTO REAL LIFE.
!!
ガバ
leap!!
THIS IDEA... MUST BE USED FOR GOOD, NOT EVIL!!!
urk!
ビクッ
yeah!
うおおおっ
BEHOLD!
THE TRANS-POSI-TION-ATOR!!
THE CAMERA UNIT ACQUIRES THE TARGET...
click
カシャ
AND THEN WIRELESSLY TRANSMITS IT TO A 3D PRINTER...!
clank!
ガガガガガ
clunk!
HOLY (MED-IUM RARE) COW!
MM-MMM! TRANS-POSI-TION-ATED!!
blurt!
んべっ
shingg!

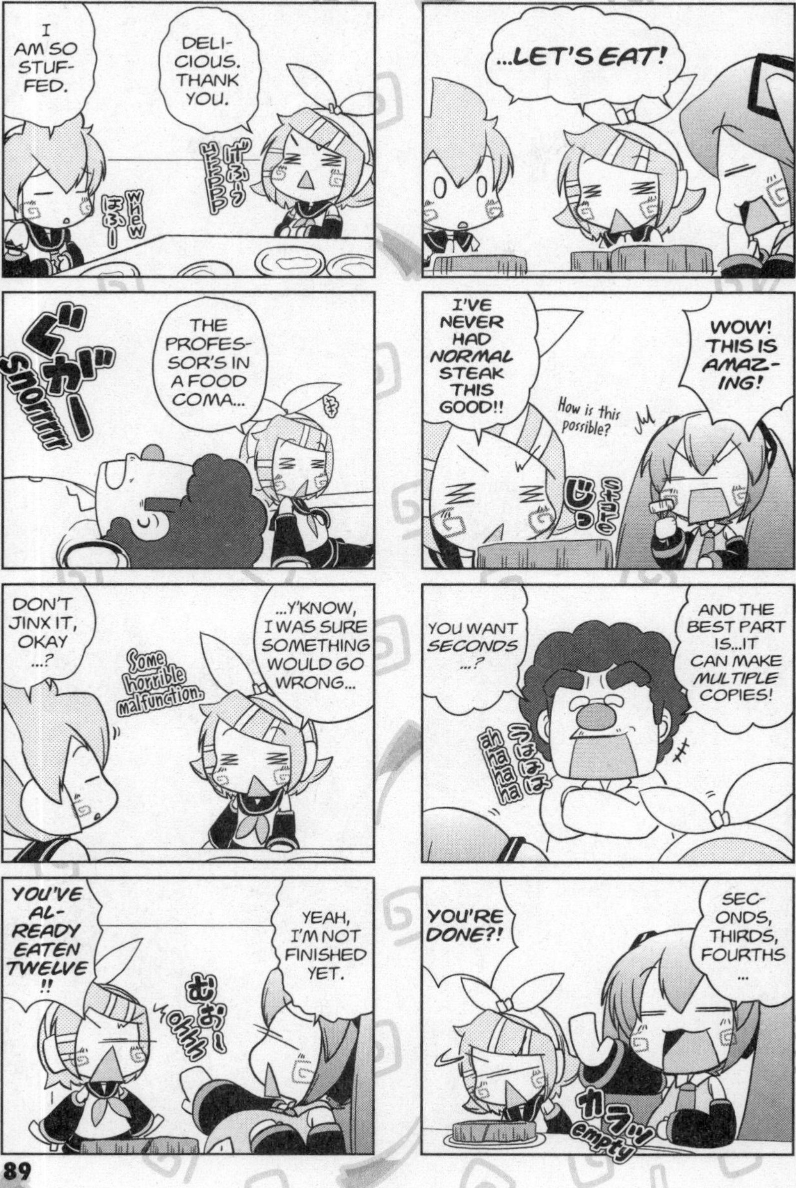
...LET'S EAT!
WOW! THIS IS AMAZING!
I'VE NEVER HAD NORMAL STEAK THIS GOOD!!
How is this possible?
じっ stare
AND THE BEST PART IS...IT CAN MAKE MULTIPLE COPIES!
YOU WANT SECONDS ...?
うははは ahahaha
SECONDS, THIRDS, FOURTHS ...
YOU'RE DONE?!
カラッ empty
DELICIOUS. THANK YOU.
げふーっ burrrp
I AM SO STUFFED.
はふー whew
THE PROFESSOR'S IN A FOOD COMA...
ぐがー snorrrrr
...Y'KNOW, I WAS SURE SOMETHING WOULD GO WRONG...
Some horrible malfunction.
DON'T JINX IT, OKAY ...?
YEAH, I'M NOT FINISHED YET.
むおー ohhh
YOU'VE ALREADY EATEN TWELVE!!

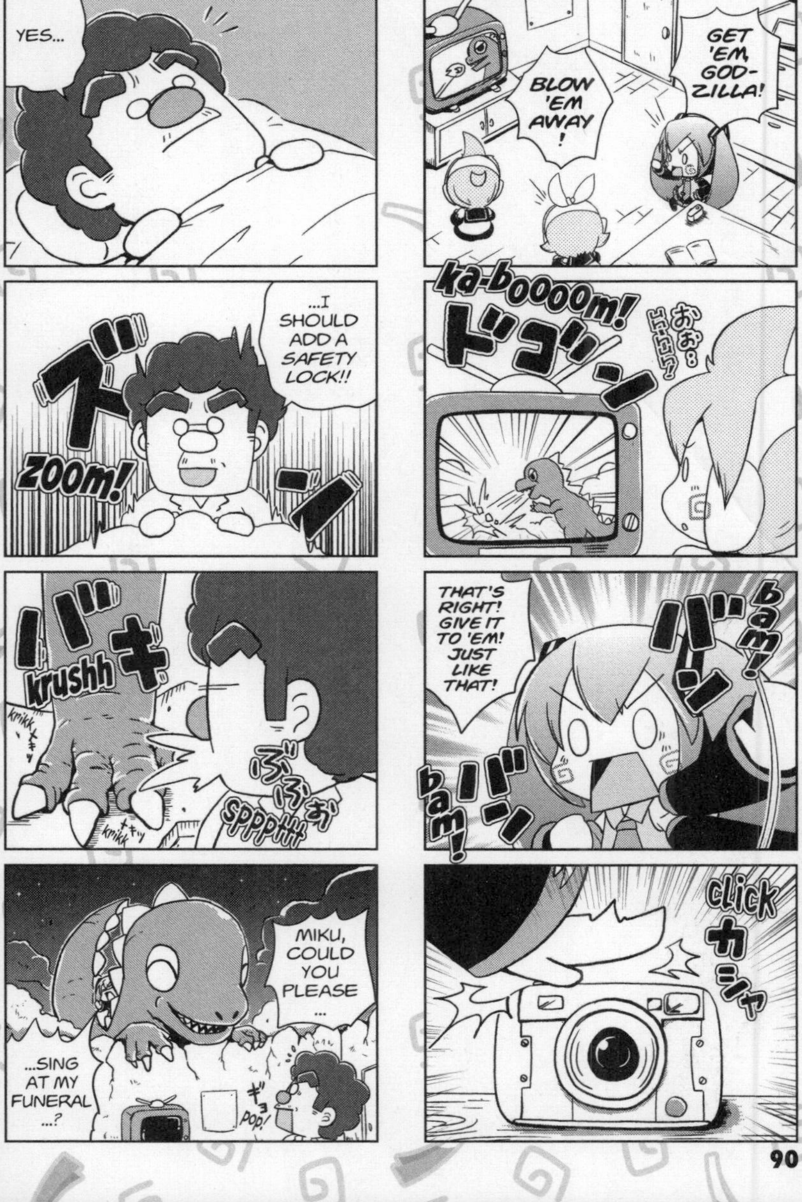
GET 'EM, GOD-ZILLA!
BLOW 'EM AWAY!
YES...
ka-boooom!
ドゴッン
...I SHOULD ADD A SAFETY LOCK!!
zoom!
THAT'S RIGHT! GIVE IT TO 'EM! JUST LIKE THAT!
bam!
bam!
krushh
krikk
krikk
sppptttt
click
カシャ
MIKU, COULD YOU PLEASE ...
...SING AT MY FUNERAL ...?
pop!

HATSUNE MIKU

MIKUBON

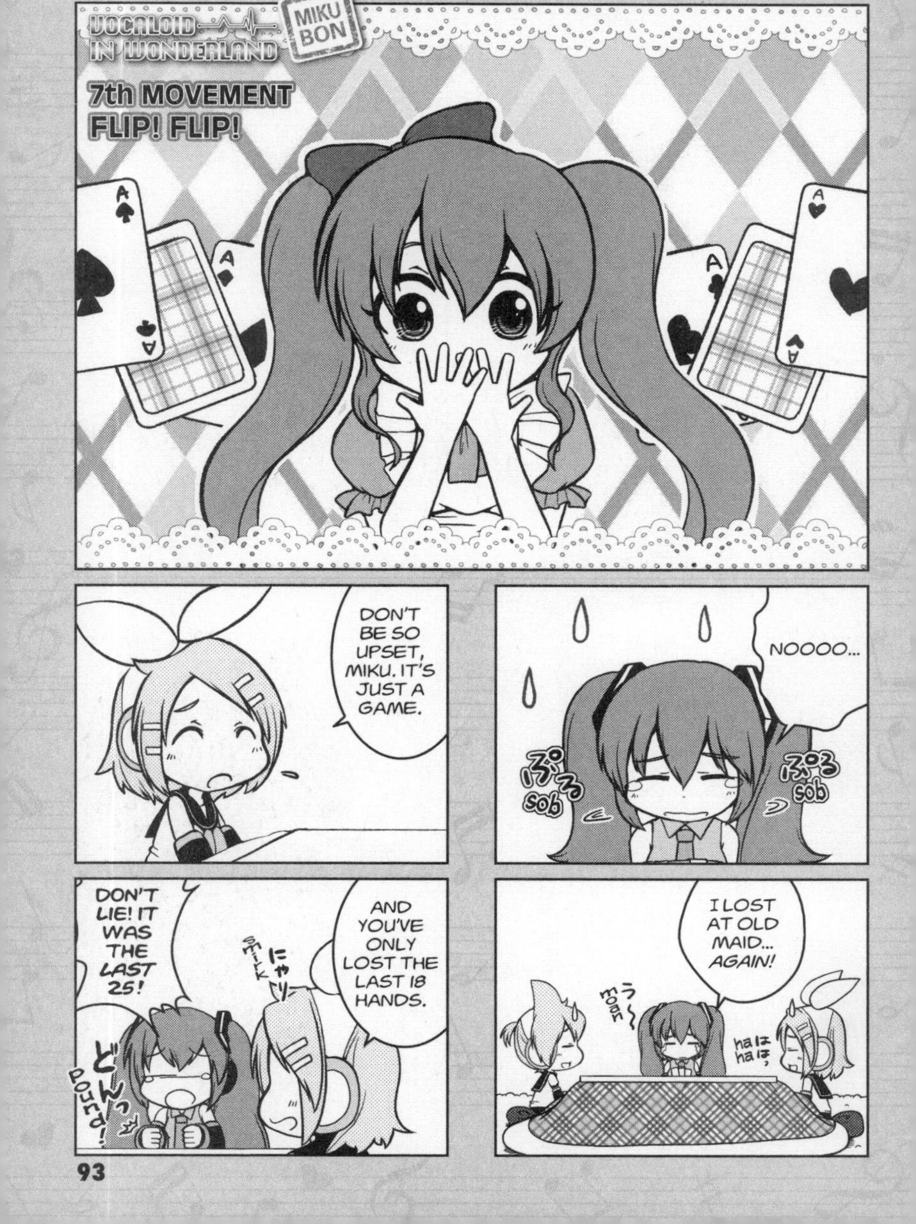
VOCALOID IN WONDERLAND
MIKU BON
7th MOVEMENT
FLIP! FLIP!
NOOOO...
ぷるぷる sob sob
DON'T BE SO UPSET, MIKU. IT'S JUST A GAME.
I LOST AT OLD MAID... AGAIN!
う~ moan
haはhaは
AND YOU'VE ONLY LOST THE LAST 18 HANDS.
にやり smirk
DON'T LIE! IT WAS THE LAST 25!
どんっ pound!

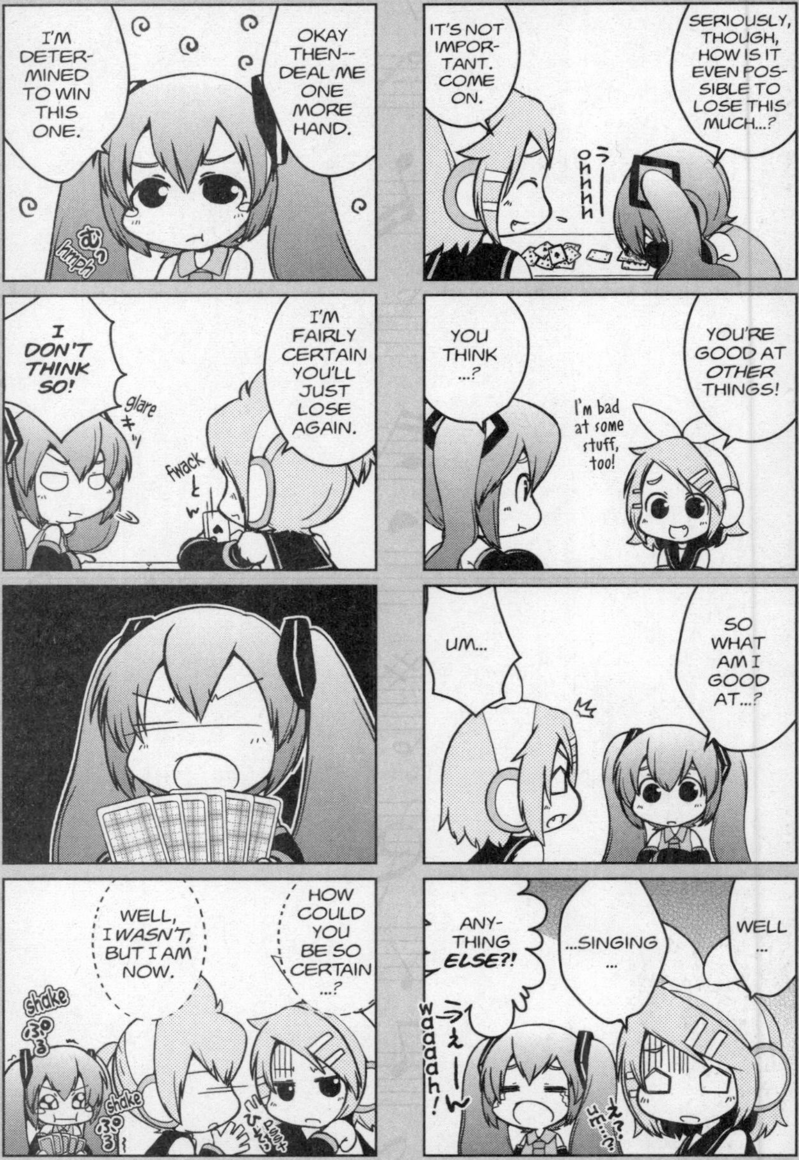
SERIOUSLY, THOUGH, HOW IS IT EVEN POSSIBLE TO LOSE THIS MUCH...?
ohhhh
IT'S NOT IMPORTANT. COME ON.
YOU'RE GOOD AT OTHER THINGS!
I'm bad at some stuff, too!
YOU THINK ...?
SO WHAT AM I GOOD AT...?
UM...
WELL ...
...SINGING ...
ANYTHING ELSE?!
waaaah!
uE...?
OKAY THEN-- DEAL ME ONE MORE HAND.
I'M DETERMINED TO WIN THIS ONE.
hmph
I'M FAIRLY CERTAIN YOU'LL JUST LOSE AGAIN.
fwack
glare
I DON'T THINK SO!
HOW COULD YOU BE SO CERTAIN ...?
WELL, I WASN'T, BUT I AM NOW.
shake
shake

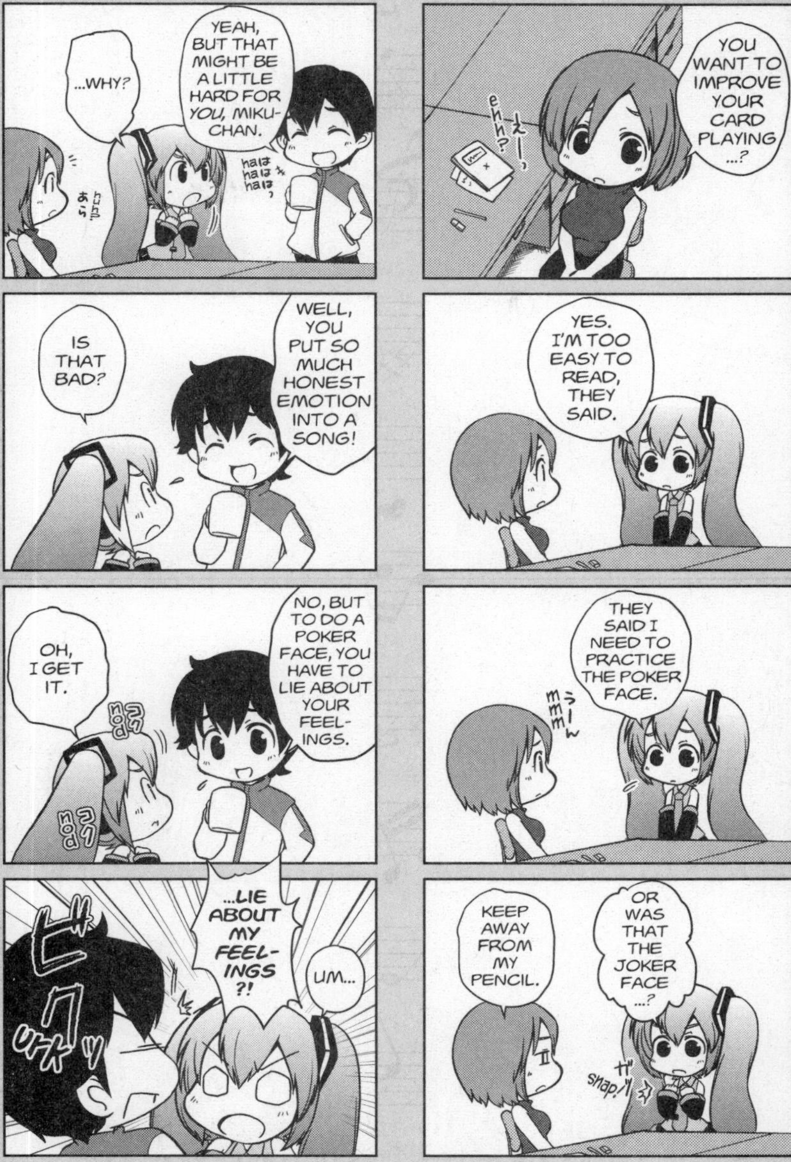
YOU WANT TO IMPROVE YOUR CARD PLAYING ...?
ehh?
YES. I'M TOO EASY TO READ, THEY SAID.
THEY SAID I NEED TO PRACTICE THE POKER FACE.
mmm
OR WAS THAT THE JOKER FACE ...?
KEEP AWAY FROM MY PENCIL.
snap!
YEAH, BUT THAT MIGHT BE A LITTLE HARD FOR YOU, MIKU-CHAN.
...WHY?
ha ha ha
huh?
WELL, YOU PUT SO MUCH HONEST EMOTION INTO A SONG!
IS THAT BAD?
NO, BUT TO DO A POKER FACE, YOU HAVE TO LIE ABOUT YOUR FEEL- INGS.
OH, I GET IT.
nod
nod
...LIE ABOUT MY FEEL- INGS ?!
UM...
urk

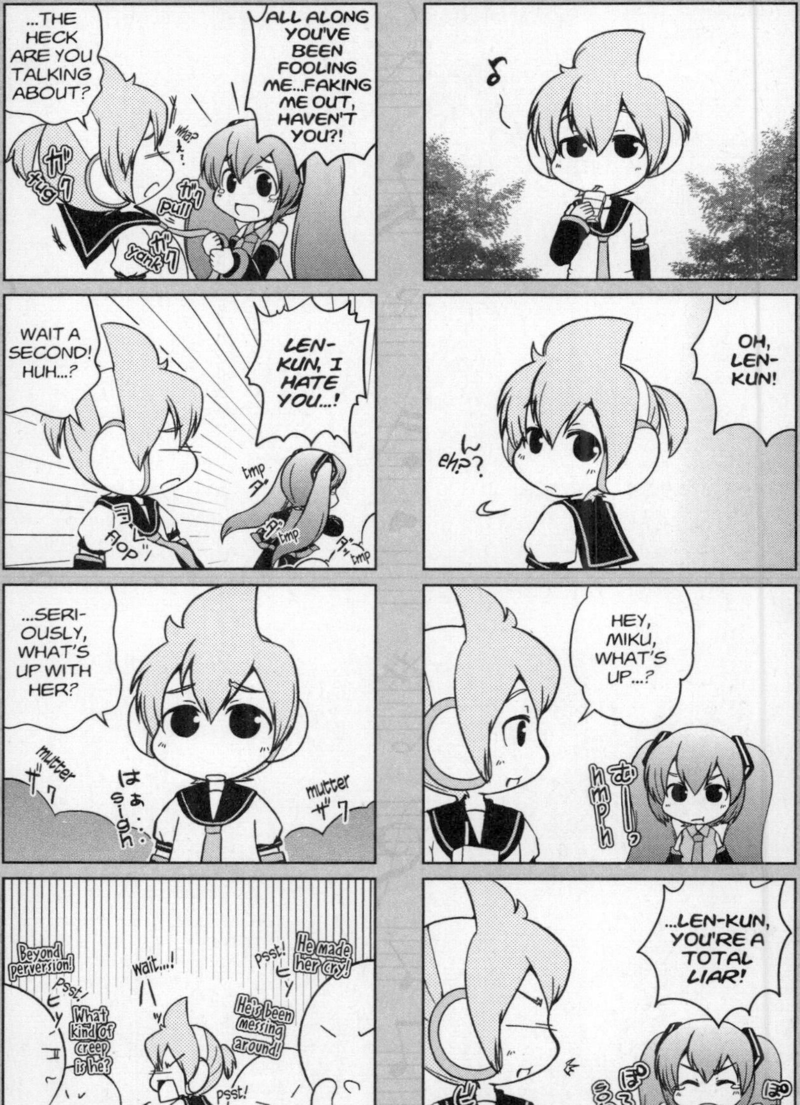

♪
ALL ALONG YOU'VE BEEN FOOLING ME...FAKING ME OUT, HAVEN'T YOU?!
...THE HECK ARE YOU TALKING ABOUT?
wha? え？
tug
pull
yank
OH, LEN-KUN!
eh?
LEN-KUN, I HATE YOU...!
WAIT A SECOND! HUH...?
tmp
tmp
tmp
flop
HEY, MIKU, WHAT'S UP...?
hmph
...SERI-OUSLY, WHAT'S UP WITH HER?
mutter
はぁ... sigh
mutter
...LEN-KUN, YOU'RE A TOTAL LIAR!
sob!
sob!
He made her cry!
psst!
He's been messing around!
wait...!
Beyond perversion!
Psst!
What kind of creep is he?
psst!
psst!

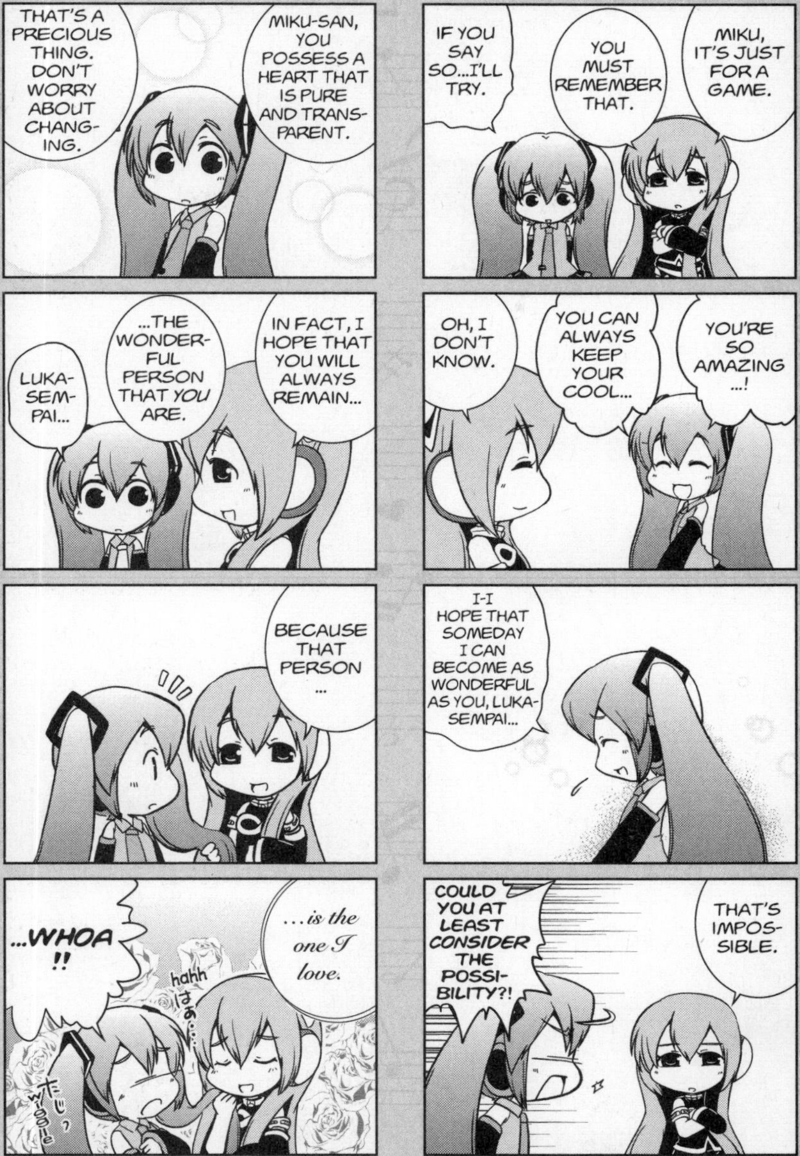
MIKU, IT'S JUST FOR A GAME.
YOU MUST REMEMBER THAT.
IF YOU SAY SO...I'LL TRY.
YOU'RE SO AMAZING ...!
YOU CAN ALWAYS KEEP YOUR COOL...
OH, I DON'T KNOW.
I-I HOPE THAT SOMEDAY I CAN BECOME AS WONDERFUL AS YOU, LUKA-SEMPAI...
THAT'S IMPOSSIBLE.
COULD YOU AT LEAST CONSIDER THE POSSIBILITY?!
MIKU-SAN, YOU POSSESS A HEART THAT IS PURE AND TRANSPARENT.
THAT'S A PRECIOUS THING. DON'T WORRY ABOUT CHANGING.
IN FACT, I HOPE THAT YOU WILL ALWAYS REMAIN...
...THE WONDERFUL PERSON THAT *YOU* ARE.
LUKA-SEMPAI...
BECAUSE THAT PERSON ...
...is the one I love.
hahh
...WHOA !!
wiggle

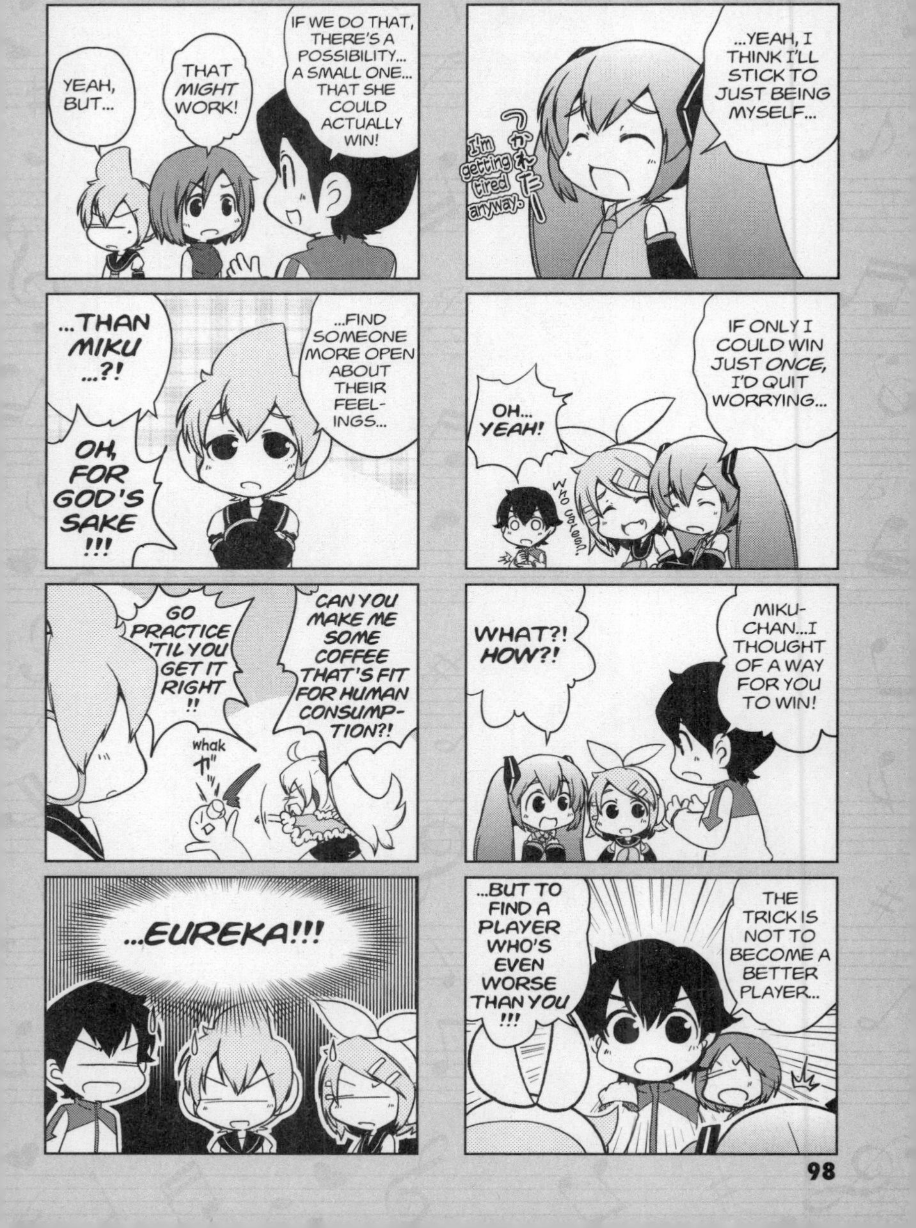
...YEAH, I THINK I'LL STICK TO JUST BEING MYSELF...
I'm getting tired anyway.
つかれた～
IF ONLY I COULD WIN JUST ONCE, I'D QUIT WORRYING...
OH... YEAH!
Who cares?
MIKU-CHAN...I THOUGHT OF A WAY FOR YOU TO WIN!
WHAT?! HOW?!
THE TRICK IS NOT TO BECOME A BETTER PLAYER...
...BUT TO FIND A PLAYER WHO'S EVEN WORSE THAN YOU!!!
IF WE DO THAT, THERE'S A POSSIBILITY... A SMALL ONE... THAT SHE COULD ACTUALLY WIN!
THAT MIGHT WORK!
YEAH, BUT...
...FIND SOMEONE MORE OPEN ABOUT THEIR FEEL-INGS...
...THAN MIKU...?!
OH, FOR GOD'S SAKE!!!
CAN YOU MAKE ME SOME COFFEE THAT'S FIT FOR HUMAN CONSUMP-TION?!
GO PRACTICE 'TIL YOU GET IT RIGHT!!
whak
ガッ
...EUREKA!!!

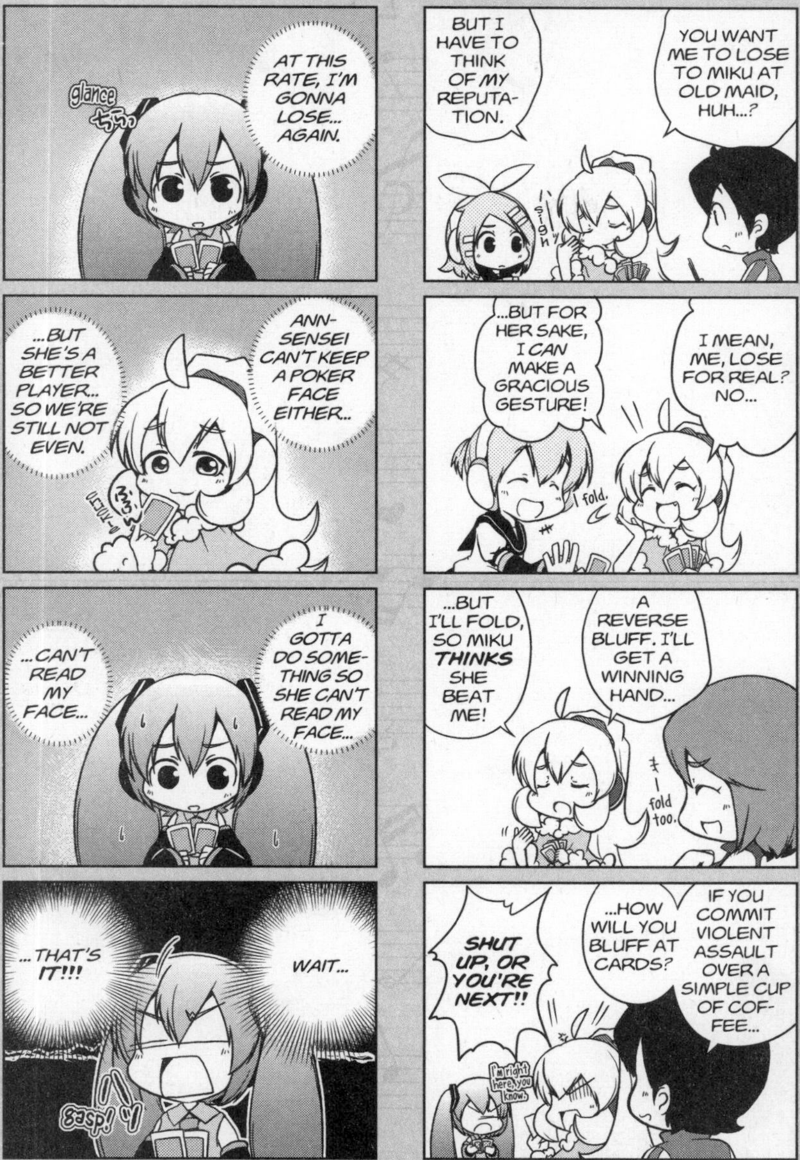
YOU WANT ME TO LOSE TO MIKU AT OLD MAID, HUH...?
BUT I HAVE TO THINK OF MY REPUTATION.
sigh
I MEAN, ME, LOSE FOR REAL? NO...
...BUT FOR HER SAKE, I CAN MAKE A GRACIOUS GESTURE!
I fold.
A REVERSE BLUFF. I'LL GET A WINNING HAND...
...BUT I'LL FOLD, SO MIKU *THINKS* SHE BEAT ME!
fold too.
IF YOU COMMIT VIOLENT ASSAULT OVER A SIMPLE CUP OF COFFEE...
...HOW WILL YOU BLUFF AT CARDS?
SHUT UP, OR YOU'RE NEXT!!
I'm right here, you know.
AT THIS RATE, I'M GONNA LOSE... AGAIN.
glance
ANN-SENSEI CAN'T KEEP A POKER FACE EITHER...
...BUT SHE'S A BETTER PLAYER... SO WE'RE STILL NOT EVEN.
I GOTTA DO SOMETHING SO SHE CAN'T READ MY FACE...
...CAN'T READ MY FACE...
WAIT...
...THAT'S *IT*!!!
gasp!

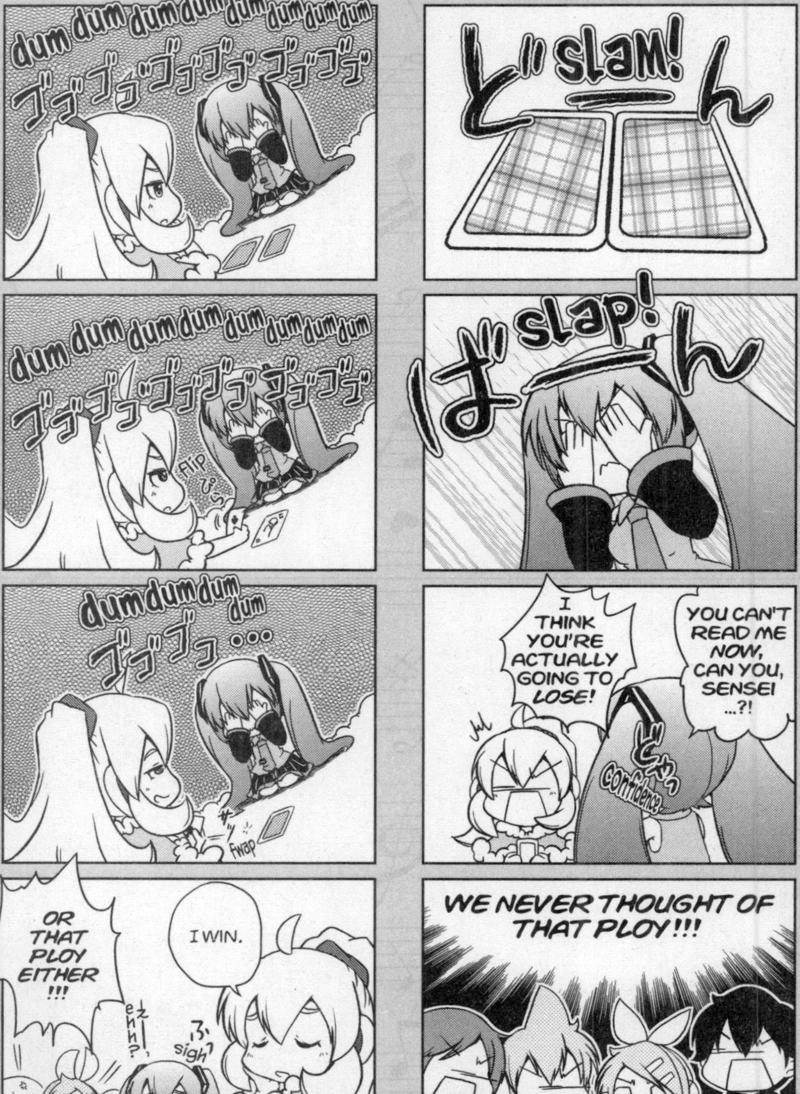

ど
slam!
ーん
dum dum dum dum dum dum dum dum
ゴゴゴゴゴゴゴゴ
ばーん
slap!
dum dum dum dum dum dum dum dum
ゴゴゴゴゴゴゴゴ
Flip
ぴら
YOU CAN'T READ ME NOW, CAN YOU, SENSEI ...?!
I THINK YOU'RE ACTUALLY GOING TO LOSE!
どやっ
confidence
dum dum dum dum
ゴゴゴ…
fwap
WE NEVER THOUGHT OF THAT PLOY!!!
I WIN.
ふ
sigh
OR THAT PLOY EITHER!!!
えー!?
ehh?

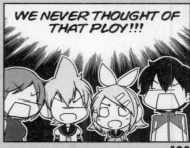

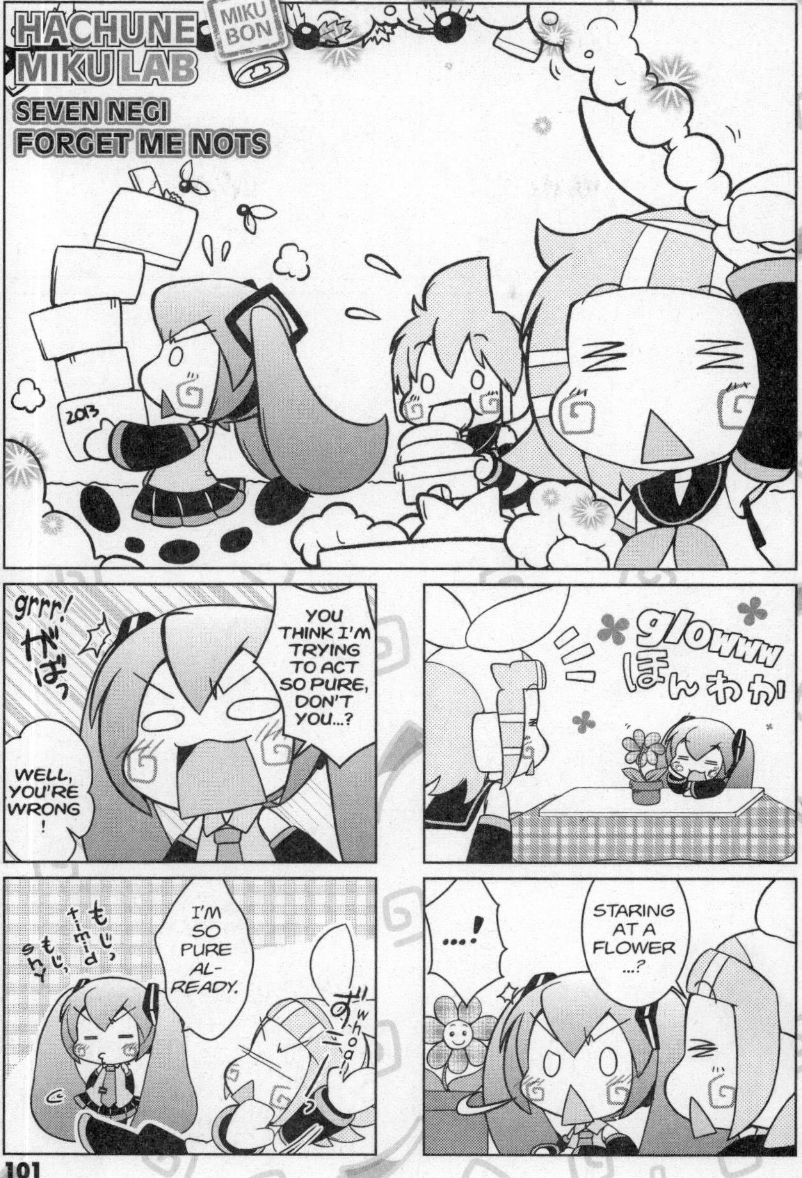
HACHUNE MIKU LAB
MIKU BON
SEVEN NEGI
FORGET ME NOTS
2013
glowww
ほんわか
grrr!
がばっ
YOU THINK I'M TRYING TO ACT SO PURE, DON'T YOU...?
WELL, YOU'RE WRONG!
...!
STARING AT A FLOWER ...?
もじっ
timid
もじっ
shy
I'M SO PURE AL-READY.
ずっ
whoa!!

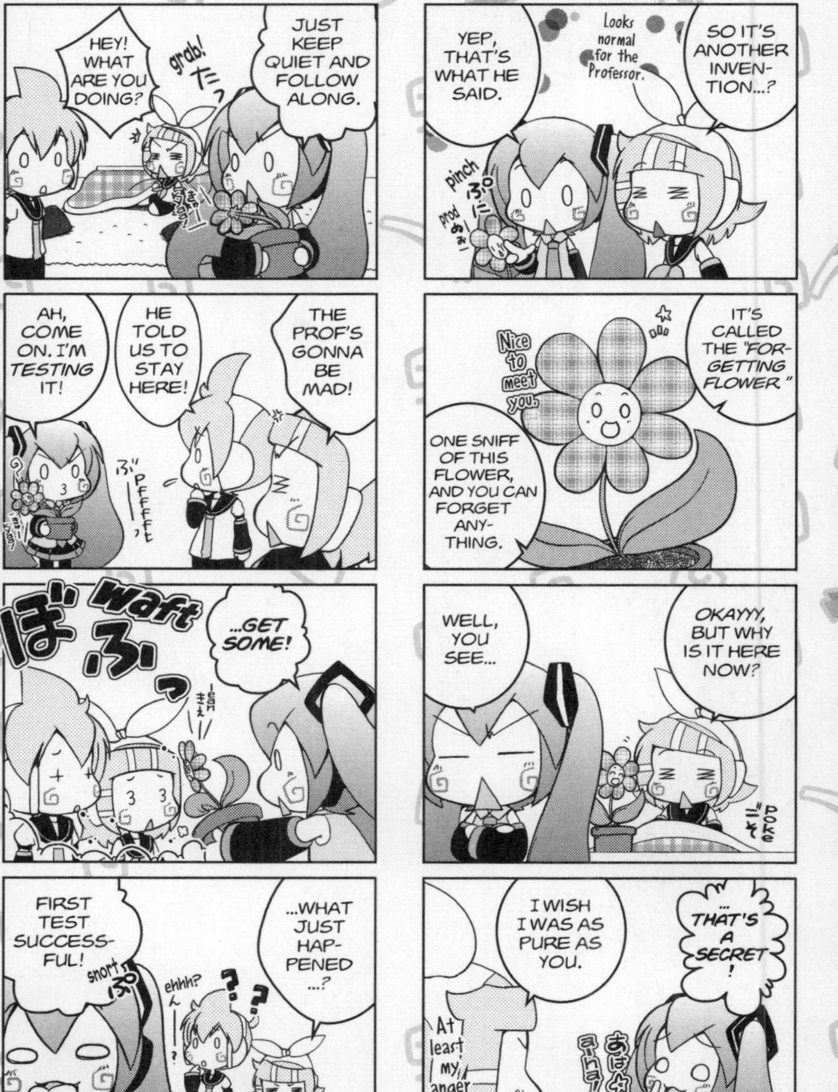
SO IT'S ANOTHER INVEN-TION...?
Looks normal for the Professor.
YEP, THAT'S WHAT HE SAID.
pinch ぷに
prod
IT'S CALLED THE "FOR-GETTING FLOWER."
Nice to meet you.
ONE SNIFF OF THIS FLOWER, AND YOU CAN FORGET ANY-THING.
OKAYYY, BUT WHY IS IT HERE NOW?
WELL, YOU SEE...
poke
... THAT'S A SECRET!
I WISH I WAS AS PURE AS YOU.
あは☆ a-ha!
At least my anger is pure.
JUST KEEP QUIET AND FOLLOW ALONG.
grab! たっ
HEY! WHAT ARE YOU DOING?
THE PROF'S GONNA BE MAD!
HE TOLD US TO STAY HERE!
AH, COME ON. I'M TESTING IT!
ぶ Pfffft
...GET SOME!
waft ぼふっ
lean
...WHAT JUST HAP-PENED ...?
ehhh? ん
FIRST TEST SUCCESS-FUL!
snort ぷ

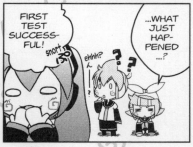

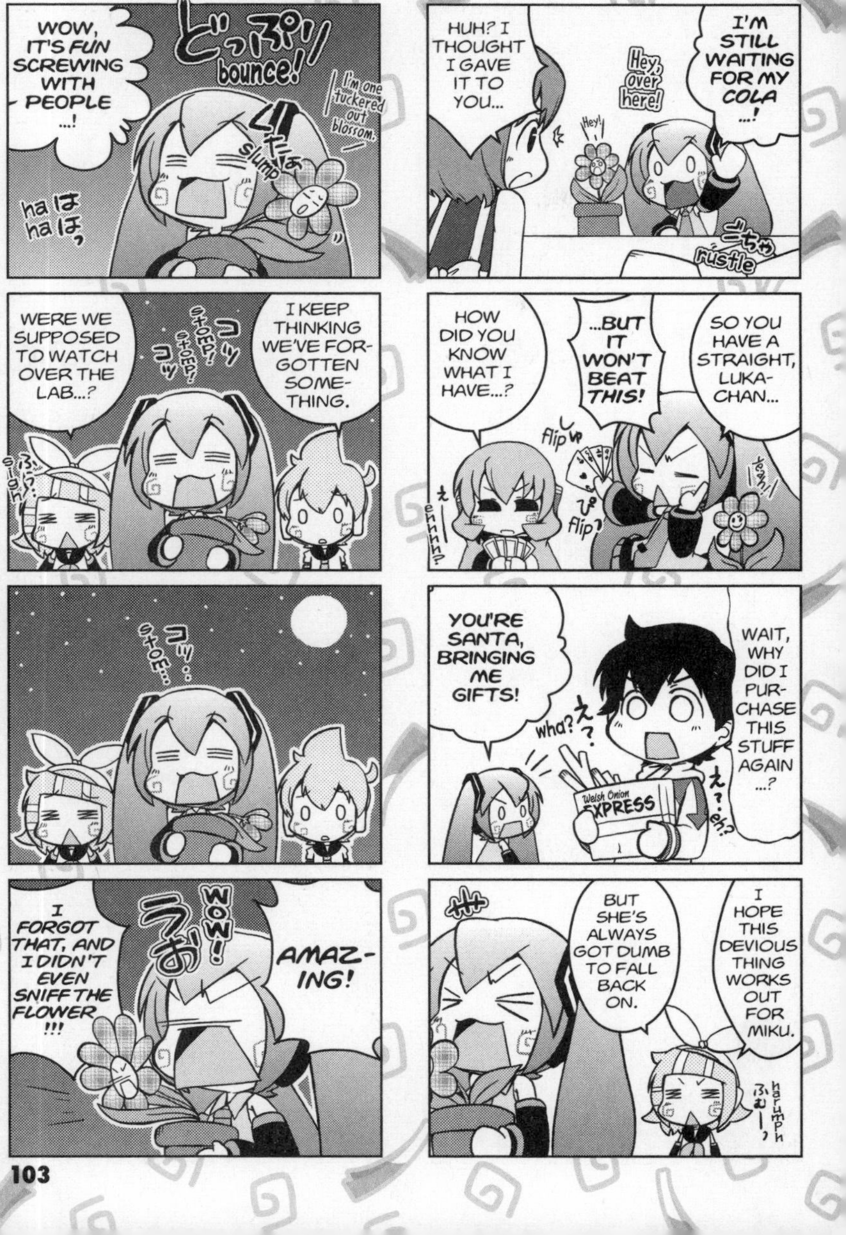

I'M STILL WAITING FOR MY COLA ...!
Hey, over here!
Hey!
HUH? I THOUGHT I GAVE IT TO YOU...
ごちゃ
rustle
どっぷり
bounce!
I'm one tuckered out blossom.
くたぁ
slump
WOW, IT'S FUN SCREWING WITH PEOPLE ...!
ha は ha ほ
SO YOU HAVE A STRAIGHT, LUKA-CHAN...
...BUT IT WON'T BEAT THIS!
HOW DID YOU KNOW WHAT I HAVE...?
flip up
ぴ flip
え ehhhh?
I KEEP THINKING WE'VE FORGOTTEN SOMETHING.
コツ stomp! コツ stomp!
WERE WE SUPPOSED TO WATCH OVER THE LAB...?
ふぅ... sigh
WAIT, WHY DID I PURCHASE THIS STUFF AGAIN...?
YOU'RE SANTA, BRINGING ME GIFTS!
え? wha?
Welsh Onion EXPRESS
え? eh?
コツ... stomp...
I HOPE THIS DEVIOUS THING WORKS OUT FOR MIKU.
BUT SHE'S ALWAYS GOT DUMB TO FALL BACK ON.
ふむー harumph
うぉ WOW!
AMAZING!
I FORGOT THAT, AND I DIDN'T EVEN SNIFF THE FLOWER !!!

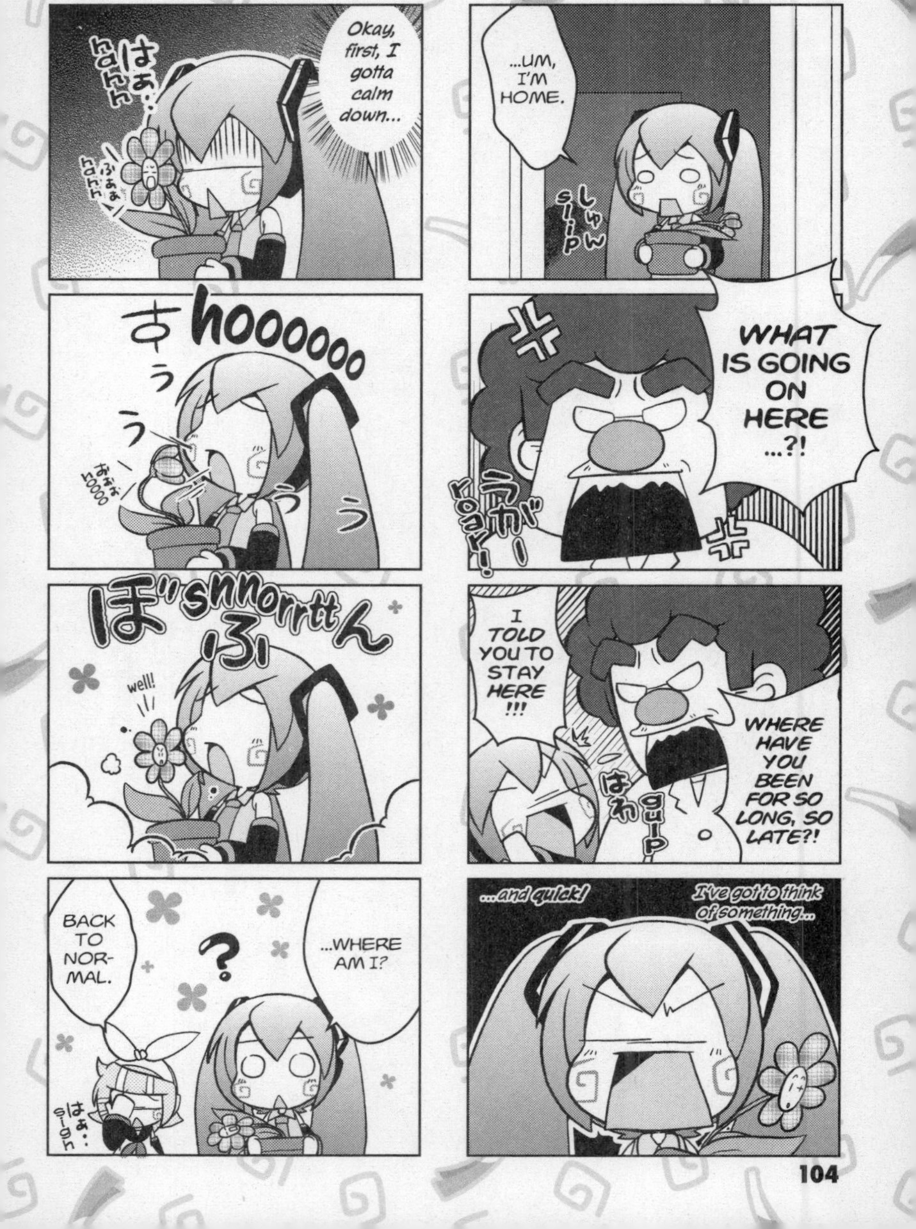

...UM, I'M HOME.
しゅ slip
Okay, first, I gotta calm down...
はぁ hahh
ふぁぁ hahh
WHAT IS GOING ON HERE ...?!
うがー roar!
すhooooooo
うううう
おぉぉ hoooo
I TOLD YOU TO STAY HERE !!!
WHERE HAVE YOU BEEN FOR SO LONG, SO LATE?!
はわ gulp
ぼ"snnorrttふん
well!
I've got to think of something...
...and quick!
...WHERE AM I?
?
BACK TO NOR-MAL.
はぁ・・ sigh

HATSUNE MIKU

MIKUBON

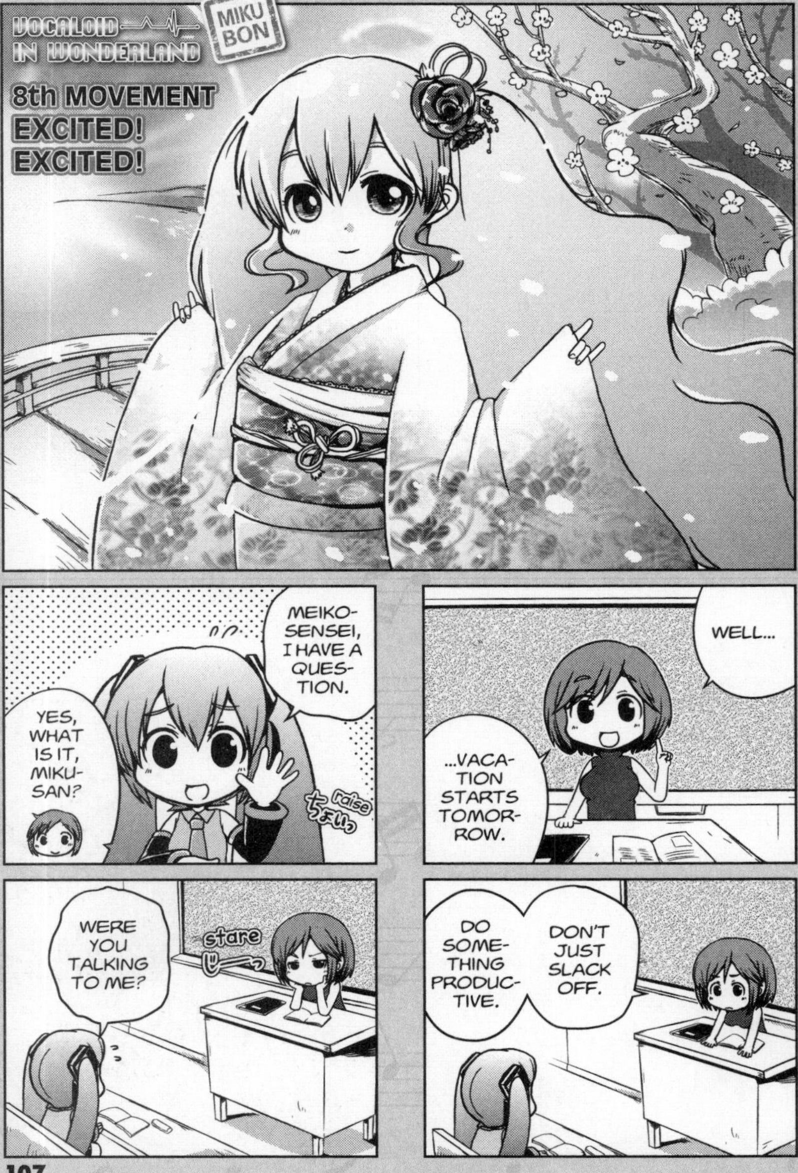
VOCALOID IN WONDERLAND
MIKU BON
8th MOVEMENT
EXCITED! EXCITED!
WELL...
...VACATION STARTS TOMORROW.
DON'T JUST SLACK OFF.
DO SOMETHING PRODUCTIVE.
MEIKO-SENSEI, I HAVE A QUESTION.
YES, WHAT IS IT, MIKU-SAN?
raise
WERE YOU TALKING TO ME?
stare

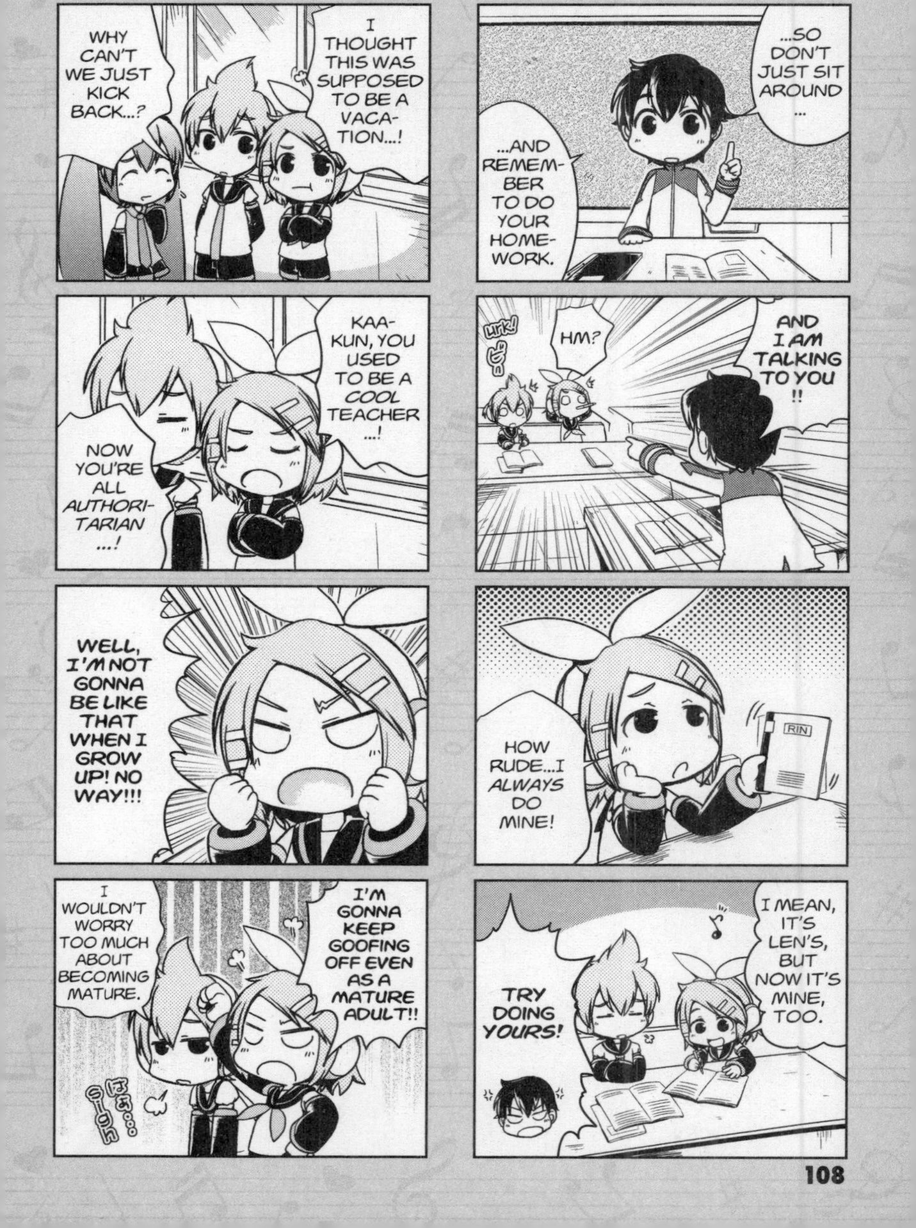
...SO DON'T JUST SIT AROUND ...
...AND REMEMBER TO DO YOUR HOMEWORK.
I THOUGHT THIS WAS SUPPOSED TO BE A VACATION...!
WHY CAN'T WE JUST KICK BACK...?
AND I AM TALKING TO YOU !!
HM?
urk!
KAA-KUN, YOU USED TO BE A COOL TEACHER ...!
NOW YOU'RE ALL AUTHORITARIAN ...!
RIN
HOW RUDE...I ALWAYS DO MINE!
WELL, I'M NOT GONNA BE LIKE THAT WHEN I GROW UP! NO WAY!!!
I MEAN, IT'S LEN'S, BUT NOW IT'S MINE, TOO.
TRY DOING YOURS!
I'M GONNA KEEP GOOFING OFF EVEN AS A MATURE ADULT!!
I WOULDN'T WORRY TOO MUCH ABOUT BECOMING MATURE.
はぁ... sigh

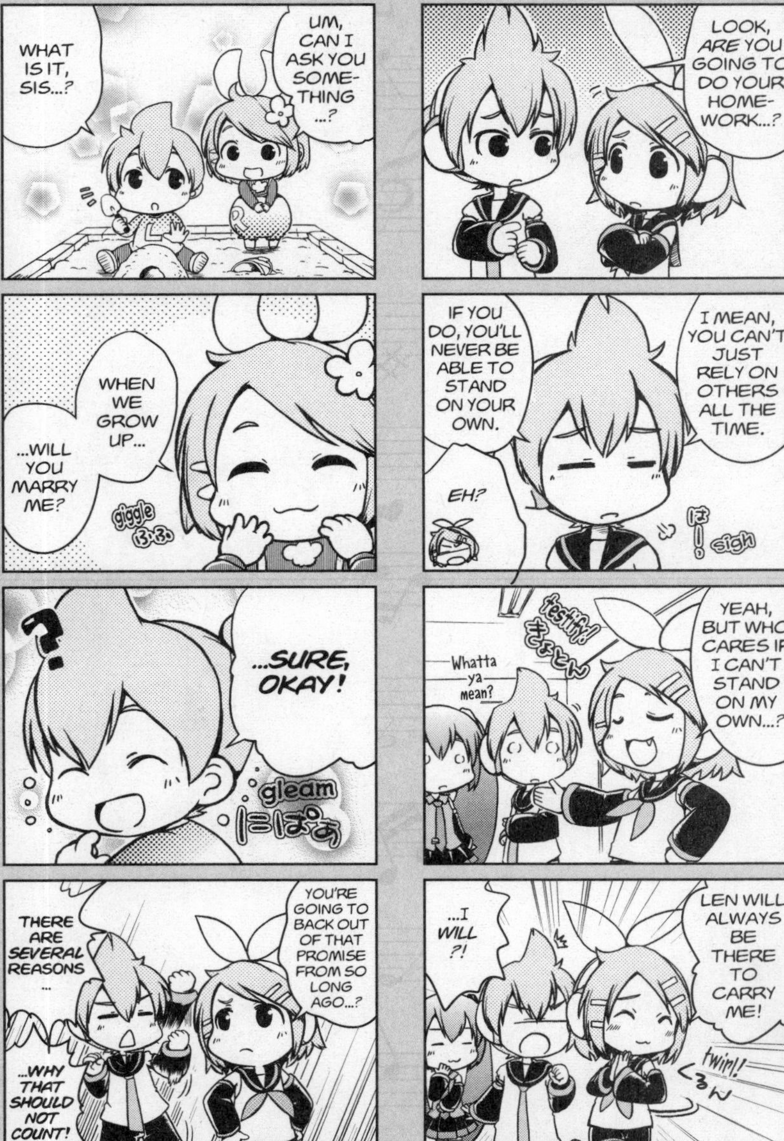
LOOK, ARE YOU GOING TO DO YOUR HOMEWORK...?
I MEAN, YOU CAN'T JUST RELY ON OTHERS ALL THE TIME.
IF YOU DO, YOU'LL NEVER BE ABLE TO STAND ON YOUR OWN.
EH?
はー! sigh
YEAH, BUT WHO CARES IF I CAN'T STAND ON MY OWN...?
testify! きょとん
Whatta ya mean?
LEN WILL ALWAYS BE THERE TO CARRY ME!
...I WILL ?!
twirl! くるん
UM, CAN I ASK YOU SOMETHING ...?
WHAT IS IT, SIS...?
WHEN WE GROW UP...
...WILL YOU MARRY ME?
giggle ふふ
...SURE, OKAY!
gleam にぱぁ
YOU'RE GOING TO BACK OUT OF THAT PROMISE FROM SO LONG AGO...?
THERE ARE SEVERAL REASONS ...
...WHY THAT SHOULD NOT COUNT!

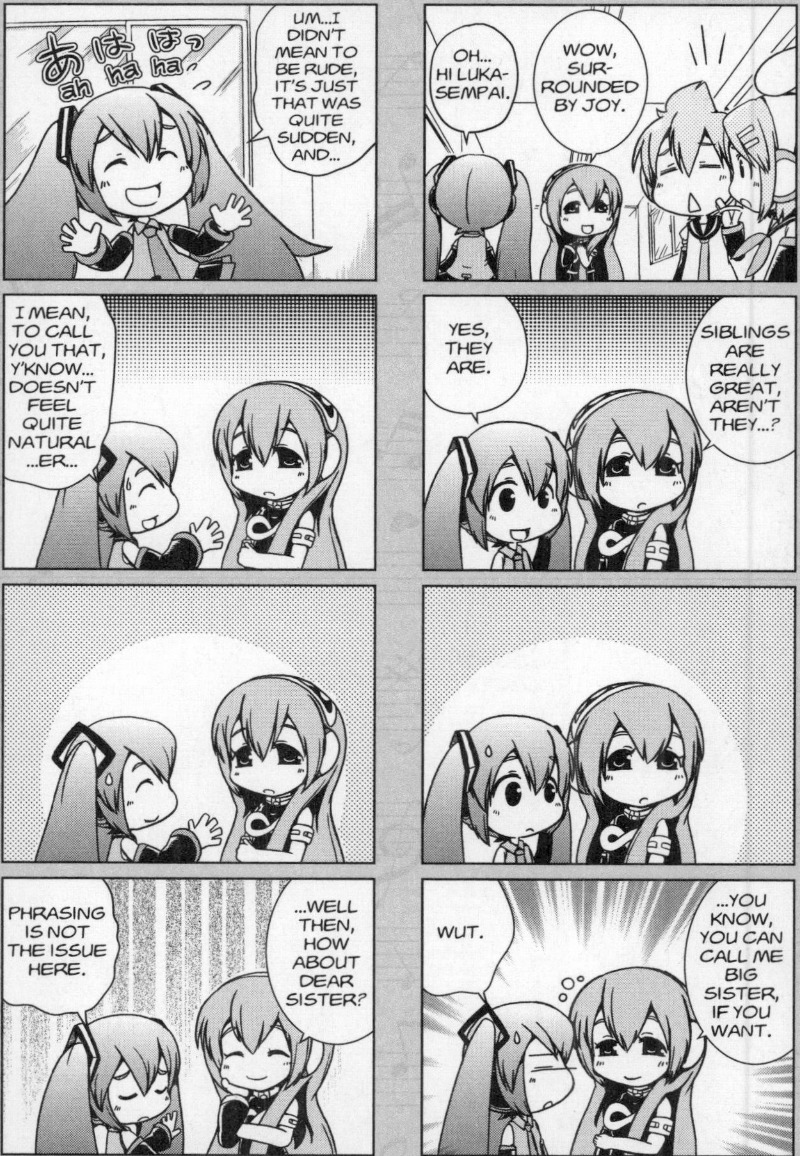
WOW, SUR-ROUNDED BY JOY.
OH... HI LUKA-SEMPAI.
UM...I DIDN'T MEAN TO BE RUDE, IT'S JUST THAT WAS QUITE SUDDEN, AND...
あははっ
ah ha ha
SIBLINGS ARE REALLY GREAT, AREN'T THEY...?
YES, THEY ARE.
I MEAN, TO CALL YOU THAT, Y'KNOW... DOESN'T FEEL QUITE NATURAL ...ER...
...YOU KNOW, YOU CAN CALL ME BIG SISTER, IF YOU WANT.
WUT.
...WELL THEN, HOW ABOUT DEAR SISTER?
PHRASING IS NOT THE ISSUE HERE.

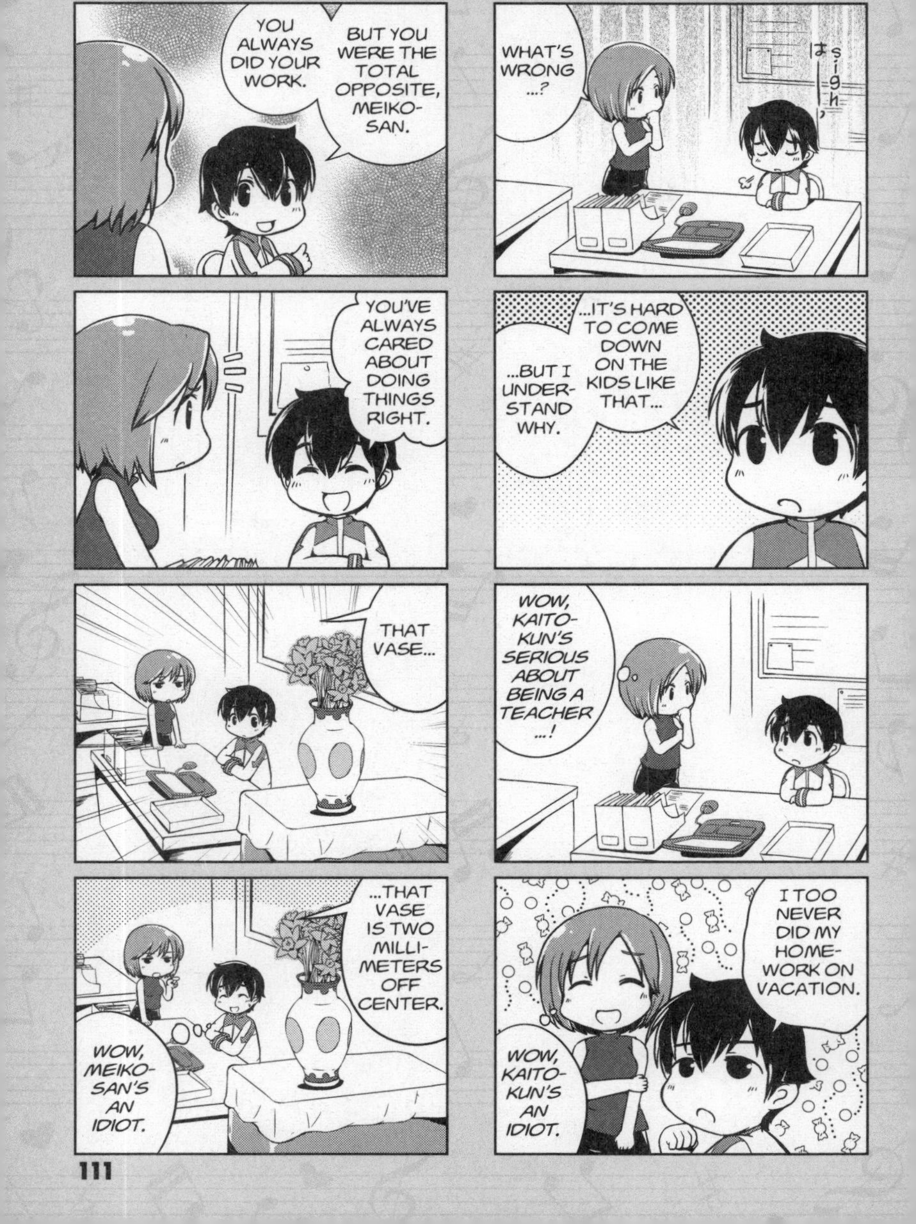
WHAT'S WRONG ...?
は sigh
...IT'S HARD TO COME DOWN ON THE KIDS LIKE THAT...
...BUT I UNDERSTAND WHY.
WOW, KAITO-KUN'S SERIOUS ABOUT BEING A TEACHER ...!
I TOO NEVER DID MY HOME-WORK ON VACATION.
WOW, KAITO-KUN'S AN IDIOT.
BUT YOU WERE THE TOTAL OPPOSITE, MEIKO-SAN.
YOU ALWAYS DID YOUR WORK.
YOU'VE ALWAYS CARED ABOUT DOING THINGS RIGHT.
THAT VASE...
...THAT VASE IS TWO MILLI-METERS OFF CENTER.
WOW, MEIKO-SAN'S AN IDIOT.

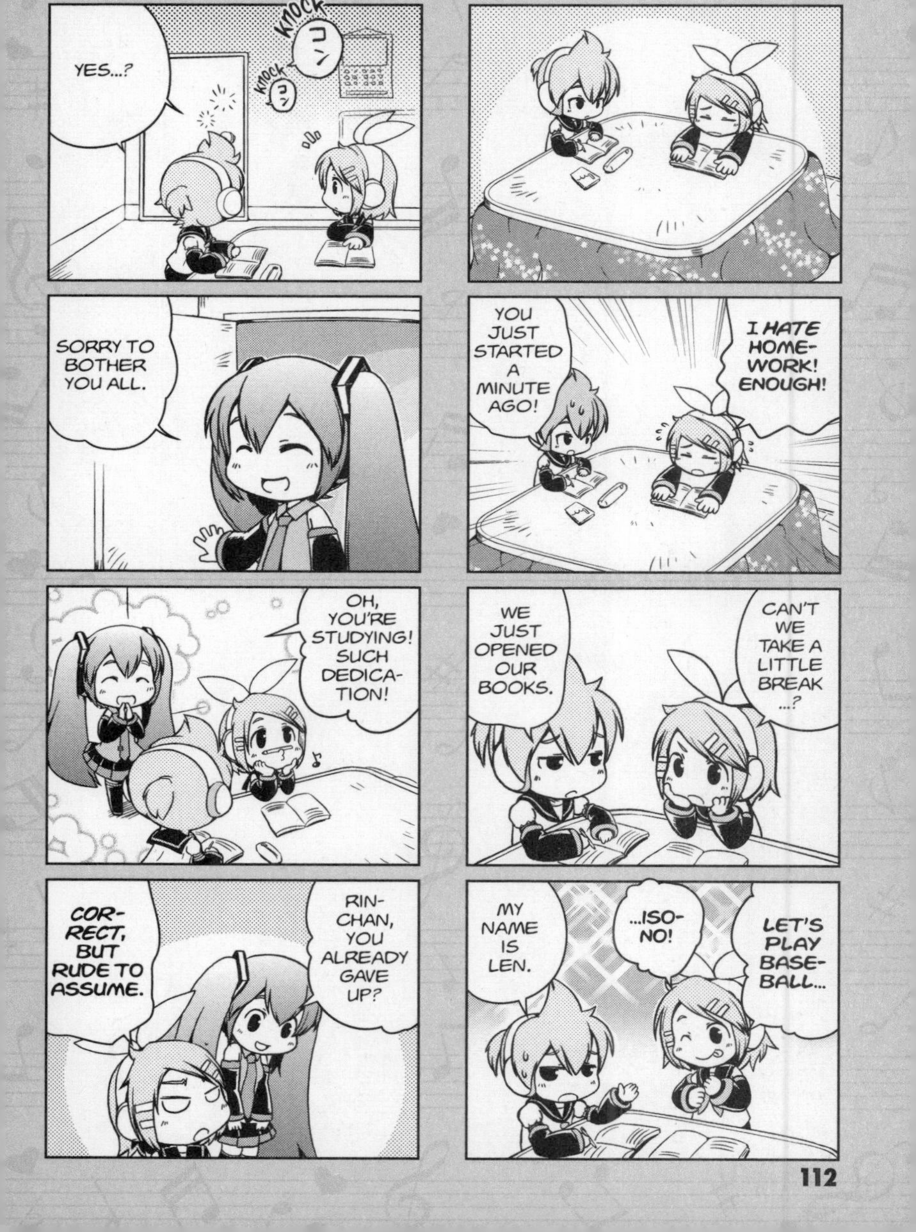
I HATE HOMEWORK! ENOUGH!
YOU JUST STARTED A MINUTE AGO!
CAN'T WE TAKE A LITTLE BREAK ...?
WE JUST OPENED OUR BOOKS.
LET'S PLAY BASEBALL...
...ISO-NO!
MY NAME IS LEN.
KNOCK
コン
KNOCK
コン
YES...?
SORRY TO BOTHER YOU ALL.
OH, YOU'RE STUDYING! SUCH DEDICATION!
RIN-CHAN, YOU ALREADY GAVE UP?
CORRECT, BUT RUDE TO ASSUME.

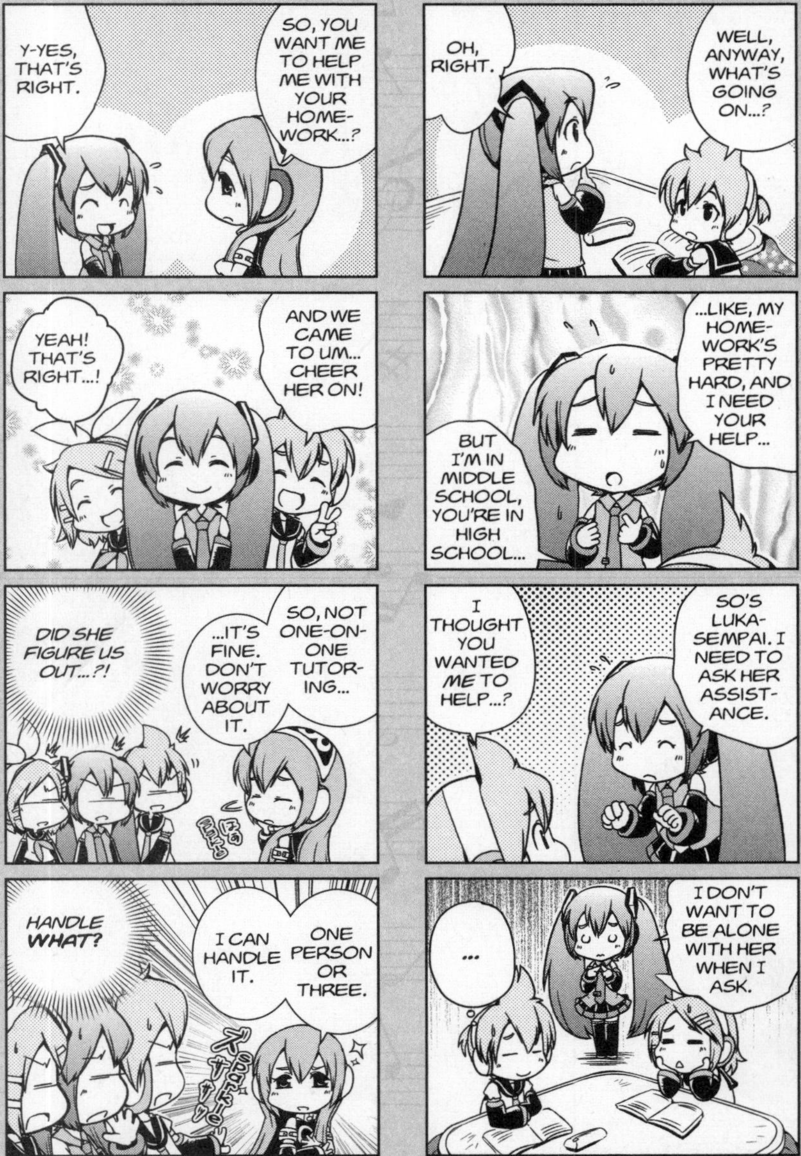
WELL, ANYWAY, WHAT'S GOING ON...?
OH, RIGHT.
...LIKE, MY HOMEWORK'S PRETTY HARD, AND I NEED YOUR HELP...
BUT I'M IN MIDDLE SCHOOL, YOU'RE IN HIGH SCHOOL...
SO'S LUKA-SEMPAI. I NEED TO ASK HER ASSISTANCE.
I THOUGHT YOU WANTED *ME* TO HELP...?
I DON'T WANT TO BE ALONE WITH HER WHEN I ASK.
...
SO, YOU WANT ME TO HELP ME WITH YOUR HOMEWORK...?
Y-YES, THAT'S RIGHT.
AND WE CAME TO UM... CHEER HER ON!
YEAH! THAT'S RIGHT...!
SO, NOT ONE-ON-ONE TUTORING...
...IT'S FINE. DON'T WORRY ABOUT IT.
DID SHE FIGURE US OUT...?!
ONE PERSON OR THREE.
I CAN HANDLE IT.
HANDLE ***WHAT?***
sparkle

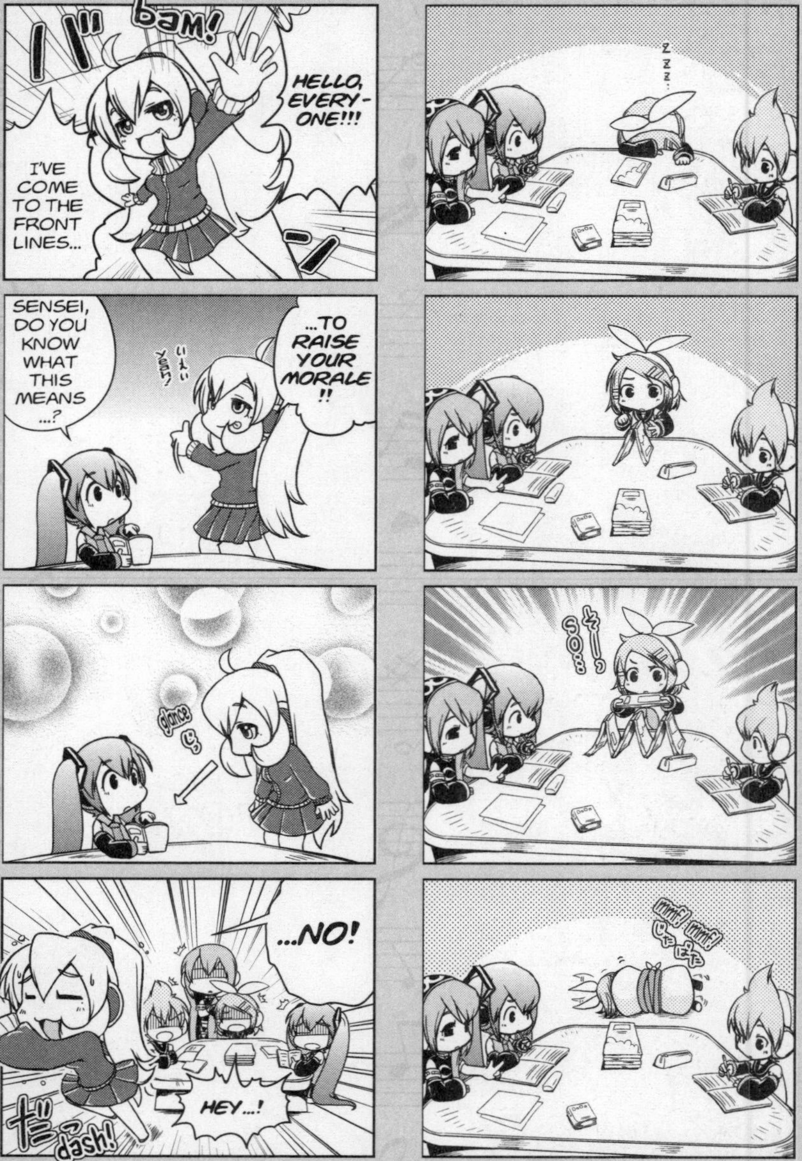
z z z
そーっ
SO...
mmf! mmf!
じたばた
バ
bam!
HELLO, EVERYONE!!!
I'VE COME TO THE FRONT LINES...
...TO RAISE YOUR MORALE!!
いえい
yeah!
SENSEI, DO YOU KNOW WHAT THIS MEANS...?
じっ
glance
...NO!
HEY...!
ダッ
dash!

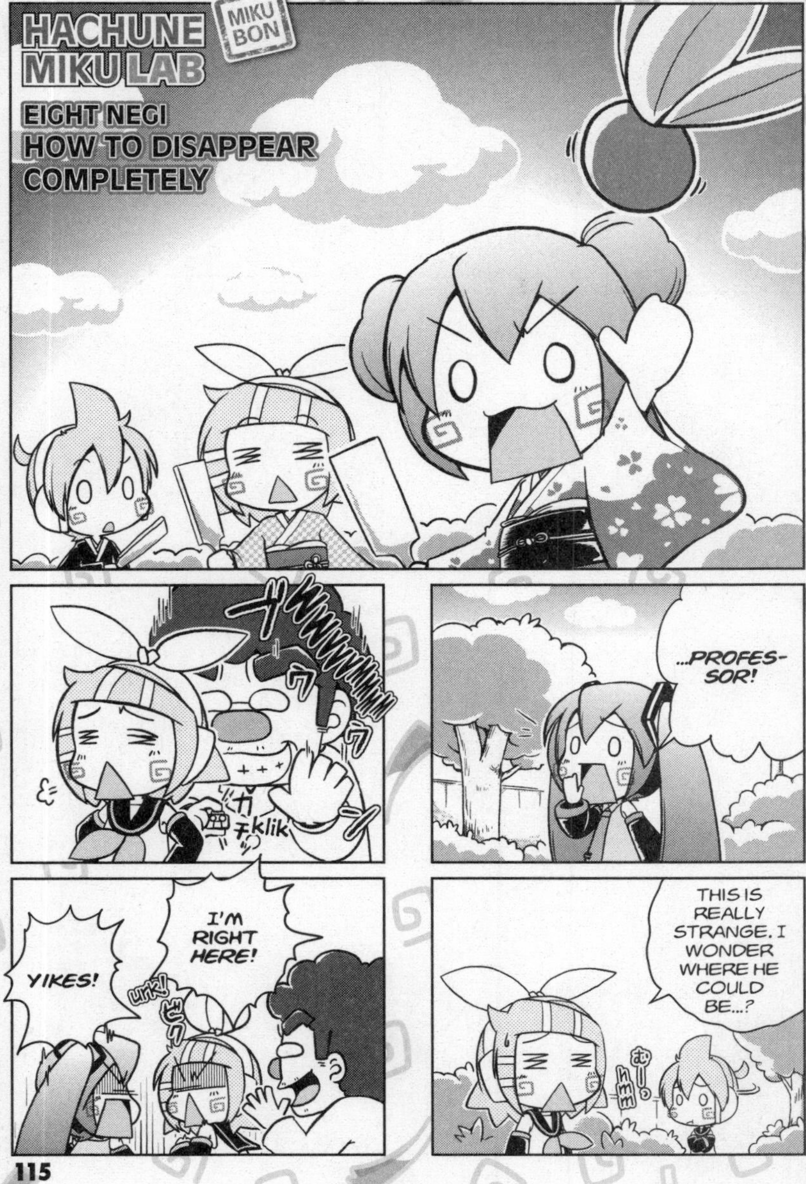
HACHUNE MIKU LAB
MIKU BON
EIGHT NEGI
HOW TO DISAPPEAR COMPLETELY
...PROFES-SOR!
klik
THIS IS REALLY STRANGE. I WONDER WHERE HE COULD BE...?
hmm
I'M RIGHT HERE!
urk!
YIKES!

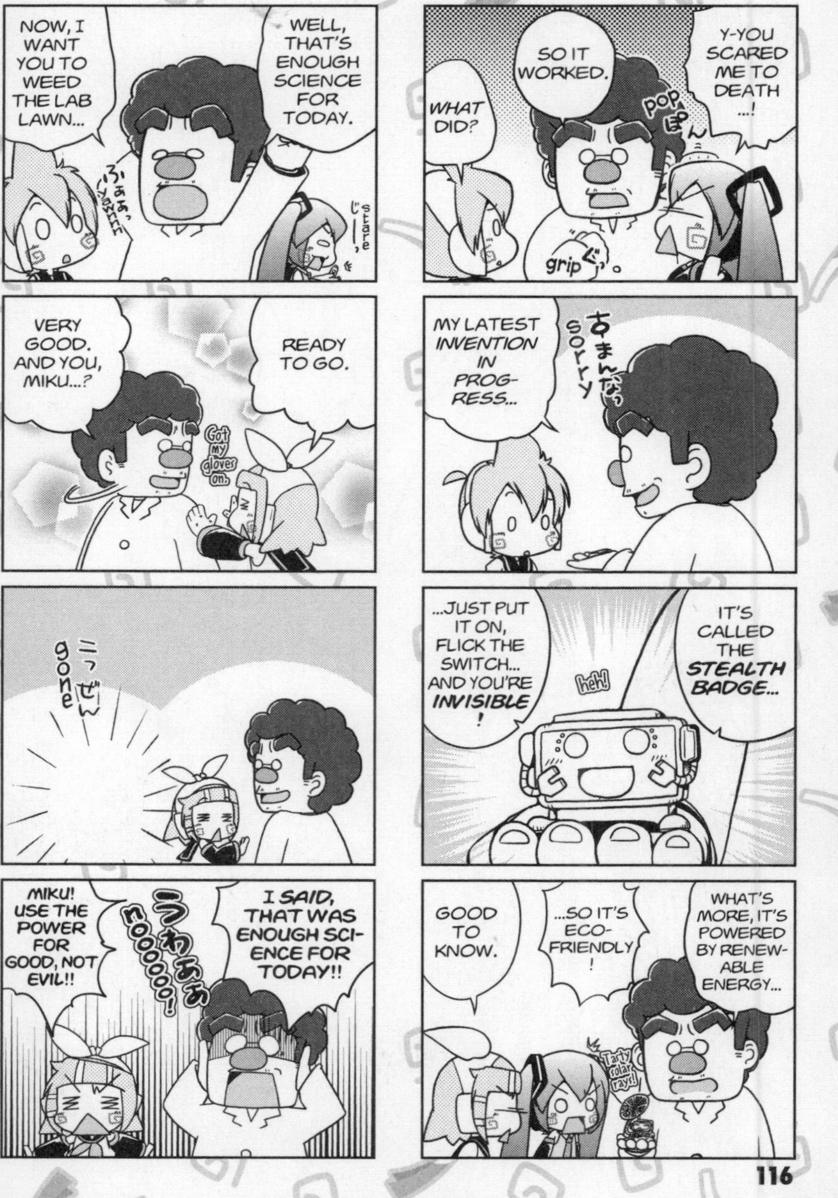
Y-YOU SCARED ME TO DEATH ...!
SO IT WORKED.
pop ぽん
WHAT DID?
grip ぐっ。
すまんな sorry
MY LATEST INVENTION IN PROGRESS...
IT'S CALLED THE STEALTH BADGE...
...JUST PUT IT ON, FLICK THE SWITCH... AND YOU'RE INVISIBLE!
heh!
WHAT'S MORE, IT'S POWERED BY RENEWABLE ENERGY...
...SO IT'S ECO-FRIENDLY!
GOOD TO KNOW.
Tarty solar rays!
WELL, THAT'S ENOUGH SCIENCE FOR TODAY.
じー stare
NOW, I WANT YOU TO WEED THE LAB LAWN...
ふぁあっ yawn
READY TO GO.
VERY GOOD. AND YOU, MIKU...?
Got my gloves on.
こつぜん gone
I SAID, THAT WAS ENOUGH SCIENCE FOR TODAY!!
うわあああ nooooooo!
MIKU! USE THE POWER FOR GOOD, NOT EVIL!!

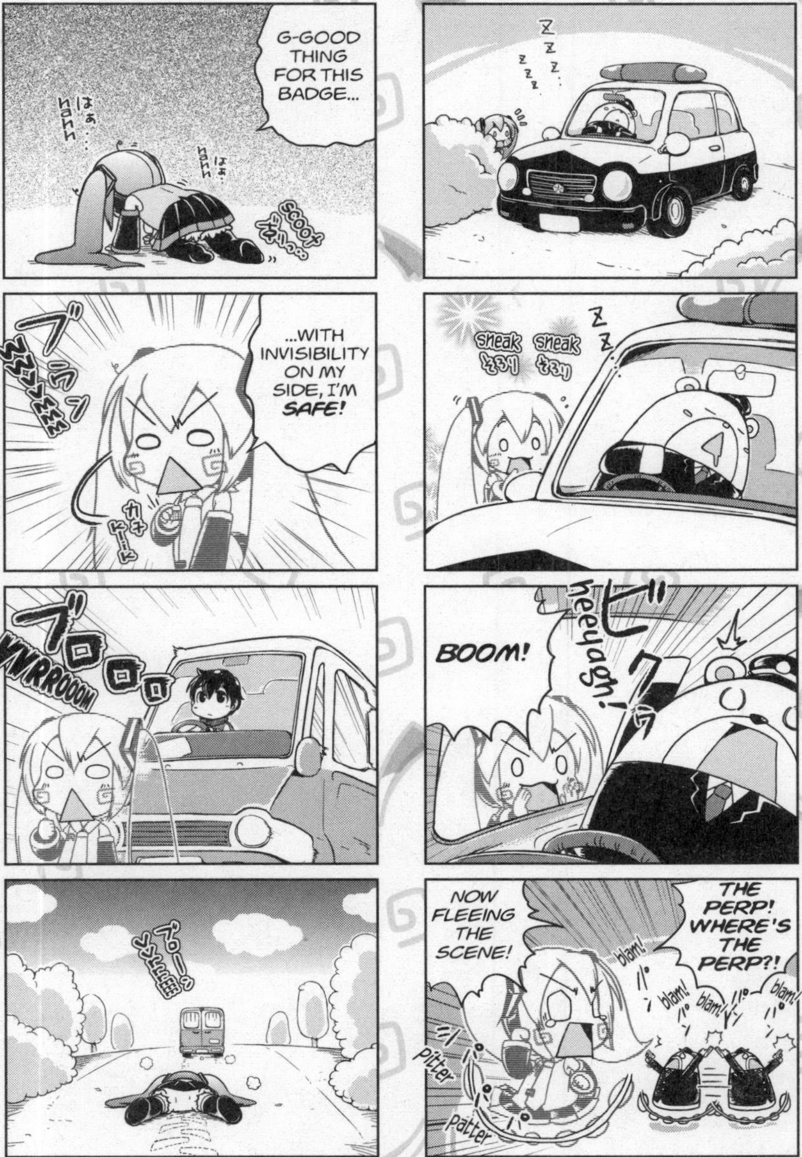
Z Z Z Z Z Z
G-GOOD THING FOR THIS BADGE...
hahh
hahh
scoot
Z Z
sneak
sneak
...WITH INVISIBILITY ON MY SIDE, I'M SAFE!
VVVVVMMM
heeyaagh!
BOOM!
VVRROOOM
ブロロロ
THE PERP! WHERE'S THE PERP?!
NOW FLEEING THE SCENE!
blam!
blam!
blam!
blam!
pitter
patter

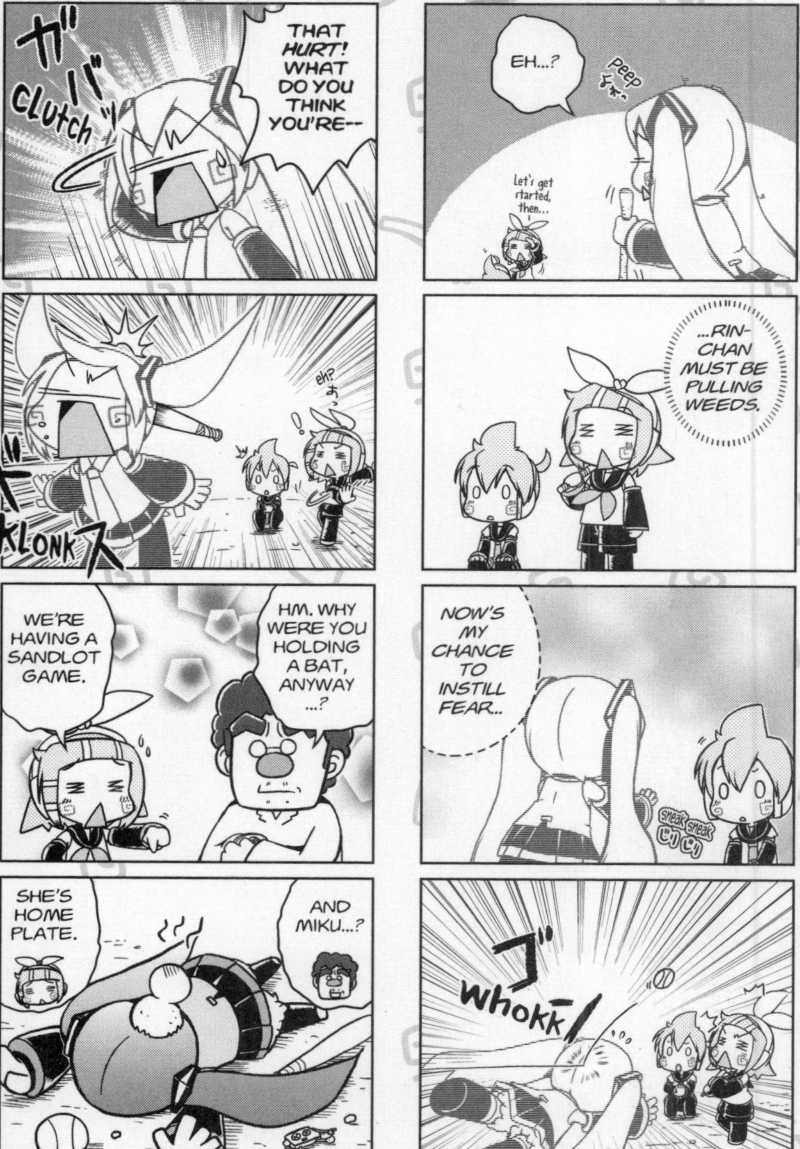

EH...?
Peep
Let's get started, then...
...RIN-CHAN MUST BE PULLING WEEDS.
NOW'S MY CHANCE TO INSTILL FEAR...
sneak sneak
Whokk
THAT HURT! WHAT DO YOU THINK YOU'RE--
Clutch
eh?
KLONK
HM. WHY WERE YOU HOLDING A BAT, ANYWAY...?
WE'RE HAVING A SANDLOT GAME.
AND MIKU...?
SHE'S HOME PLATE.

HATSUNE MIKU **MIKUBON**

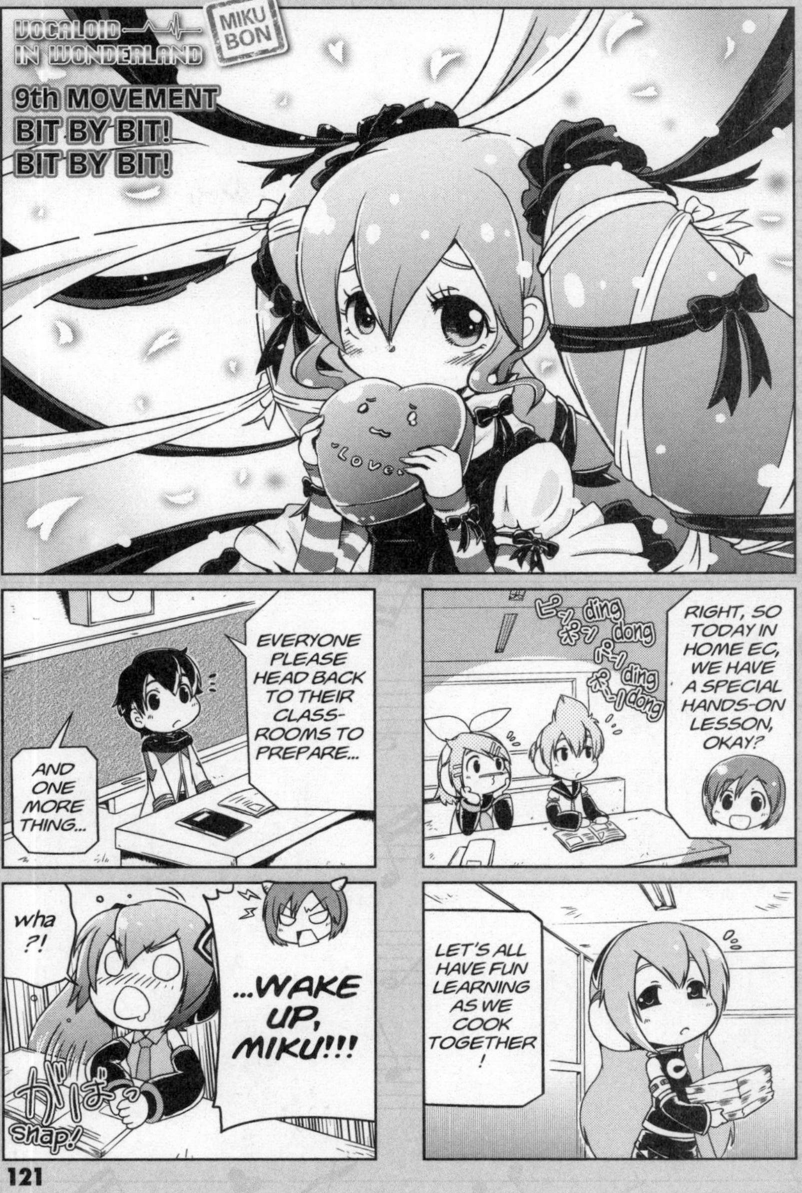
VOCALOID IN WONDERLAND
MIKU BON
9th MOVEMENT
BIT BY BIT! BIT BY BIT!
LOVE
RIGHT, SO TODAY IN HOME EC, WE HAVE A SPECIAL HANDS-ON LESSON, OKAY?
ピーンポーン ding dong
ピーンポーン ding dong
EVERYONE PLEASE HEAD BACK TO THEIR CLASS-ROOMS TO PREPARE...
AND ONE MORE THING...
LET'S ALL HAVE FUN LEARNING AS WE COOK TOGETHER!
...WAKE UP, MIKU!!!
wha?!
がばっ snap!

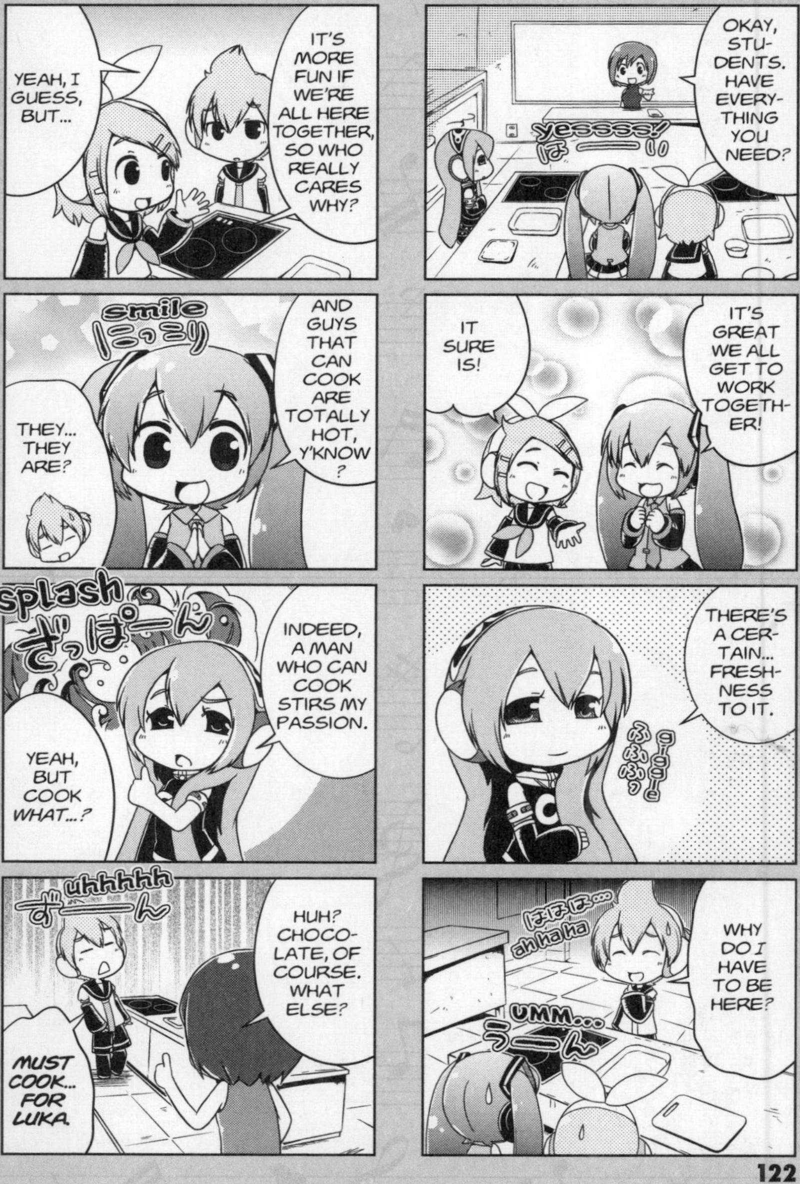
OKAY, STUDENTS. HAVE EVERYTHING YOU NEED?
yessss! はーーい
IT'S MORE FUN IF WE'RE ALL HERE TOGETHER, SO WHO REALLY CARES WHY?
YEAH, I GUESS, BUT...
IT'S GREAT WE ALL GET TO WORK TOGETHER!
IT SURE IS!
AND GUYS THAT CAN COOK ARE TOTALLY HOT, Y'KNOW?
smile にっこり
THEY... THEY ARE?
THERE'S A CERTAIN... FRESHNESS TO IT.
giggle ふふふっ
INDEED, A MAN WHO CAN COOK STIRS MY PASSION.
splash ざっぱーん
YEAH, BUT COOK WHAT...?
WHY DO I HAVE TO BE HERE?
ははは… ah ha ha
UMM... うーん
HUH? CHOCOLATE, OF COURSE. WHAT ELSE?
uhhhhh ずーーん
MUST COOK... FOR LUKA.

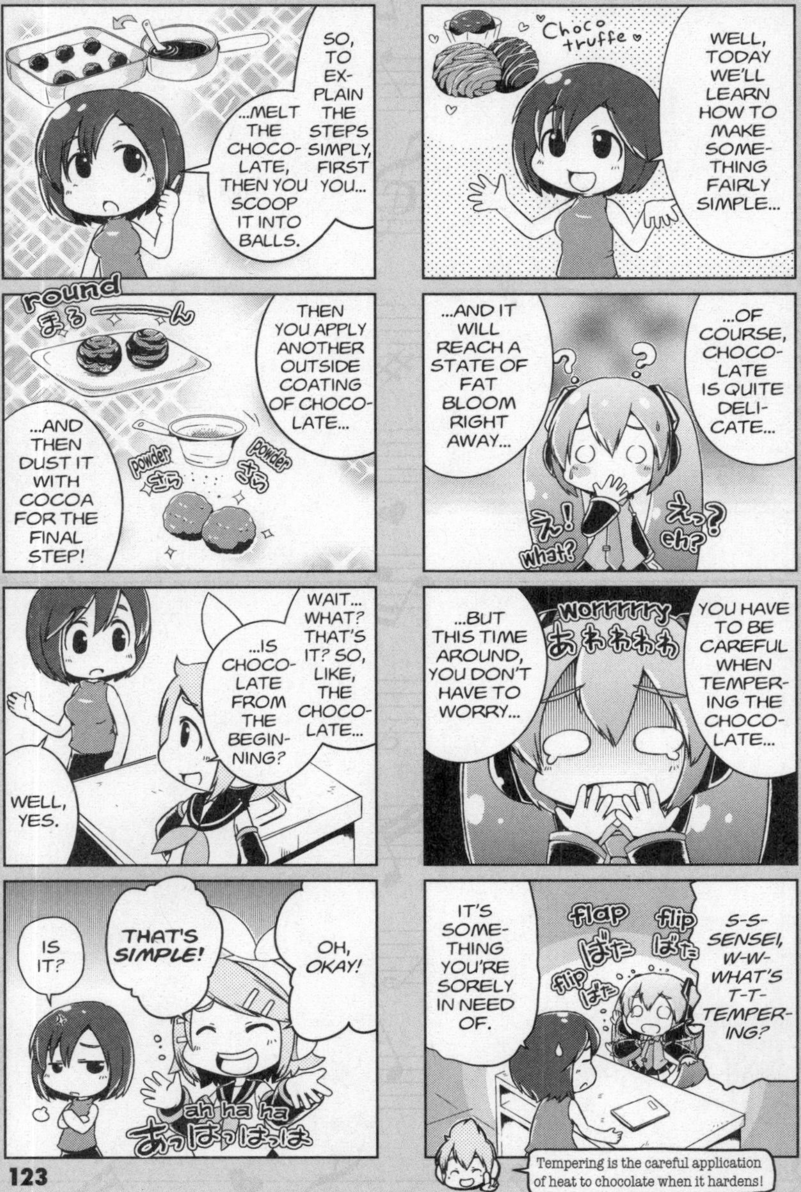
Choco truffe
WELL, TODAY WE'LL LEARN HOW TO MAKE SOMETHING FAIRLY SIMPLE...
SO, TO EXPLAIN THE STEPS SIMPLY, FIRST YOU...
...MELT THE CHOCOLATE, THEN YOU SCOOP IT INTO BALLS.
...OF COURSE, CHOCOLATE IS QUITE DELICATE...
...AND IT WILL REACH A STATE OF FAT BLOOM RIGHT AWAY...
えっ? eh?
え! what?
THEN YOU APPLY ANOTHER OUTSIDE COATING OF CHOCOLATE...
round まる———ん
powder さら
powder さら
...AND THEN DUST IT WITH COCOA FOR THE FINAL STEP!
YOU HAVE TO BE CAREFUL WHEN TEMPERING THE CHOCOLATE...
worrrrry あわわわわ
...BUT THIS TIME AROUND, YOU DON'T HAVE TO WORRY...
WAIT... WHAT? THAT'S IT? SO, LIKE, THE CHOCOLATE...
...IS CHOCOLATE FROM THE BEGINNING?
WELL, YES.
S-S-SENSEI, W-W-WHAT'S T-T-TEMPERING?
flip ばた
flap ばた
flip ばた
IT'S SOMETHING YOU'RE SORELY IN NEED OF.
Tempering is the careful application of heat to chocolate when it hardens!
OH, OKAY!
THAT'S SIMPLE!
IS IT?
ah ha ha あっはっはっは

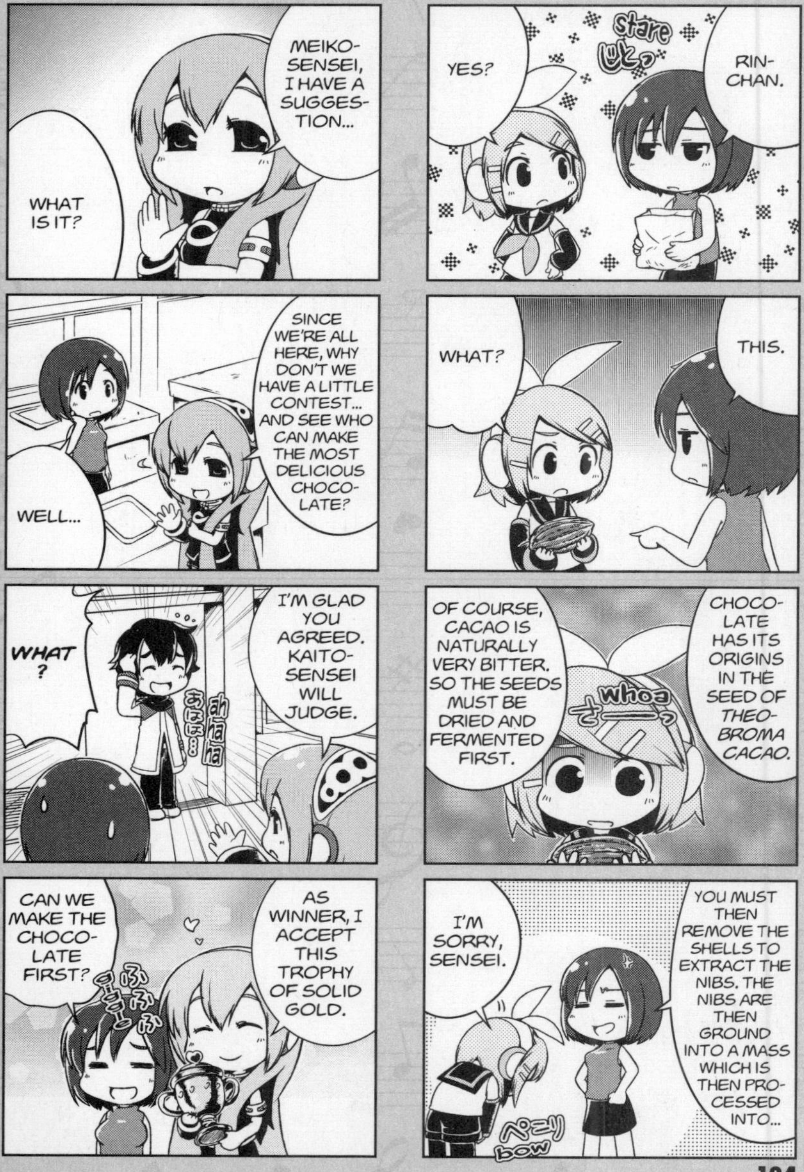
RIN-CHAN.
stare
じとっ
YES?
THIS.
WHAT?
CHOCO-LATE HAS ITS ORIGINS IN THE SEED OF *THEO-BROMA CACAO.*
whoa
さーっ
OF COURSE, CACAO IS NATURALLY VERY BITTER. SO THE SEEDS MUST BE DRIED AND FERMENTED FIRST.
YOU MUST THEN REMOVE THE SHELLS TO EXTRACT THE NIBS. THE NIBS ARE THEN GROUND INTO A MASS WHICH IS THEN PRO-CESSED INTO...
I'M SORRY, SENSEI.
ぺこり
bow
MEIKO-SENSEI, I HAVE A SUGGES-TION...
WHAT IS IT?
SINCE WE'RE ALL HERE, WHY DON'T WE HAVE A LITTLE CONTEST... AND SEE WHO CAN MAKE THE MOST DELICIOUS CHOCO-LATE?
WELL...
I'M GLAD YOU AGREED. KAITO-SENSEI WILL JUDGE.
ah ha ha
あはは…
WHAT?
AS WINNER, I ACCEPT THIS TROPHY OF SOLID GOLD.
ふふふ
CAN WE MAKE THE CHOCO-LATE FIRST?

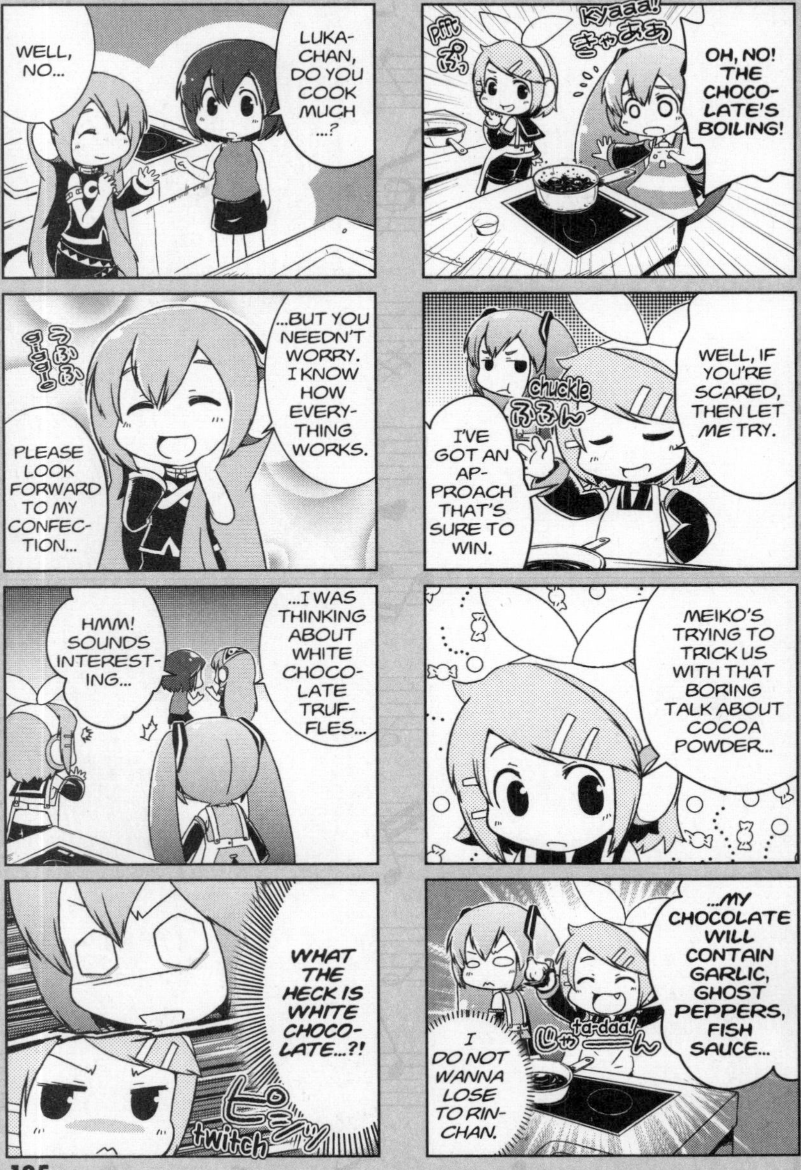
Kyaaa! きゃああ
pfft ぷっ
OH, NO! THE CHOCO-LATE'S BOILING!
LUKA-CHAN, DO YOU COOK MUCH ...?
WELL, NO...
WELL, IF YOU'RE SCARED, THEN LET ME TRY.
chuckle ふふん
I'VE GOT AN AP-PROACH THAT'S SURE TO WIN.
...BUT YOU NEEDN'T WORRY. I KNOW HOW EVERY-THING WORKS.
うふふ
PLEASE LOOK FORWARD TO MY CONFEC-TION...
MEIKO'S TRYING TO TRICK US WITH THAT BORING TALK ABOUT COCOA POWDER...
...I WAS THINKING ABOUT WHITE CHOCO-LATE TRUF-FLES...
HMM! SOUNDS INTEREST-ING...
...MY CHOCOLATE WILL CONTAIN GARLIC, GHOST PEPPERS, FISH SAUCE...
ta-daa! じゃ——ん
I DO NOT WANNA LOSE TO RIN-CHAN.
WHAT THE HECK IS WHITE CHOCO-LATE...?!
twitch ピシッ

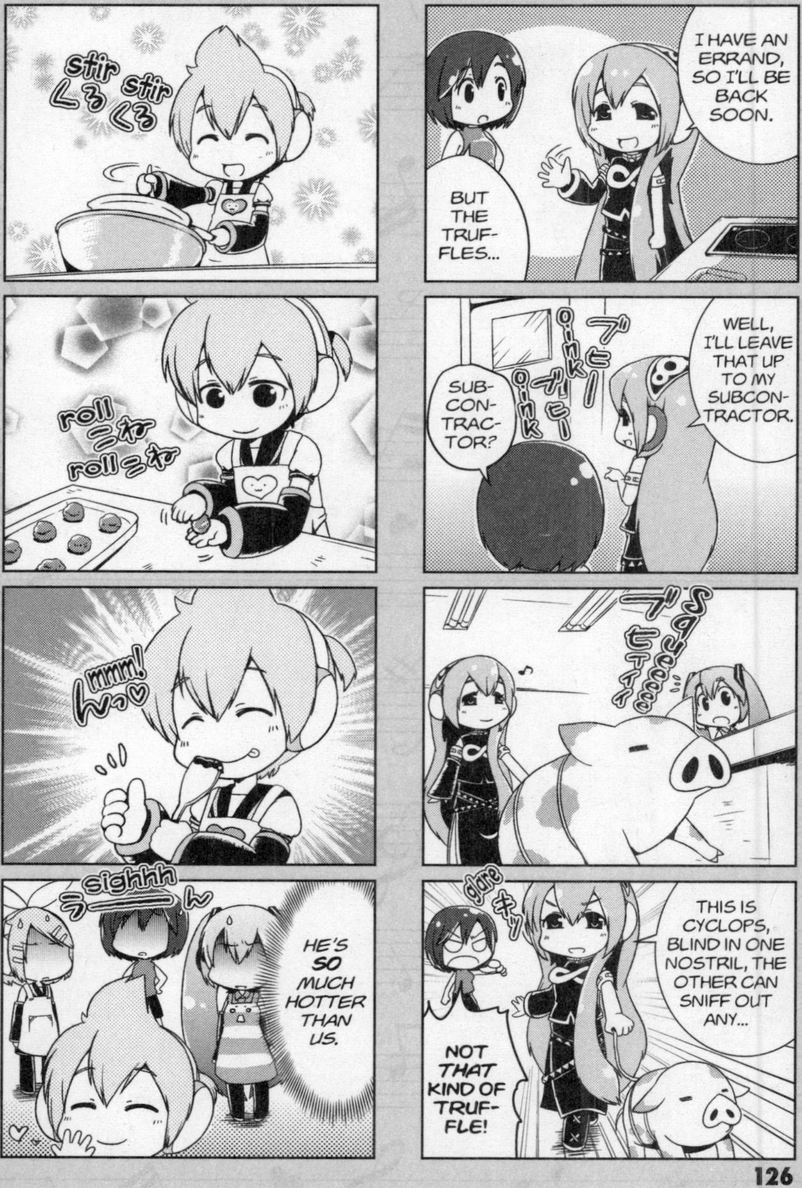
I HAVE AN ERRAND, SO I'LL BE BACK SOON.
BUT THE TRUF-FLES...
WELL, I'LL LEAVE THAT UP TO MY SUBCON-TRACTOR.
oink ブヒー oink ブヒー
SUB-CON-TRAC-TOR?
squeeee ブヒィィ
glare キッ
THIS IS CYCLOPS, BLIND IN ONE NOSTRIL, THE OTHER CAN SNIFF OUT ANY...
NOT THAT KIND OF TRUF-FLE!
stir stir くるくる
roll こね roll こね
mmm! んっ♡
sighhh う———ん
HE'S SO MUCH HOTTER THAN US.

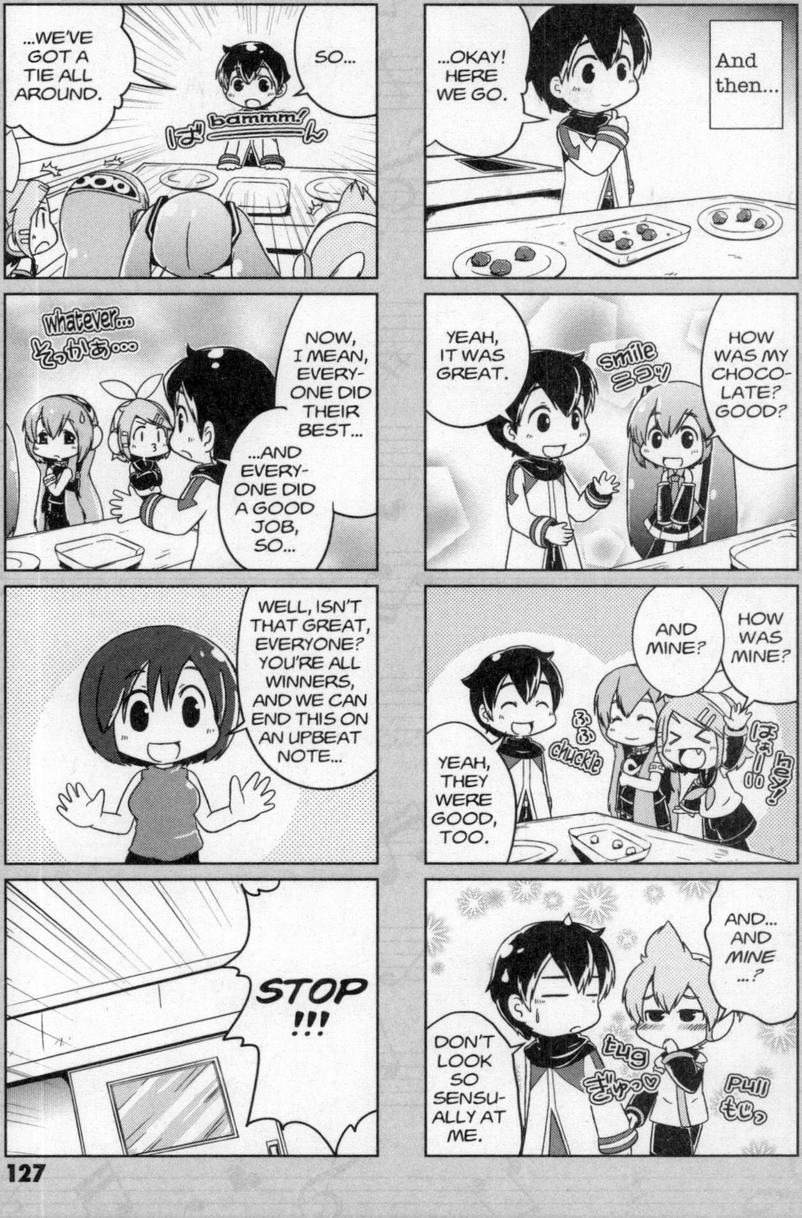
And then...
...OKAY! HERE WE GO.
HOW WAS MY CHOCOLATE? GOOD?
smile
ニコッ
YEAH, IT WAS GREAT.
HOW WAS MINE?
AND MINE?
hey!
はーい!!
ふふ
chuckle
YEAH, THEY WERE GOOD, TOO.
AND... AND MINE ...?
pull
もじっ
tug
ぎゅっ♡
DON'T LOOK SO SENSUALLY AT ME.
SO...
...WE'VE GOT A TIE ALL AROUND.
bammm!
ば——ん
NOW, I MEAN, EVERYONE DID THEIR BEST...
...AND EVERYONE DID A GOOD JOB, SO...
whatever...
そっかぁ…
WELL, ISN'T THAT GREAT, EVERYONE? YOU'RE ALL WINNERS, AND WE CAN END THIS ON AN UPBEAT NOTE...
STOP!!!

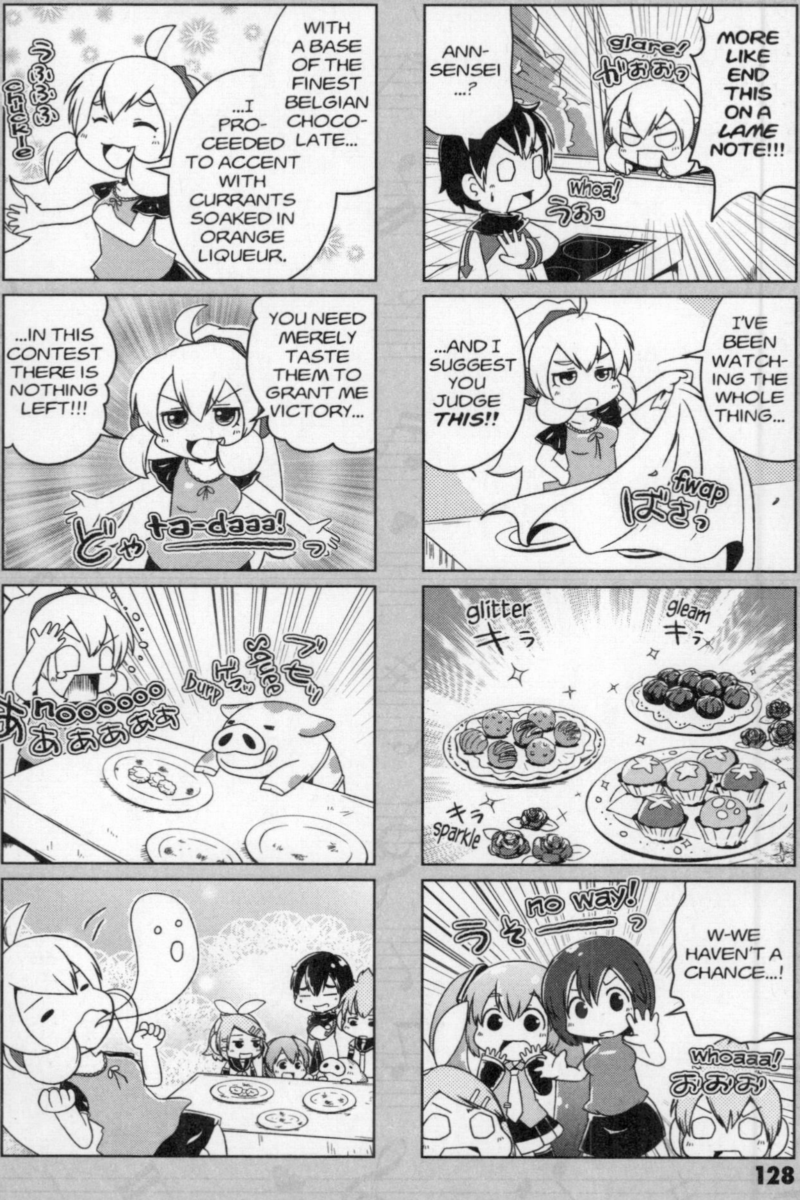
MORE LIKE END THIS ON A *LAME* NOTE!!!
glare! がおおっ
ANN-SENSEI ...?
whoa! うおっ
WITH A BASE OF THE FINEST BELGIAN CHOCOLATE...
...I PROCEEDED TO ACCENT WITH CURRANTS SOAKED IN ORANGE LIQUEUR.
うふふふ chuckle
I'VE BEEN WATCHING THE WHOLE THING...
...AND I SUGGEST YOU JUDGE *THIS!!*
fwap ばさっ
YOU NEED MERELY TASTE THEM TO GRANT ME VICTORY...
...IN THIS CONTEST THERE IS NOTHING LEFT!!!
どやっ ta-daaa!
gleam キラ
glitter キラ
キラ sparkle
ブピッ squee
げふっ burp
あああああ noooooo
W-WE HAVEN'T A CHANCE...!
うそーっ no way!
whoaaa! おおお

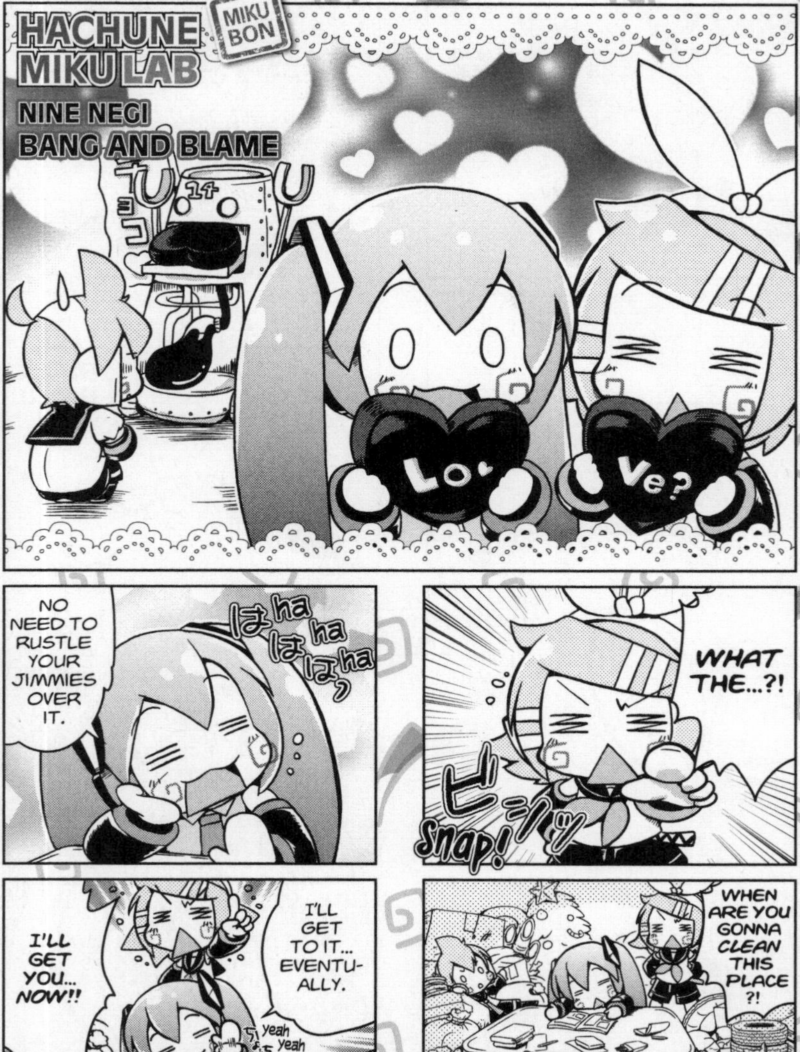
HACHUNE MIKU LAB
MIKU BON
NINE NEGI
BANG AND BLAME
LOve?
WHAT THE...?!
ピシッ
SNAP!
NO NEED TO RUSTLE YOUR JIMMIES OVER IT.
はははっ
ha ha ha
WHEN ARE YOU GONNA CLEAN THIS PLACE?!
ごちゃあぁ…
squalor
I'LL GET TO IT... EVENTUALLY.
yeah yeah
I'LL GET YOU... NOW!!

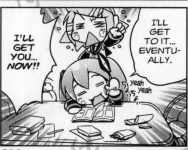

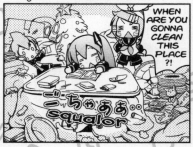

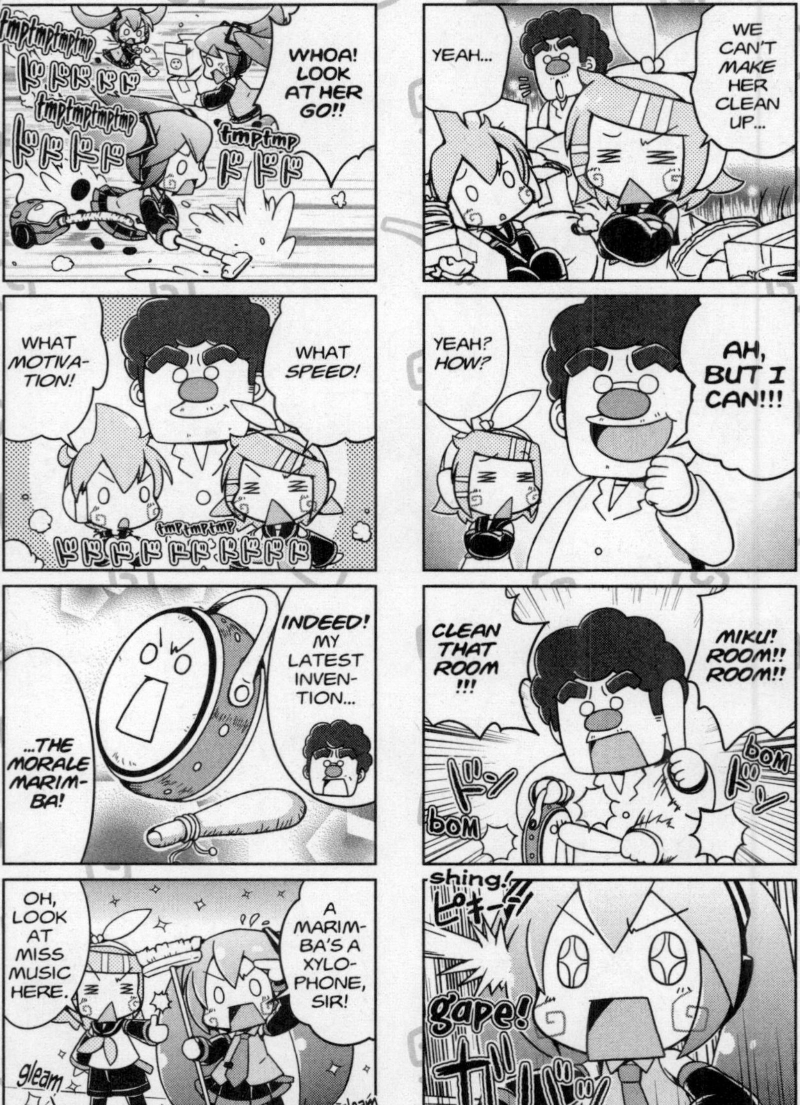
WE CAN'T MAKE HER CLEAN UP...
YEAH...
WHOA! LOOK AT HER GO!!
tmptmptmptmp
ドドドドド
tmptmptmptmp
ドドドド
tmptmp
ドドド
AH, BUT I CAN!!!
YEAH? HOW?
WHAT SPEED!
WHAT MOTIVATION!
tmptmptmp
ドドドドドドドドド
MIKU! ROOM!! ROOM!!
CLEAN THAT ROOM!!!
bom
ドン
bom
ドン
INDEED! MY LATEST INVENTION...
...THE MORALE MARIMBA!
shing!
ピキーン!
gape!
ガバッ
A MARIMBA'S A XYLOPHONE, SIR!
OH, LOOK AT MISS MUSIC HERE.
gleam
キラ
gleam
キラ

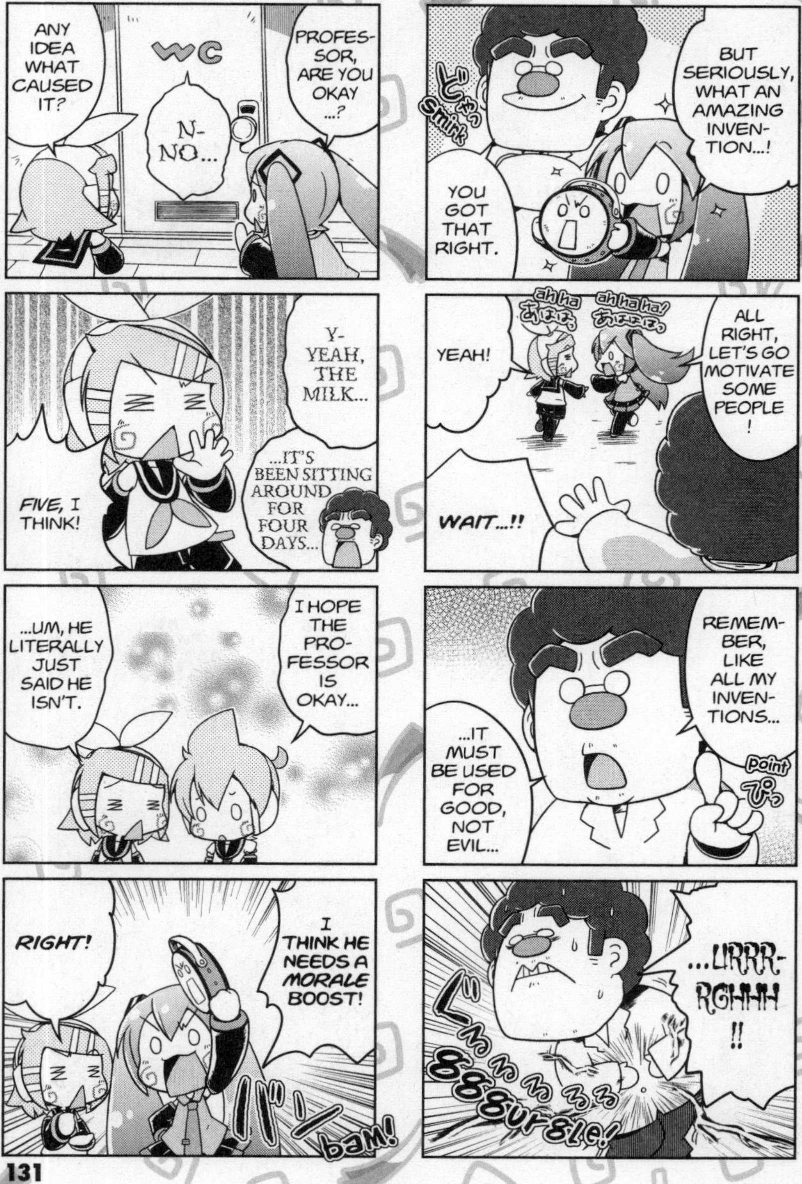
BUT SERIOUSLY, WHAT AN AMAZING INVEN-TION...!
どやっ smirk
YOU GOT THAT RIGHT.
ALL RIGHT, LET'S GO MOTIVATE SOME PEOPLE !
ah ha ha! あははは
ah ha あはは
YEAH!
WAIT...!!
REMEM-BER, LIKE ALL MY INVEN-TIONS...
...IT MUST BE USED FOR GOOD, NOT EVIL...
point ぴっ
...URRR-RGHHH !!
gurgle!
PROFES-SOR, ARE YOU OKAY ...?
WC
N-NO...
ANY IDEA WHAT CAUSED IT?
Y-YEAH, THE MILK...
...IT'S BEEN SITTING AROUND FOR FOUR DAYS...
FIVE, I THINK!
I HOPE THE PRO-FESSOR IS OKAY...
...UM, HE LITERALLY JUST SAID HE ISN'T.
I THINK HE NEEDS A MORALE BOOST!
bam!
RIGHT!

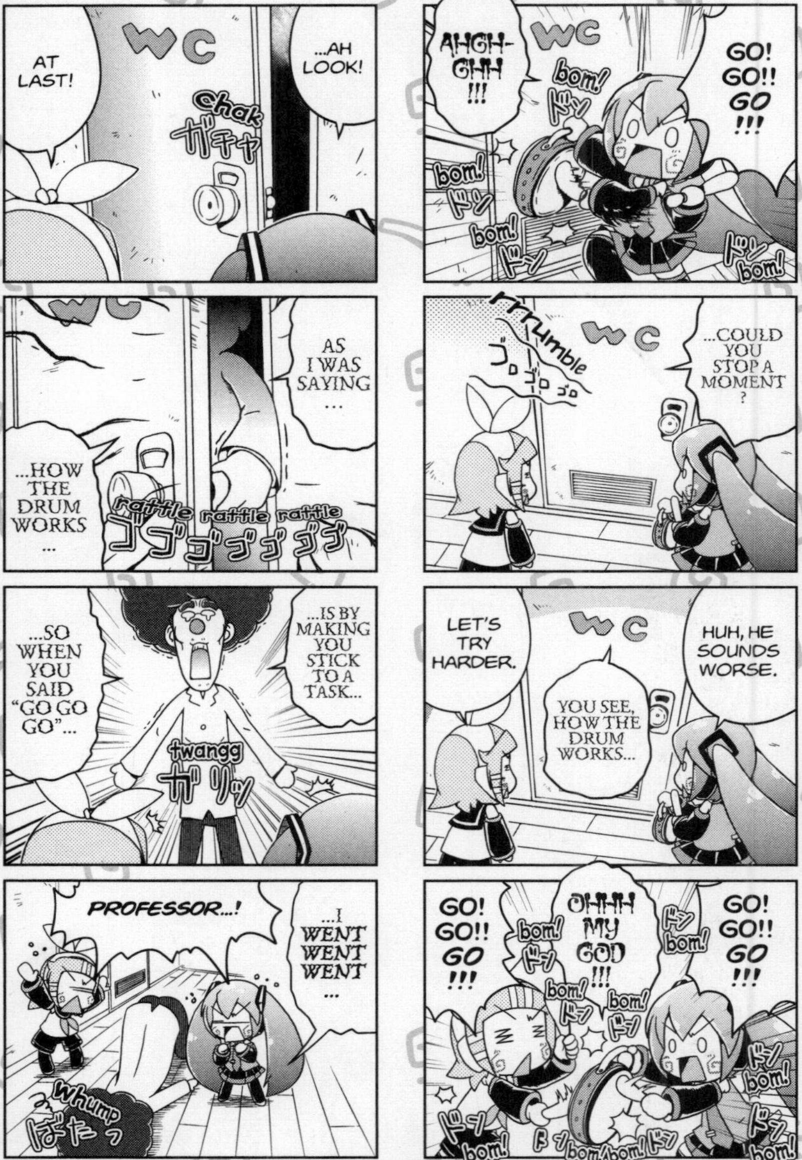
GO! GO!! GO !!!
AHGH-GHH !!!
bom! ドッ
bom! ドン
bom! ドン
ドン bom!
...COULD YOU STOP A MOMENT ?
rrrumble ゴロゴロゴロ
HUH, HE SOUNDS WORSE.
YOU SEE, HOW THE DRUM WORKS...
LET'S TRY HARDER.
GO! GO!! GO !!!
ドン bom!
OHHH MY GOD !!!
bom! ドン
bom! ドン
bom! ドン
GO! GO!! GO !!!
ドン bom!
ドン bom!
bom! bom! ドン
ドッ bom!
...AH LOOK!
chak ガチャ
AT LAST!
AS I WAS SAYING ...
...HOW THE DRUM WORKS ...
rattle rattle rattle
...IS BY MAKING YOU STICK TO A TASK...
...SO WHEN YOU SAID "GO GO GO"...
twangg ガリッ
...I WENT WENT WENT ...
PROFESSOR...!
whump ばたっ

HATSUNE MIKU MIKUBON

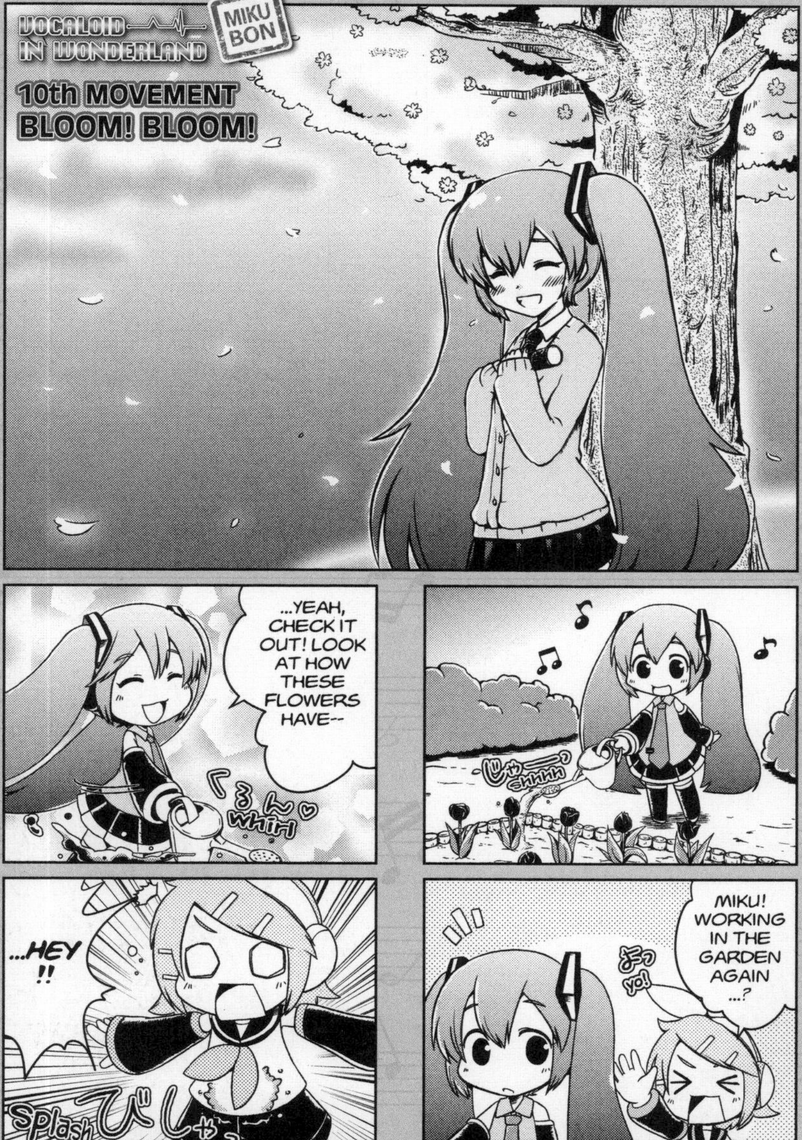
VOCALOID IN WONDERLAND
MIKU BON
10th MOVEMENT
BLOOM! BLOOM!
じゅーっ shhhh
よっ yo!
MIKU! WORKING IN THE GARDEN AGAIN ...?
...YEAH, CHECK IT OUT! LOOK AT HOW THESE FLOWERS HAVE--
くるん♡ whirl
...HEY !!
びしゃっ splash

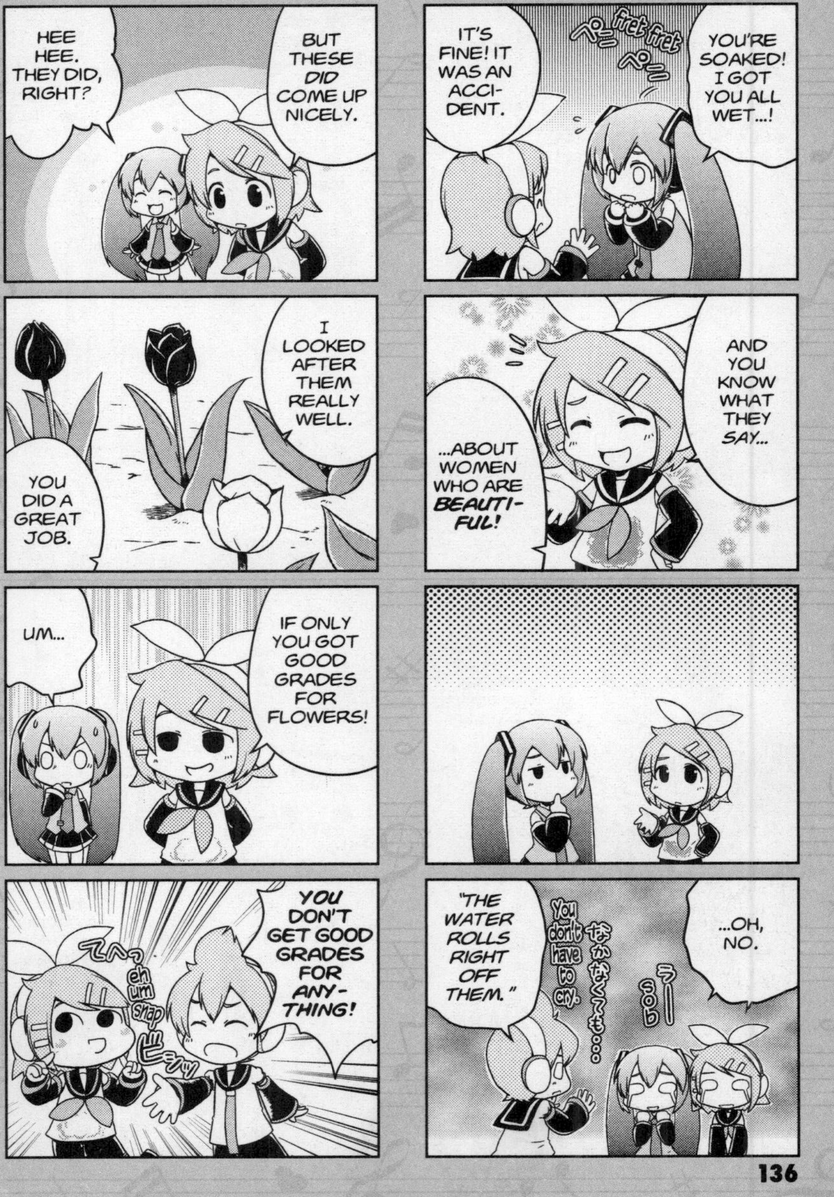
YOU'RE SOAKED! I GOT YOU ALL WET...!
fret fret
IT'S FINE! IT WAS AN ACCI-DENT.
BUT THESE *DID* COME UP NICELY.
HEE HEE. THEY DID, RIGHT?
AND YOU KNOW WHAT THEY *SAY*...
...ABOUT WOMEN WHO ARE ***BEAUTIFUL!***
I LOOKED AFTER THEM REALLY WELL.
YOU DID A GREAT JOB.
IF ONLY YOU GOT GOOD GRADES FOR FLOWERS!
UM...
...OH, NO.
sob
You don't have to cry.
なかなくても…
"THE WATER ROLLS RIGHT OFF THEM."
YOU **DON'T GET GOOD GRADES FOR** ***ANY-THING!***
eh um
snap

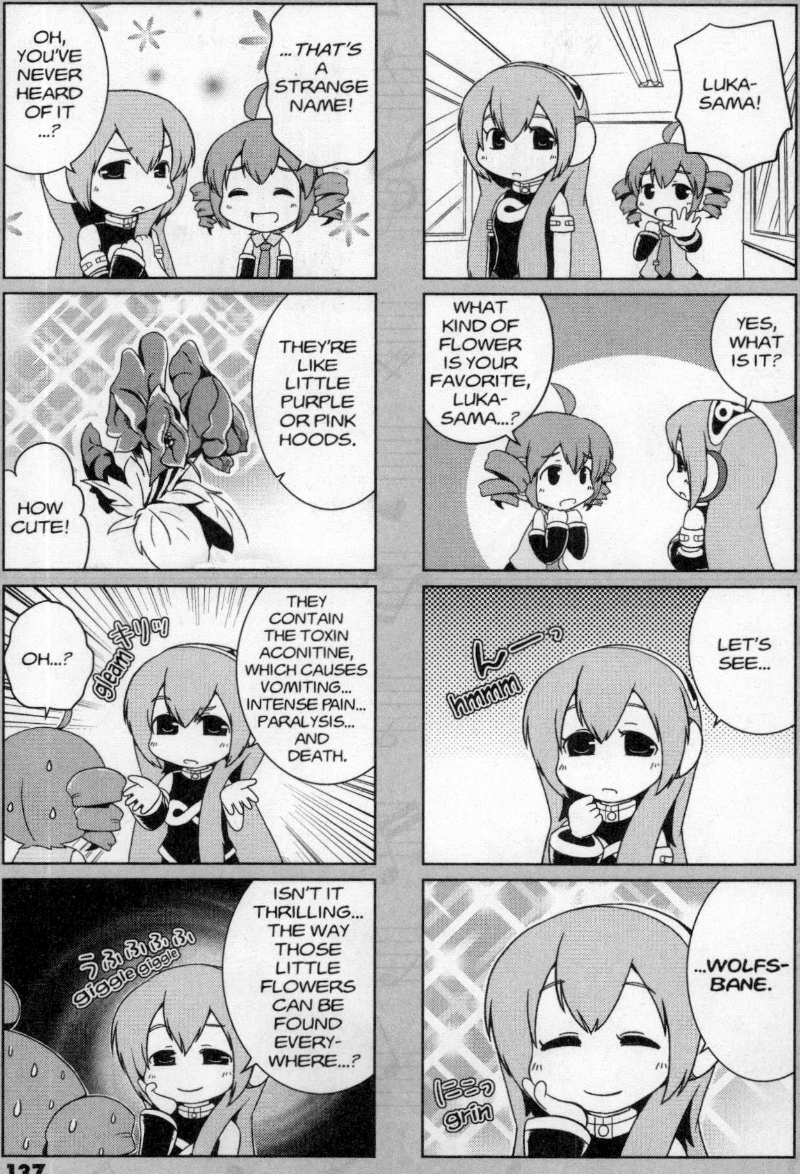
LUKA-SAMA!
YES, WHAT IS IT?
WHAT KIND OF FLOWER IS YOUR FAVORITE, LUKA-SAMA...?
LET'S SEE...
ん〜っ
hmmm
...WOLFS-BANE.
にこっ
grin
...THAT'S A STRANGE NAME!
OH, YOU'VE NEVER HEARD OF IT ...?
THEY'RE LIKE LITTLE PURPLE OR PINK HOODS.
HOW CUTE!
THEY CONTAIN THE TOXIN ACONITINE, WHICH CAUSES VOMITING... INTENSE PAIN... PARALYSIS... AND DEATH.
キリッ
gleam
OH...?
ISN'T IT THRILLING... THE WAY THOSE LITTLE FLOWERS CAN BE FOUND EVERY-WHERE...?
うふふふふ
giggle giggle

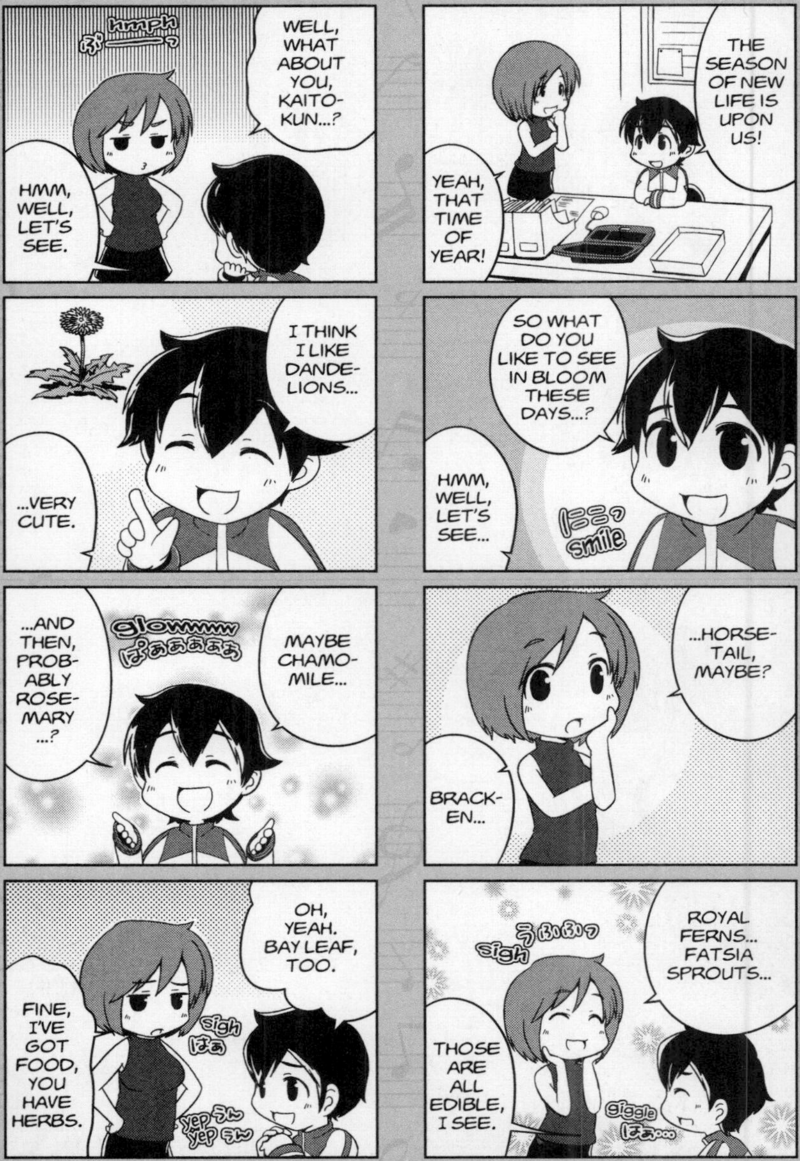
THE SEASON OF NEW LIFE IS UPON US!
YEAH, THAT TIME OF YEAR!
SO WHAT DO YOU LIKE TO SEE IN BLOOM THESE DAYS...?
HMM, WELL, LET'S SEE...
にこっ smile
...HORSE-TAIL, MAYBE?
BRACK-EN...
ROYAL FERNS... FATSIA SPROUTS...
うふふっ sigh
THOSE ARE ALL EDIBLE, I SEE.
giggle はぁ…
WELL, WHAT ABOUT YOU, KAITO-KUN...?
hmph ぷーっ
HMM, WELL, LET'S SEE.
I THINK I LIKE DANDE-LIONS...
...VERY CUTE.
MAYBE CHAMO-MILE...
glowwww ぱぁぁぁぁぁ
...AND THEN, PROB-ABLY ROSE-MARY ...?
OH, YEAH. BAY LEAF, TOO.
sigh はぁ
FINE, I'VE GOT FOOD, YOU HAVE HERBS.
yep うん yep うん

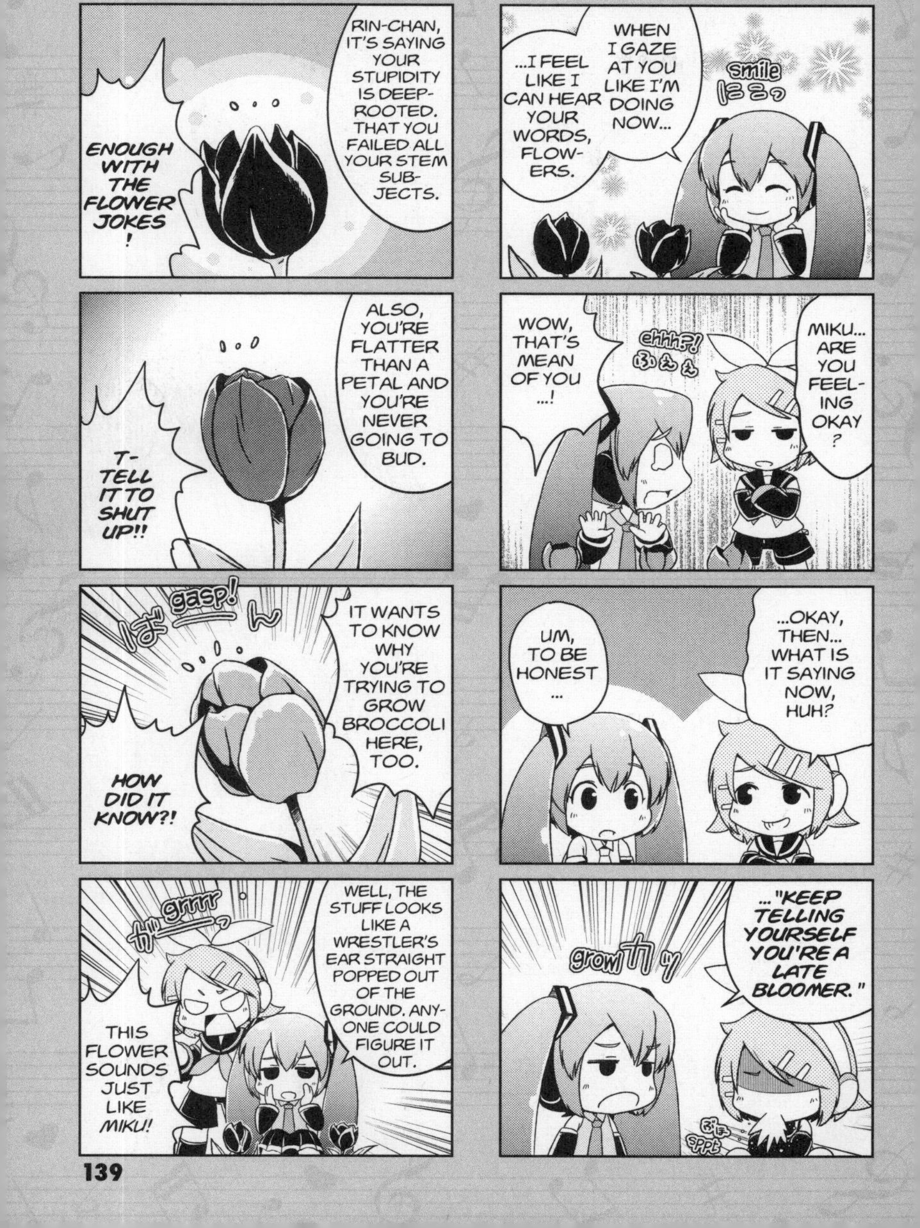
WHEN I GAZE AT YOU LIKE I'M DOING NOW...
...I FEEL LIKE I CAN HEAR YOUR WORDS, FLOWERS.
smile にこっ
MIKU... ARE YOU FEELING OKAY?
WOW, THAT'S MEAN OF YOU ...!
ehhh?! ふぇぇ
...OKAY, THEN... WHAT IS IT SAYING NOW, HUH?
UM, TO BE HONEST ...
..."KEEP TELLING YOURSELF YOU'RE A LATE BLOOMER."
growl カッ
sppt
RIN-CHAN, IT'S SAYING YOUR STUPIDITY IS DEEP-ROOTED. THAT YOU FAILED ALL YOUR STEM SUBJECTS.
ENOUGH WITH THE FLOWER JOKES!
ALSO, YOU'RE FLATTER THAN A PETAL AND YOU'RE NEVER GOING TO BUD.
T-TELL IT TO SHUT UP!!
gasp!
IT WANTS TO KNOW WHY YOU'RE TRYING TO GROW BROCCOLI HERE, TOO.
HOW DID IT KNOW?!
grrrr
WELL, THE STUFF LOOKS LIKE A WRESTLER'S EAR STRAIGHT POPPED OUT OF THE GROUND. ANYONE COULD FIGURE IT OUT.
THIS FLOWER SOUNDS JUST LIKE MIKU!

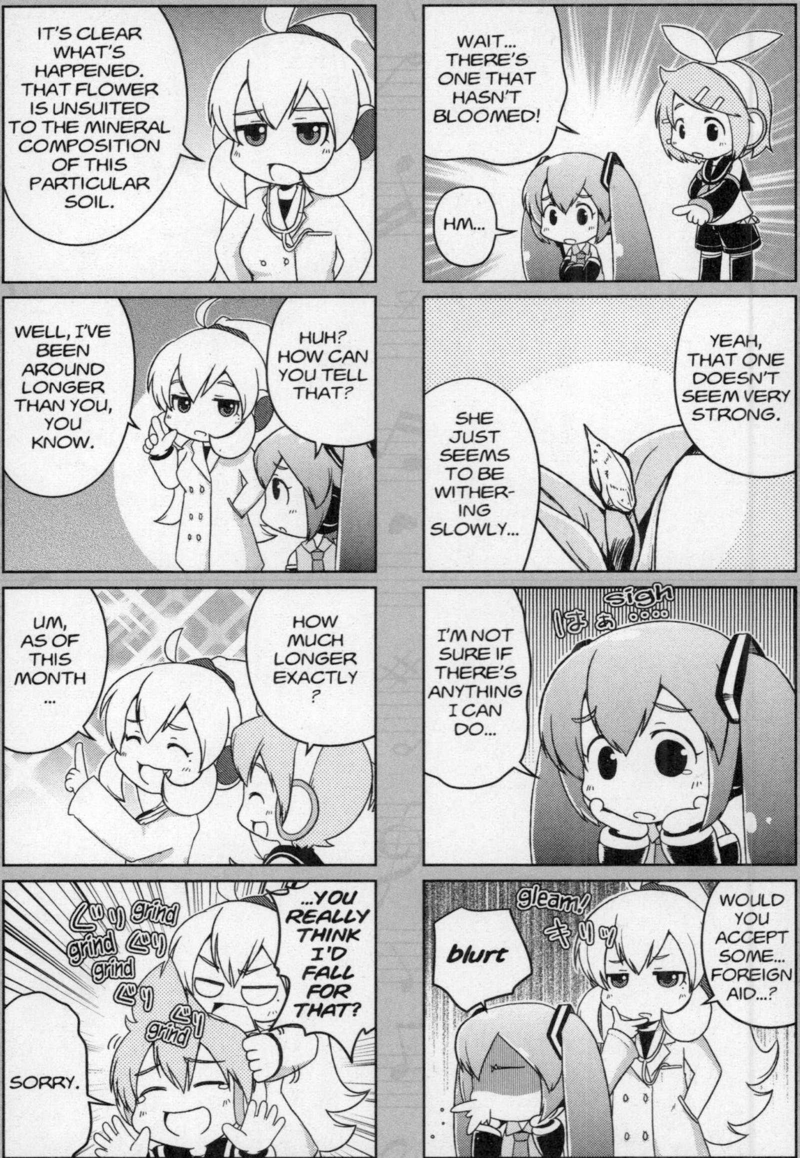
WAIT... THERE'S ONE THAT HASN'T BLOOMED!
HM...
IT'S CLEAR WHAT'S HAPPENED. THAT FLOWER IS UNSUITED TO THE MINERAL COMPOSITION OF THIS PARTICULAR SOIL.
YEAH, THAT ONE DOESN'T SEEM VERY STRONG.
SHE JUST SEEMS TO BE WITHER-ING SLOWLY...
HUH? HOW CAN YOU TELL THAT?
WELL, I'VE BEEN AROUND LONGER THAN YOU, YOU KNOW.
sigh
はぁ…
I'M NOT SURE IF THERE'S ANYTHING I CAN DO...
HOW MUCH LONGER EXACTLY?
UM, AS OF THIS MONTH...
gleam!
キリッ
WOULD YOU ACCEPT SOME... FOREIGN AID...?
blurt
...YOU REALLY THINK I'D FALL FOR THAT?
ぐりぐりgrind grind ぐりgrind ぐり ぐり grind
SORRY.

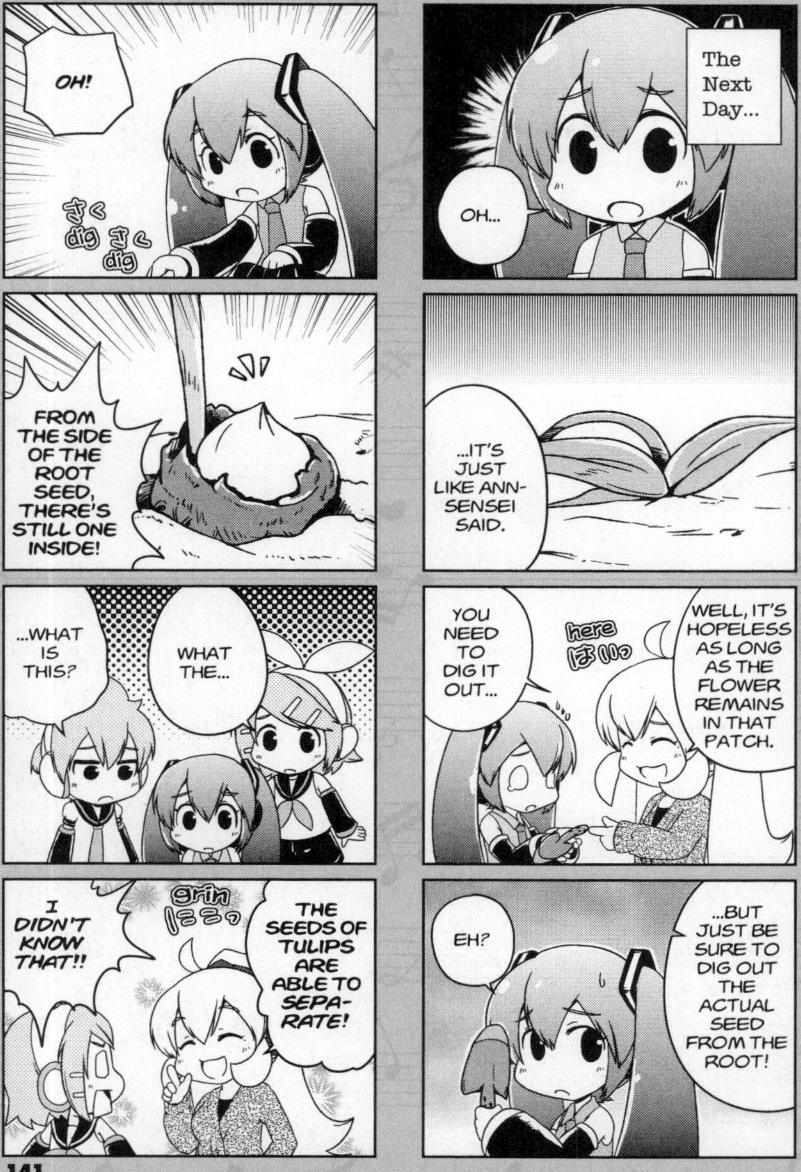
The Next Day...
OH...
...IT'S JUST LIKE ANN-SENSEI SAID.
WELL, IT'S HOPELESS AS LONG AS THE FLOWER REMAINS IN THAT PATCH.
here はいっ
YOU NEED TO DIG IT OUT...
...BUT JUST BE SURE TO DIG OUT THE ACTUAL SEED FROM THE ROOT!
EH?
OH!
さく dig さく dig
FROM THE SIDE OF THE ROOT SEED, THERE'S STILL ONE INSIDE!
WHAT THE...
...WHAT IS THIS?
THE SEEDS OF TULIPS ARE ABLE TO SEPARATE!
grin にこっ
I DIDN'T KNOW THAT!!

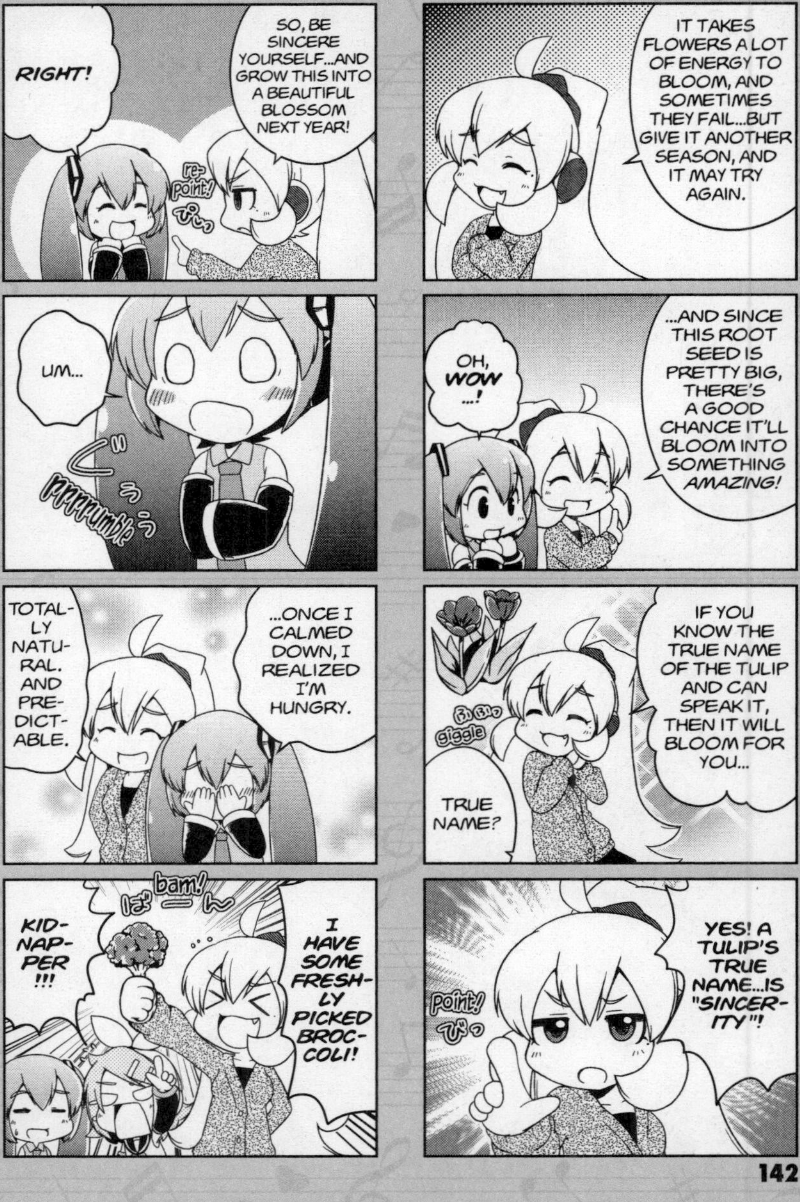
IT TAKES FLOWERS A LOT OF ENERGY TO BLOOM, AND SOMETIMES THEY FAIL...BUT GIVE IT ANOTHER SEASON, AND IT MAY TRY AGAIN.
SO, BE SINCERE YOURSELF...AND GROW THIS INTO A BEAUTIFUL BLOSSOM NEXT YEAR!
re-point! ぴっ
RIGHT!
...AND SINCE THIS ROOT SEED IS PRETTY BIG, THERE'S A GOOD CHANCE IT'LL BLOOM INTO SOMETHING *AMAZING!*
OH, **WOW** ...!
UM...
ぐぅぅ
IF YOU KNOW THE TRUE NAME OF THE TULIP AND CAN SPEAK IT, THEN IT WILL BLOOM FOR YOU...
ふふっ giggle
TRUE NAME?
...ONCE I CALMED DOWN, I REALIZED I'M HUNGRY.
TOTALLY NATURAL. AND PREDICTABLE.
YES! A TULIP'S TRUE NAME...IS "SINCERITY"!
point! びっ
bam! ばーん
I HAVE SOME FRESHLY PICKED BROCCOLI!
KIDNAPPER!!!

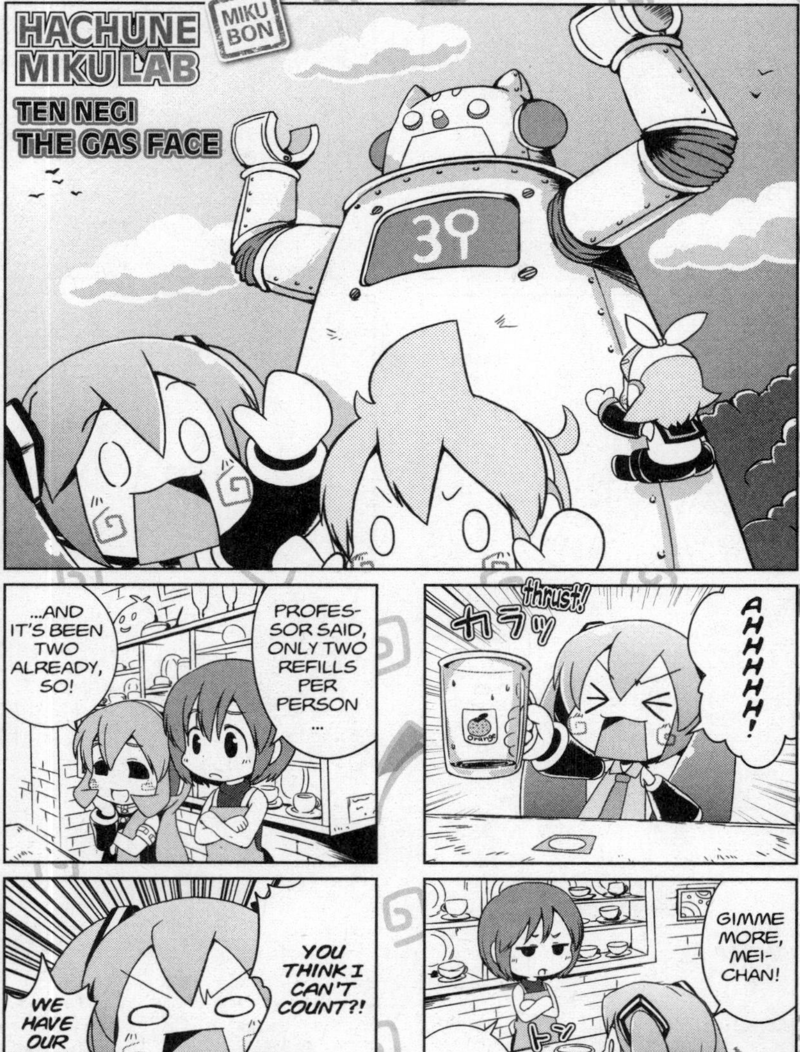
HACHUNE MIKU LAB
MIKU BON
TEN NEGI
THE GAS FACE
39
thrust!
カラッ
AHHHHH!
Orange
PROFES-SOR SAID, ONLY TWO REFILLS PER PERSON ...
...AND IT'S BEEN TWO ALREADY, SO!
GIMME MORE, MEI-CHAN!
トッ
ton
NO, YOU'RE DONE.
YOU THINK I CAN'T COUNT?!
WE HAVE OUR DOUBTS!
ど——ん
wham!

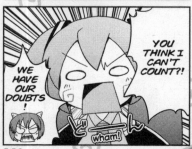

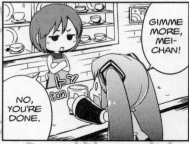

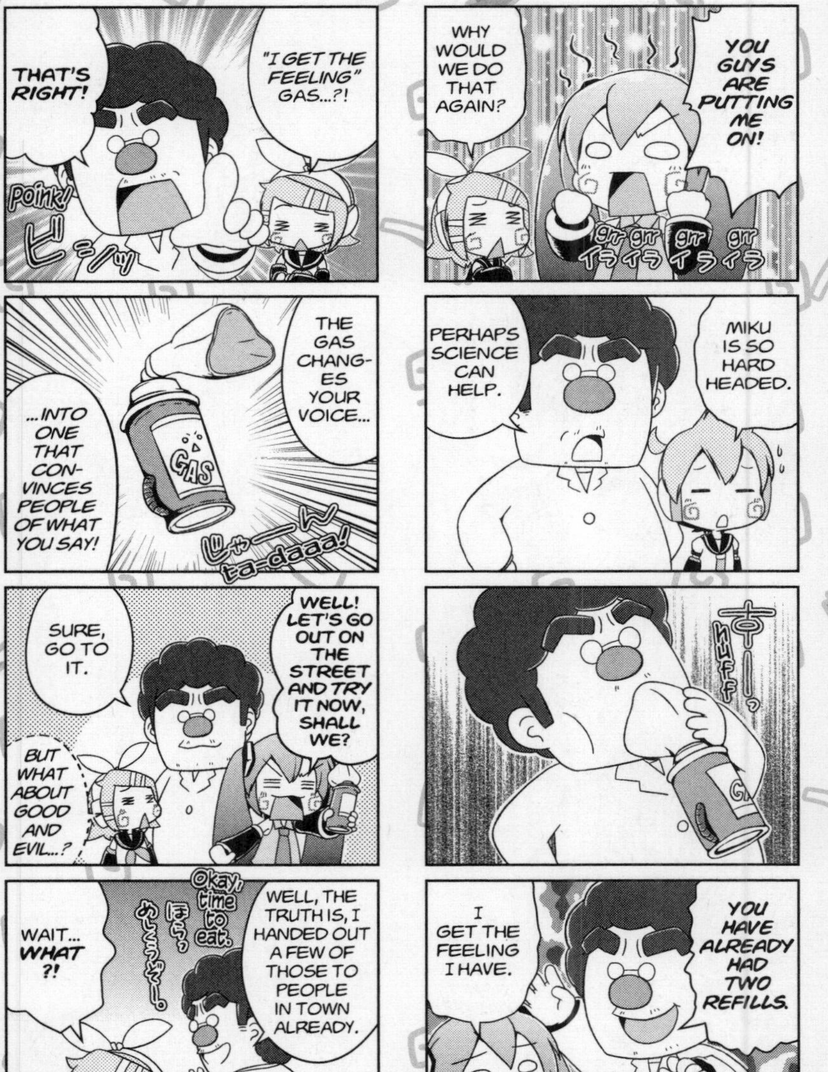
YOU GUYS ARE PUTTING ME ON!
WHY WOULD WE DO THAT AGAIN?
grr grr grr grr
イライライライラ
"I GET THE FEELING" GAS...?!
THAT'S RIGHT!
Poink!
ピシッ
MIKU IS SO HARD HEADED.
PERHAPS SCIENCE CAN HELP.
THE GAS CHANGES YOUR VOICE...
...INTO ONE THAT CONVINCES PEOPLE OF WHAT YOU SAY!
GAS
じゃーん
ta-daaa!
すーっ
huff
WELL! LET'S GO OUT ON THE STREET AND TRY IT NOW, SHALL WE?
SURE, GO TO IT.
BUT WHAT ABOUT GOOD AND EVIL...?
YOU HAVE ALREADY HAD TWO REFILLS.
I GET THE FEELING I HAVE.
hahhhhh
もあああん
WELL, THE TRUTH IS, I HANDED OUT A FEW OF THOSE TO PEOPLE IN TOWN ALREADY.
Okay, time to eat.
ほらっ めしどうぞー。
WAIT... WHAT?!

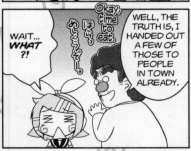

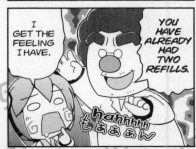

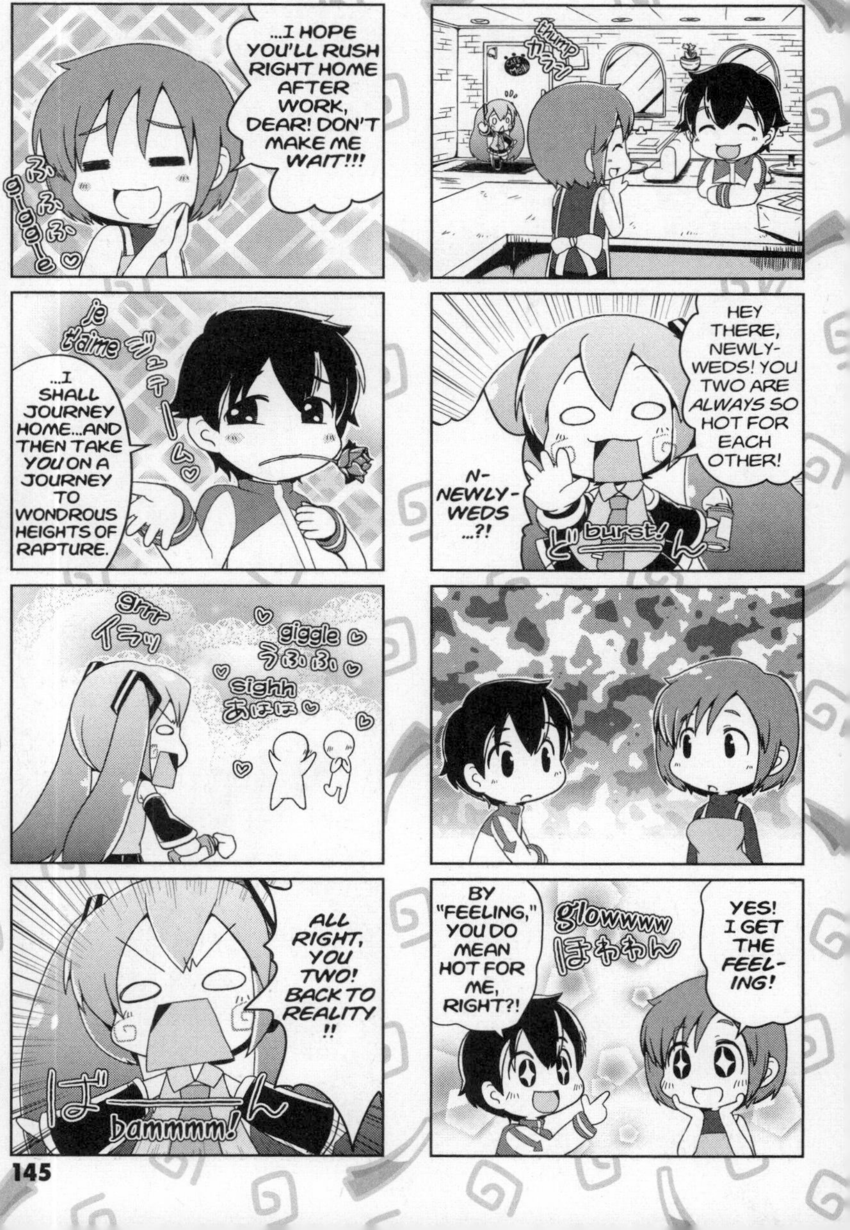
thump
カラン
...I HOPE YOU'LL RUSH RIGHT HOME AFTER WORK, DEAR! DON'T MAKE ME WAIT!!!
ふふふ
giggle
HEY THERE, NEWLY-WEDS! YOU TWO ARE ALWAYS SO HOT FOR EACH OTHER!
N-NEWLY-WEDS ...?!
burst!
どーん
je t'aime
ジュテーム
...I SHALL JOURNEY HOME...AND THEN TAKE YOU ON A JOURNEY TO WONDROUS HEIGHTS OF RAPTURE.
grrr
イラッ
giggle
うふふ
sighh
あはは
YES! I GET THE FEEL-ING!
glowwww
ほわわん
BY "FEELING," YOU DO MEAN HOT FOR ME, RIGHT?!
ALL RIGHT, YOU TWO! BACK TO REALITY!!
ばーーん
bammmm!

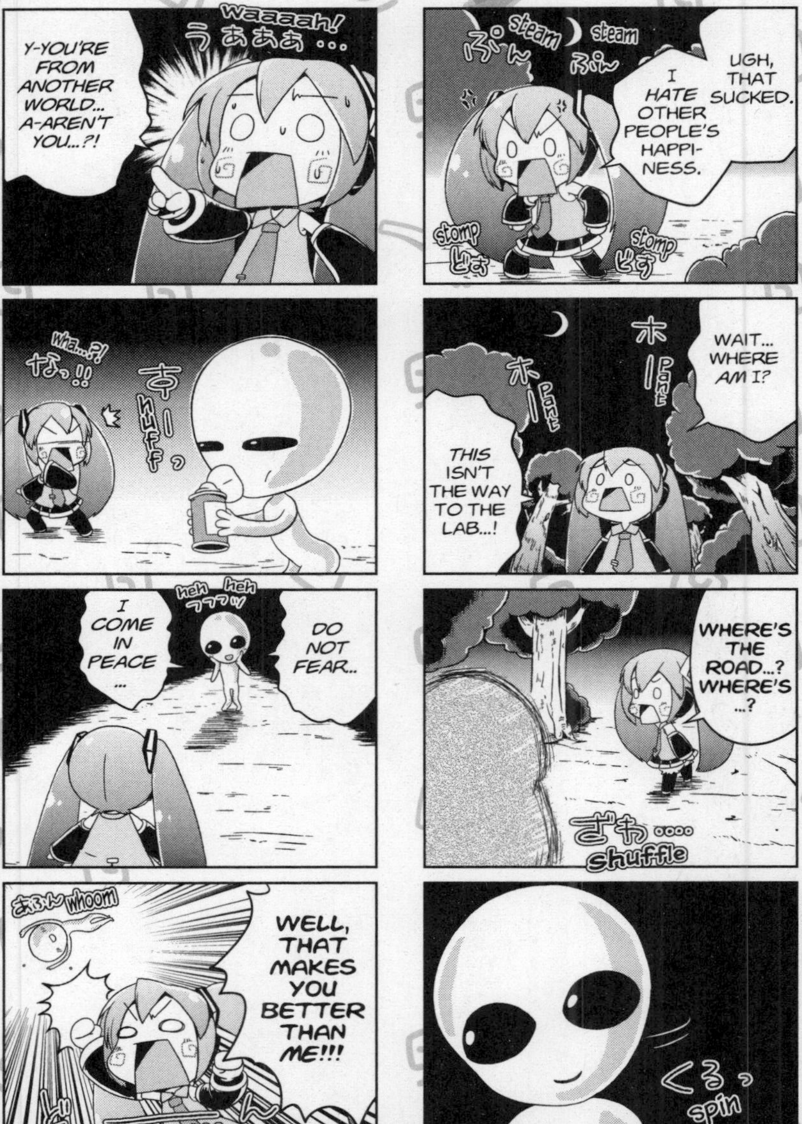
steam
ぷん
steam
ぷん
UGH, THAT SUCKED.
I HATE OTHER PEOPLE'S HAPPINESS.
stomp
stomp
ビす
waaaah!
うあああ...
Y-YOU'RE FROM ANOTHER WORLD... A-AREN'T YOU...?!
ホー
Pone
ホー
Pone
WAIT... WHERE AM I?
THIS ISN'T THE WAY TO THE LAB...!
wha...?!
なっ!!
ふー
HUFF
WHERE'S THE ROAD...? WHERE'S ...?
ざわ....
shuffle
heh heh
フフフッ
I COME IN PEACE ...
DO NOT FEAR...
くるっ
spin
whoom
WELL, THAT MAKES YOU BETTER THAN ME!!!
punch!!!

HATSUNE MIKU

MIKUBON

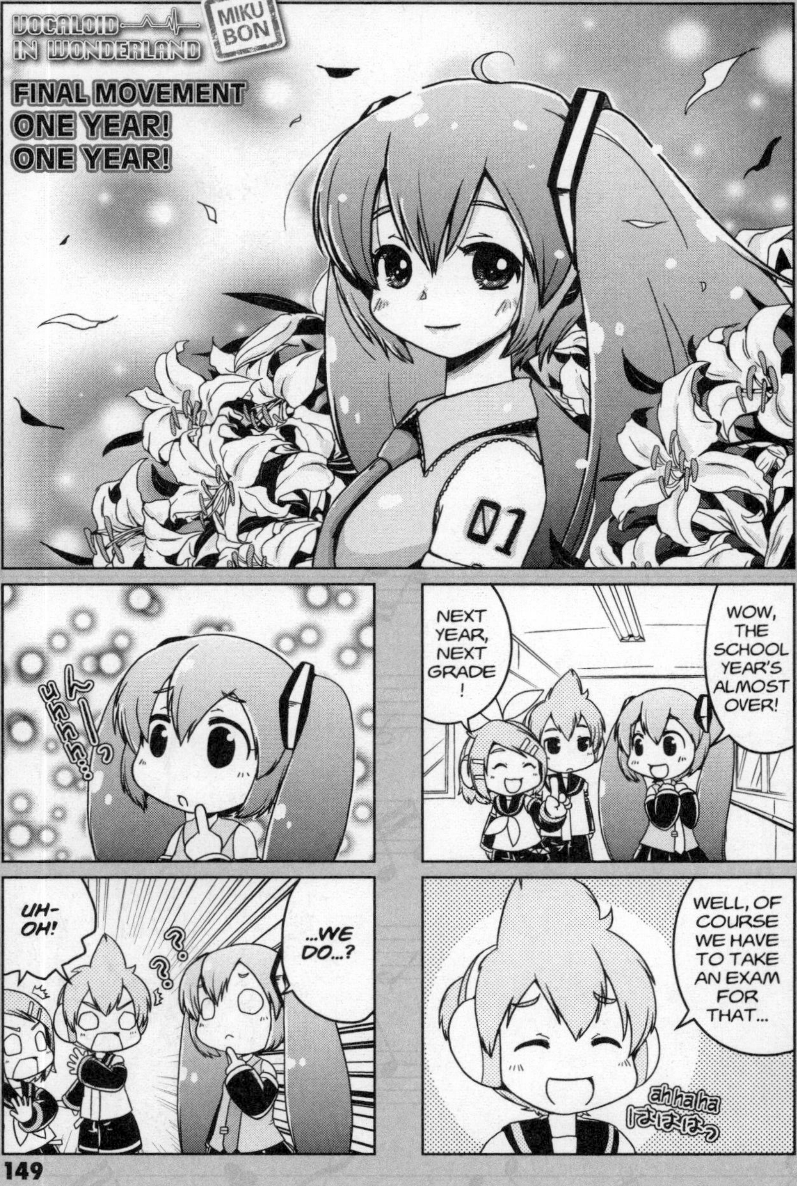
VOCALOID IN WONDERLAND
MIKU BON
FINAL MOVEMENT
ONE YEAR! ONE YEAR!
WOW, THE SCHOOL YEAR'S ALMOST OVER!
NEXT YEAR, NEXT GRADE!
WELL, OF COURSE WE HAVE TO TAKE AN EXAM FOR THAT...
ah ha ha
はははっ
...WE DO...?
UH-OH!

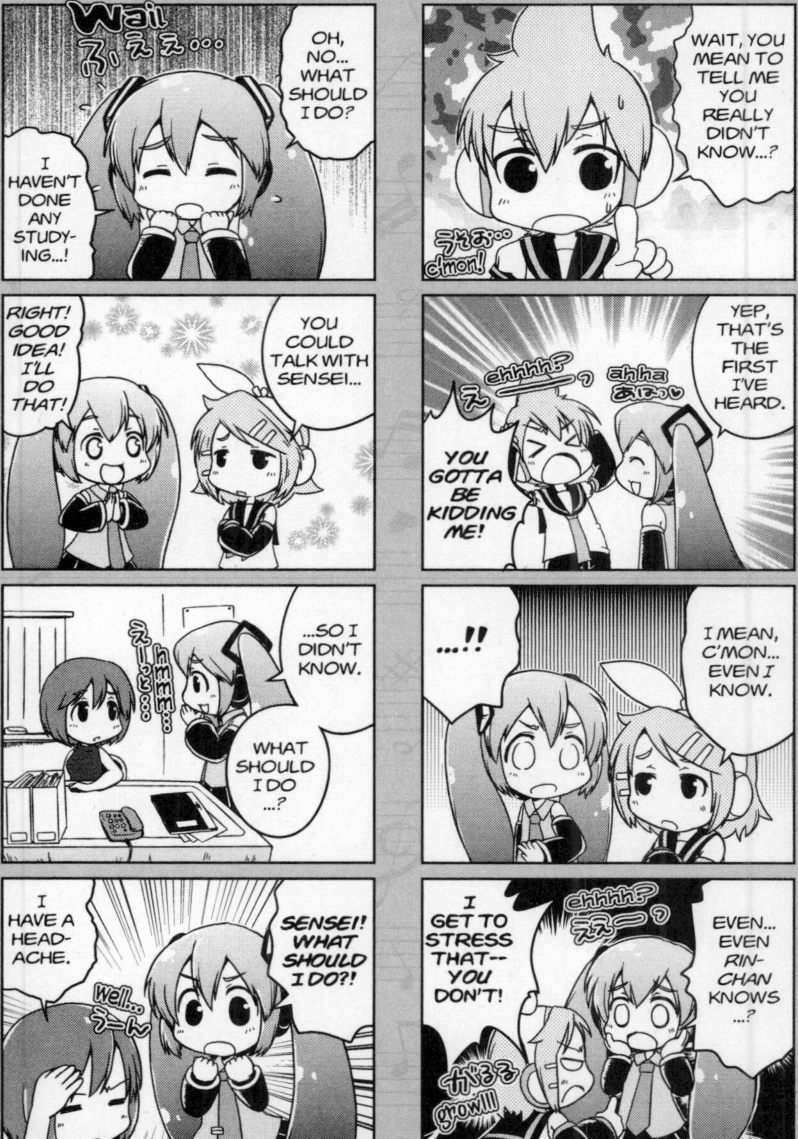
WAIT, YOU MEAN TO TELL ME YOU REALLY DIDN'T KNOW...?
うそぉ‥ c'mon!
YEP, THAT'S THE FIRST I'VE HEARD.
ahha あはっ♥
ehhhh? えー
YOU GOTTA BE KIDDING ME!
I MEAN, C'MON... EVEN I KNOW.
...!!
EVEN... EVEN RIN-CHAN KNOWS ...?
ehhhh? ええー
I GET TO STRESS THAT-- YOU DON'T!
がるるる growlll
OH, NO... WHAT SHOULD I DO?
Wail ふえぇ…
I HAVEN'T DONE ANY STUDYING...!
YOU COULD TALK WITH SENSEI...
RIGHT! GOOD IDEA! I'LL DO THAT!
...SO I DIDN'T KNOW.
hmmm... えーっと‥
WHAT SHOULD I DO ...?
SENSEI! WHAT SHOULD I DO?!
I HAVE A HEADACHE.
well... うーん

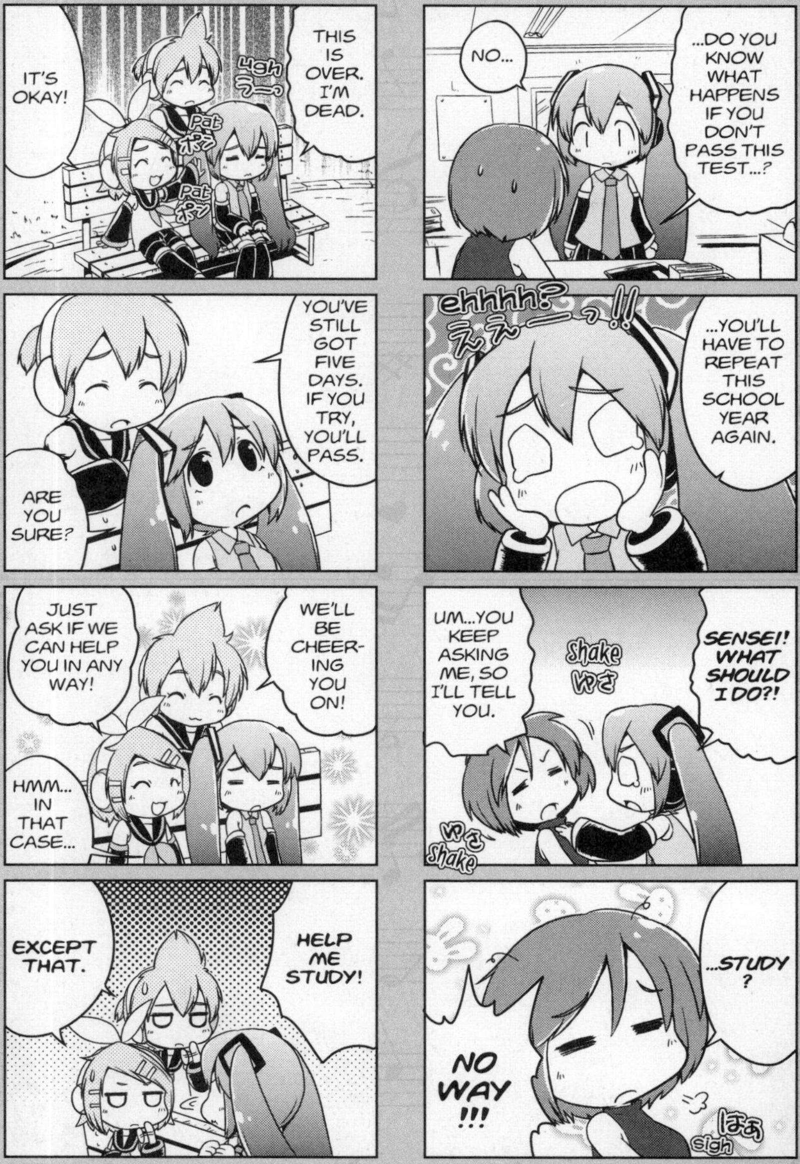

...DO YOU KNOW WHAT HAPPENS IF YOU DON'T PASS THIS TEST...?
NO...
ehhhh? ええーっ!!
...YOU'LL HAVE TO REPEAT THIS SCHOOL YEAR AGAIN.
SENSEI! WHAT SHOULD I DO?!
shake ゆさ
UM...YOU KEEP ASKING ME, SO I'LL TELL YOU.
ゆさ shake
...STUDY?
NO WAY!!!
はぁ sigh
THIS IS OVER. I'M DEAD.
ugh うーっ
Pat ポン
Pat ポン
IT'S OKAY!
YOU'VE STILL GOT FIVE DAYS. IF YOU TRY, YOU'LL PASS.
ARE YOU SURE?
WE'LL BE CHEERING YOU ON!
JUST ASK IF WE CAN HELP YOU IN ANY WAY!
HMM... IN THAT CASE...
HELP ME STUDY!
EXCEPT THAT.

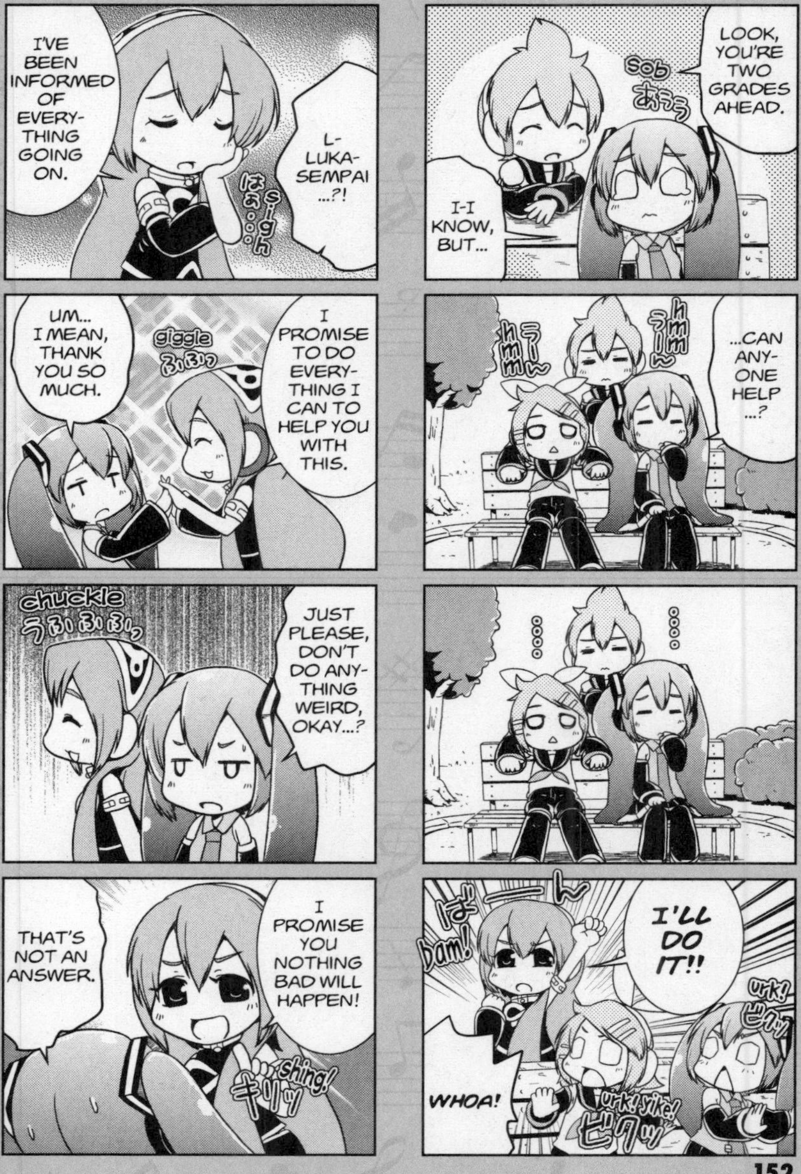

LOOK, YOU'RE TWO GRADES AHEAD.
sob
あうう
I-I KNOW, BUT...
...CAN ANY-ONE HELP ...?
hmm
うーん
hmm
うーん
....
....
I'LL DO IT!!
ばーーん
Bam!
urk!
ビクッ
urk! yike!
ビクッ
WHOA!
L-LUKA-SEMPAI ...?!
はぁ…
sigh
I'VE BEEN INFORMED OF EVERY-THING GOING ON.
I PROMISE TO DO EVERY-THING I CAN TO HELP YOU WITH THIS.
giggle
ふふっ
UM... I MEAN, THANK YOU SO MUCH.
JUST PLEASE, DON'T DO ANY-THING WEIRD, OKAY...?
chuckle
うふふふっ
I PROMISE YOU NOTHING BAD WILL HAPPEN!
shing!
キリッ
THAT'S NOT AN ANSWER.

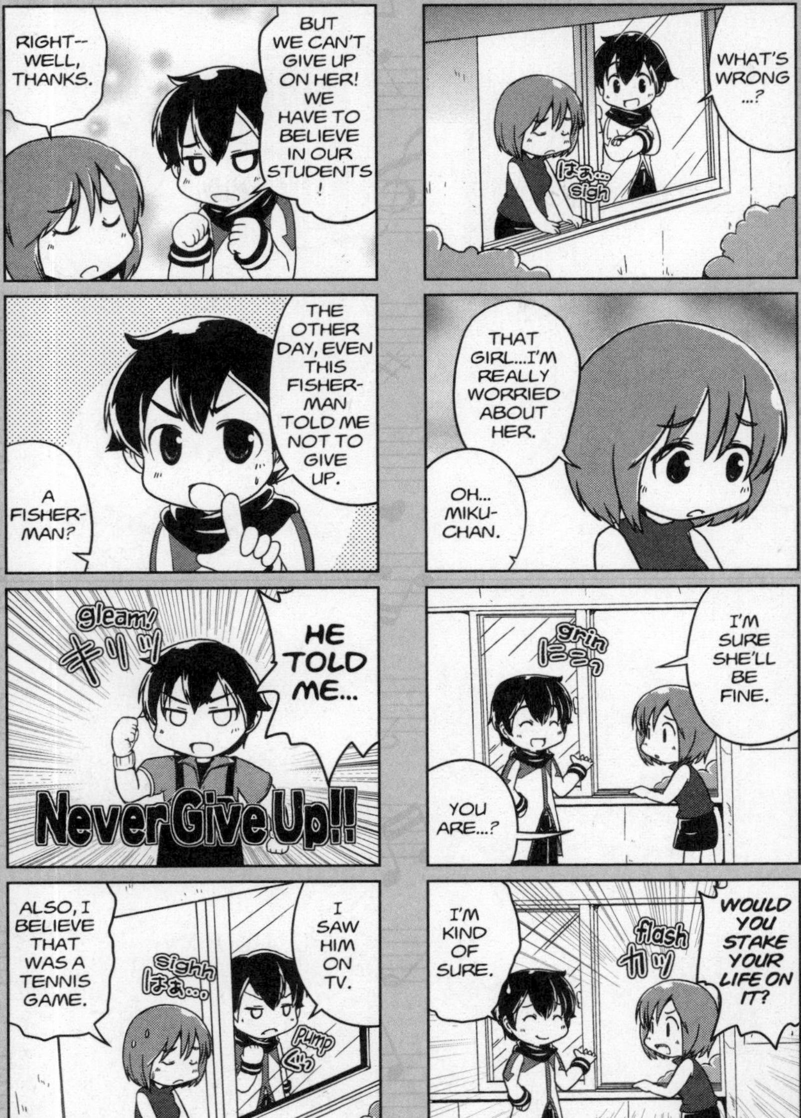
WHAT'S WRONG ...?
はぁ... sigh
THAT GIRL...I'M REALLY WORRIED ABOUT HER.
OH... MIKU-CHAN.
I'M SURE SHE'LL BE FINE.
grin にこっ
YOU ARE...?
WOULD YOU STAKE YOUR LIFE ON IT?
flash カッ
I'M KIND OF SURE.
BUT WE CAN'T GIVE UP ON HER! WE HAVE TO BELIEVE IN OUR STUDENTS!
RIGHT-- WELL, THANKS.
THE OTHER DAY, EVEN THIS FISHER-MAN TOLD ME NOT TO GIVE UP.
A FISHER-MAN?
HE TOLD ME...
gleam! キリッ
Never Give Up!!
I SAW HIM ON TV.
pump ぐっ
sighh はぁ...
ALSO, I BELIEVE THAT WAS A TENNIS GAME.

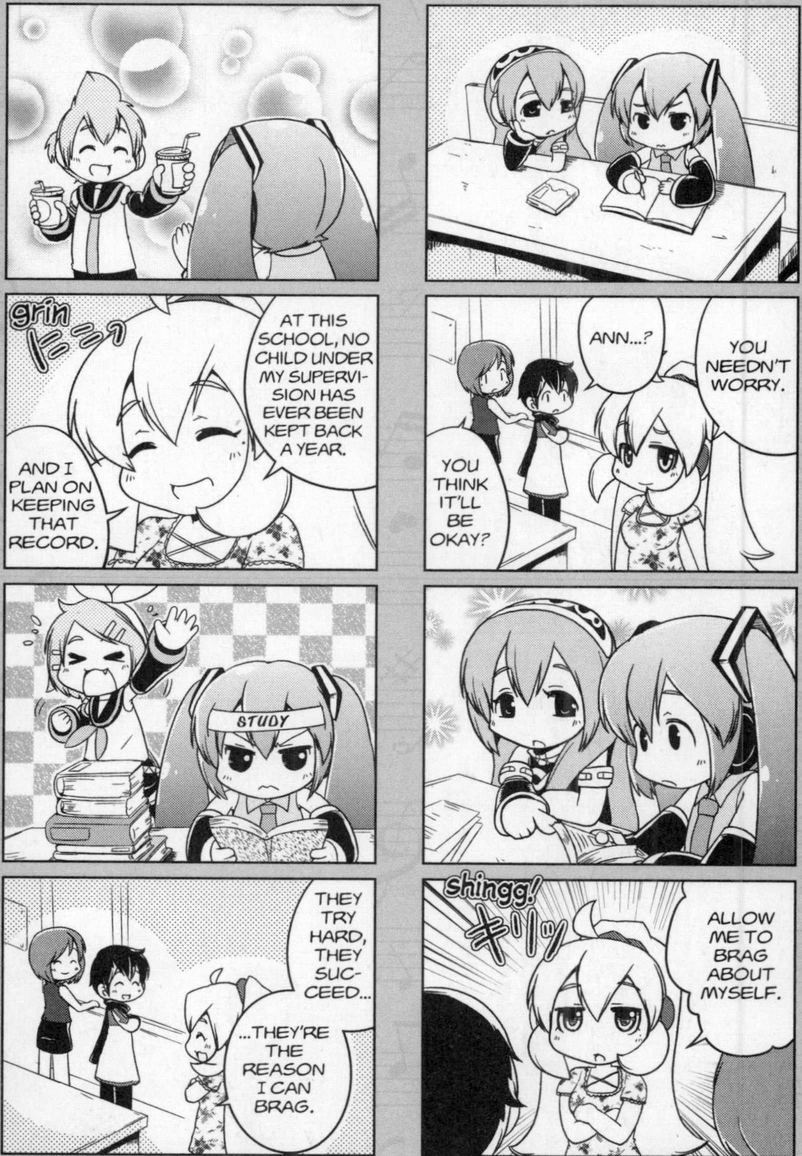
YOU NEEDN'T WORRY.
ANN...?
YOU THINK IT'LL BE OKAY?
ALLOW ME TO BRAG ABOUT MYSELF.
shingg! キリッ
AT THIS SCHOOL, NO CHILD UNDER MY SUPERVISION HAS EVER BEEN KEPT BACK A YEAR.
grin
AND I PLAN ON KEEPING THAT RECORD.
STUDY
THEY TRY HARD, THEY SUCCEED...
...THEY'RE THE REASON I CAN BRAG.

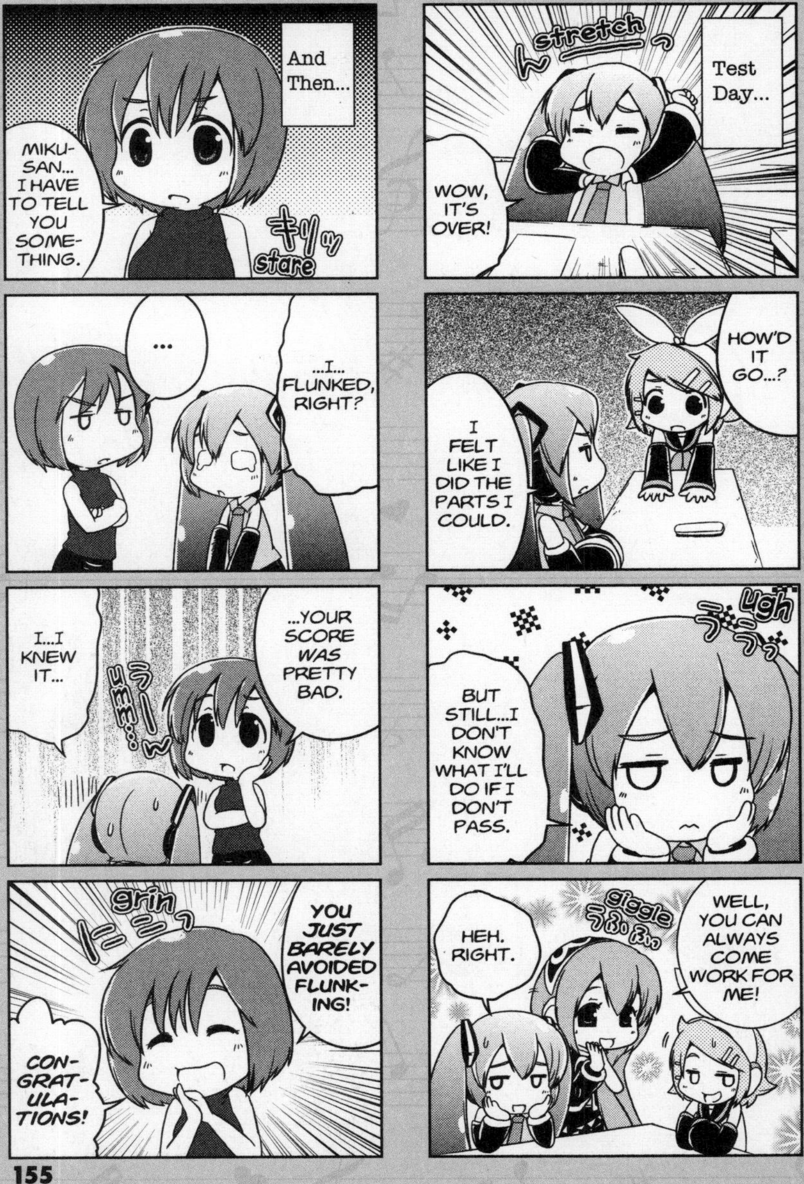
Test Day...
stretch
WOW, IT'S OVER!
HOW'D IT GO...?
I FELT LIKE I DID THE PARTS I COULD.
ugh
BUT STILL...I DON'T KNOW WHAT I'LL DO IF I DON'T PASS.
WELL, YOU CAN ALWAYS COME WORK FOR ME!
giggle
HEH. RIGHT.
And Then...
MIKU-SAN... I HAVE TO TELL YOU SOMETHING.
stare
...I... FLUNKED, RIGHT?
...
...YOUR SCORE WAS PRETTY BAD.
umm...
I...I KNEW IT...
YOU JUST BARELY AVOIDED FLUNKING!
grin
CONGRATULATIONS!

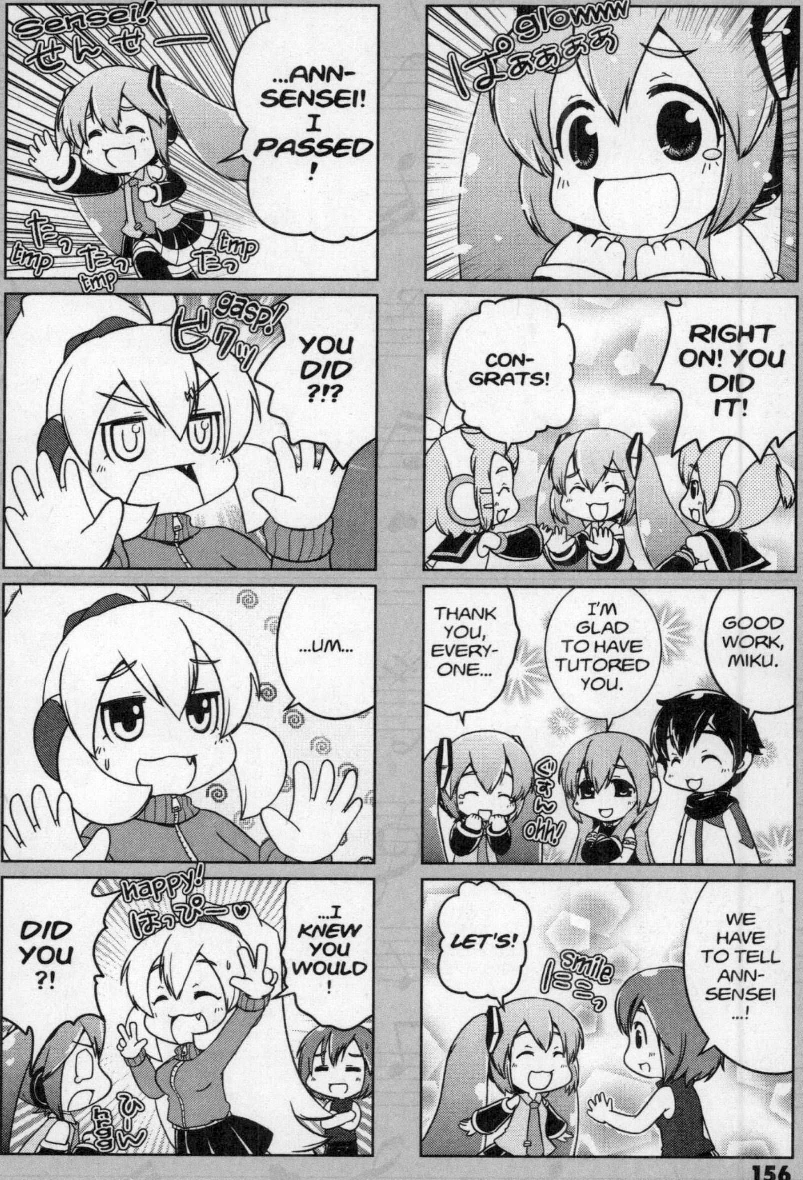

glowww
ぱあああああ
RIGHT ON! YOU DID IT!
CON-GRATS!
GOOD WORK, MIKU.
I'M GLAD TO HAVE TUTORED YOU.
THANK YOU, EVERY-ONE...
ぐすん ohh!
WE HAVE TO TELL ANN-SENSEI ...!
smile にこっ
LET'S!
Sensei! せんせー
...ANN-SENSEI! I PASSED!
たっ tmp たっ tmp たっ tmp
gasp! ビクッ
YOU DID ?!?
...UM...
...I KNEW YOU WOULD!
happy! はっぴー♥
DID YOU ?!
ひーん

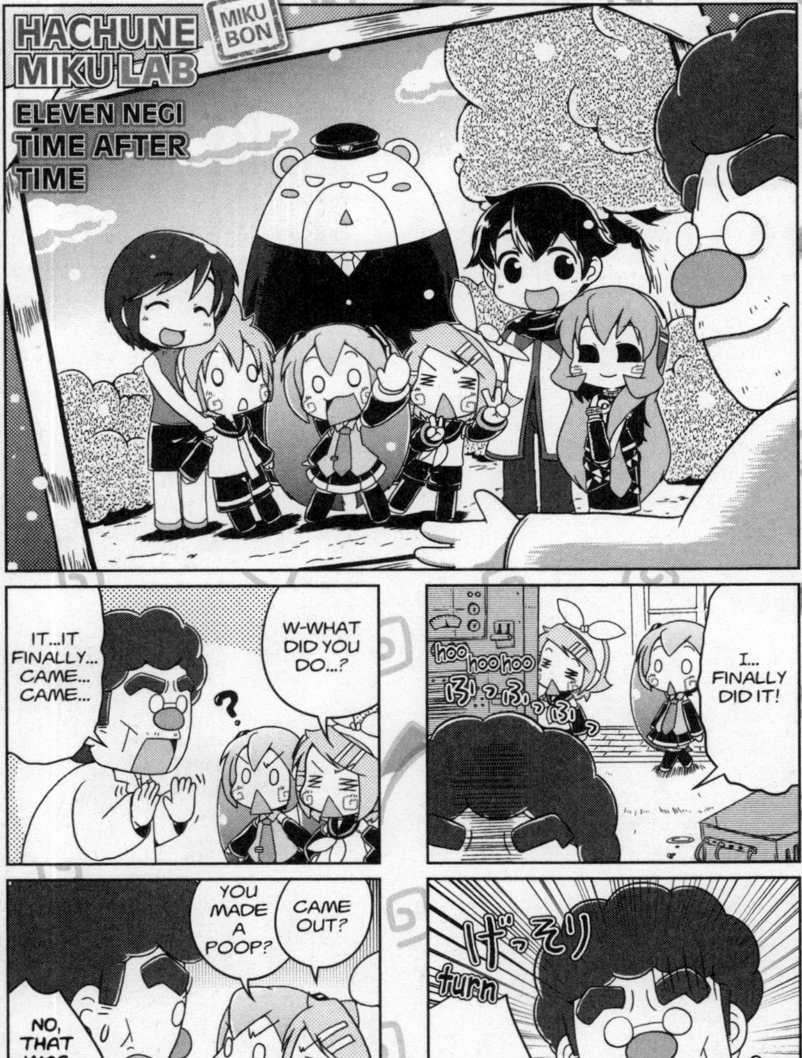
HACHUNE MIKU LAB
MIKU BON
ELEVEN NEGI TIME AFTER TIME
hoo hoo hoo
ふっふっふっ
I... FINALLY DID IT!
W-WHAT DID YOU DO...?
IT...IT FINALLY... CAME... CAME...
?
げっそり
turn
PROFES-SOR...?!
snap!
ビシッ
CAME OUT?
YOU MADE A POOP?
NO, THAT WAS THE OTHER TIME!!

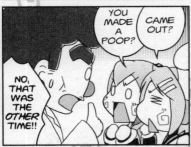

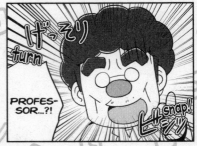

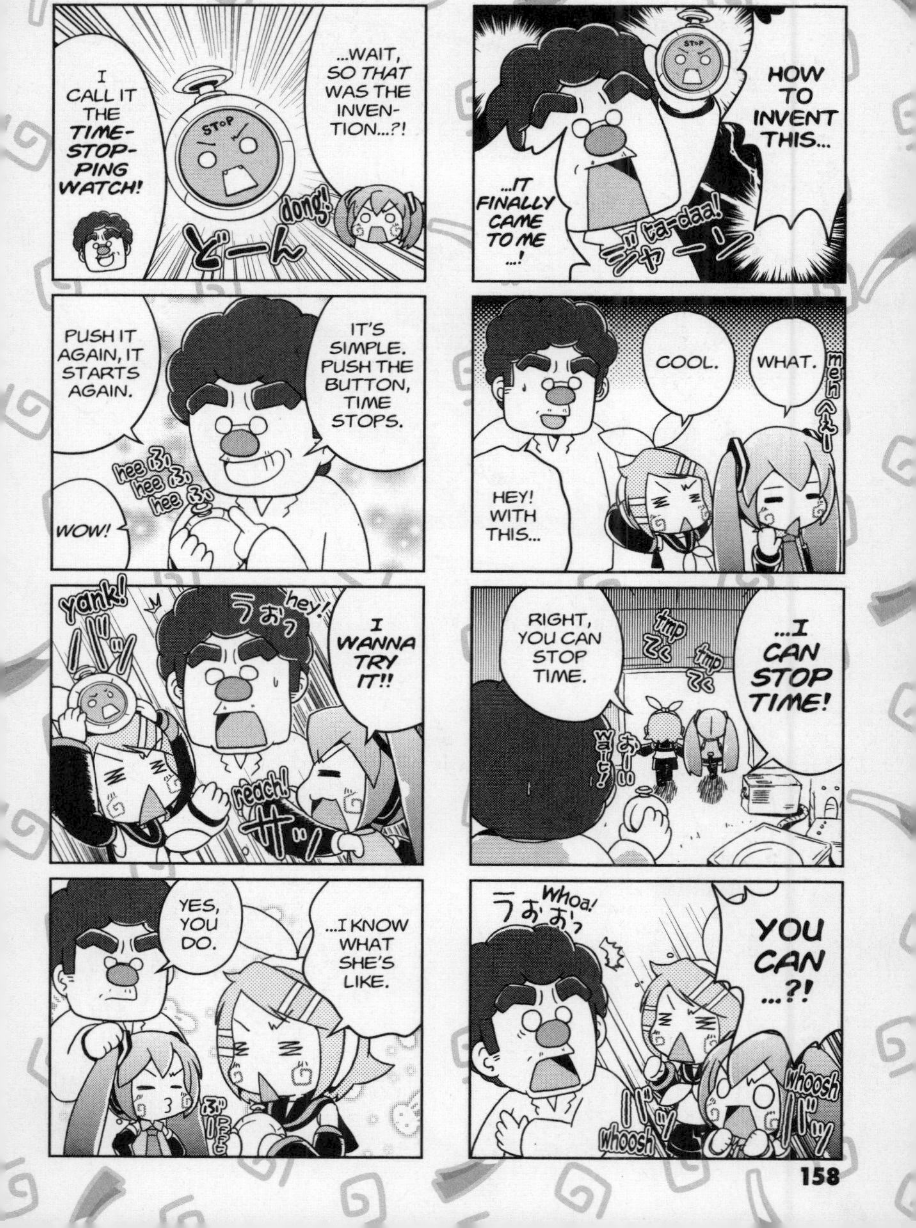
HOW TO INVENT THIS...
...IT FINALLY CAME TO ME ...!
ta-daa! ジャーン
WHAT.
meh へぇー
COOL.
HEY! WITH THIS...
...I CAN STOP TIME!
RIGHT, YOU CAN STOP TIME.
fmp てく
fmp てく
wait! おーい
YOU CAN ...?!
Whoa! うおおっ
whoosh バッ
whoosh バッ
...WAIT, SO THAT WAS THE INVENTION...?!
I CALL IT THE TIME-STOPPING WATCH!
STOP
dong! どーん
IT'S SIMPLE. PUSH THE BUTTON, TIME STOPS.
PUSH IT AGAIN, IT STARTS AGAIN.
hee ふ hee ふ hee ふ
WOW!
I WANNA TRY IT!!
hey! うおっ
yank! バッ
reach! サッ
...I KNOW WHAT SHE'S LIKE.
YES, YOU DO.

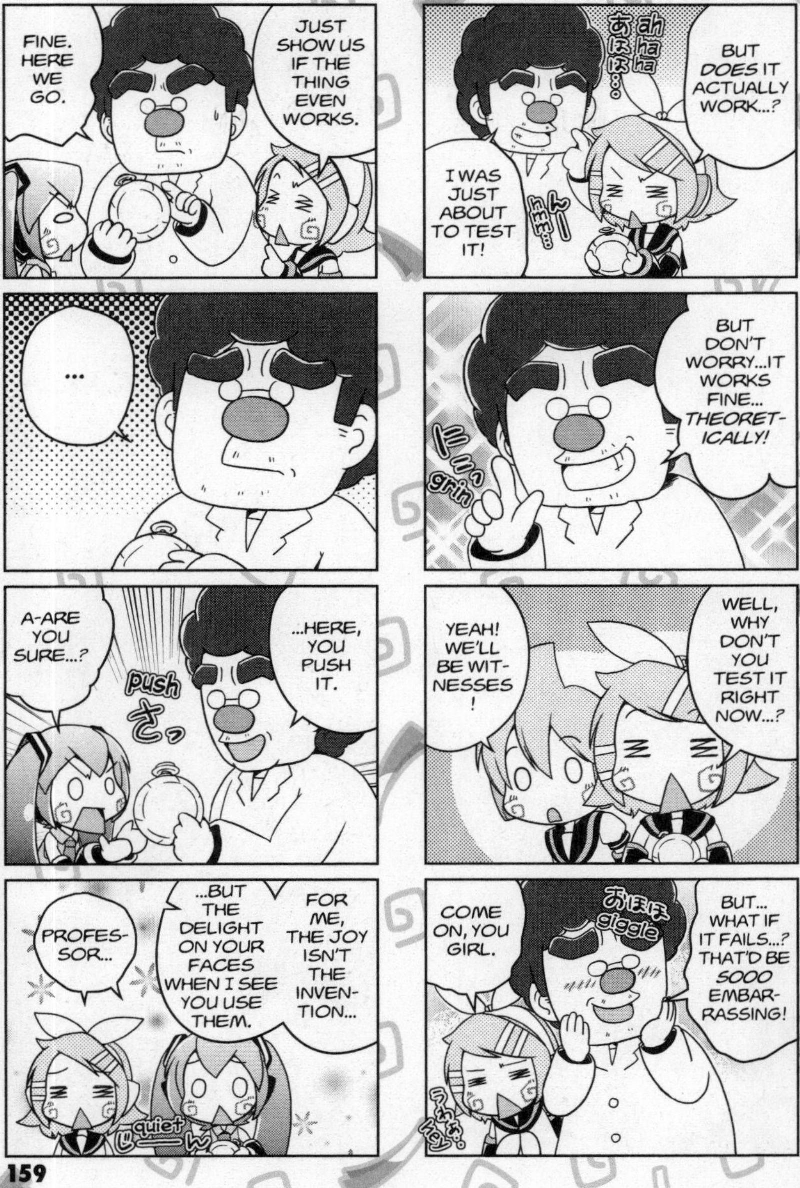
BUT DOES IT ACTUALLY WORK...?
あははは… ah ha ha
I WAS JUST ABOUT TO TEST IT!
んーー hmm...
JUST SHOW US IF THE THING EVEN WORKS.
FINE. HERE WE GO.
BUT DON'T WORRY...IT WORKS FINE... THEORETICALLY!
ニッ grin
...
WELL, WHY DON'T YOU TEST IT RIGHT NOW...?
YEAH! WE'LL BE WITNESSES!
...HERE, YOU PUSH IT.
push さっ
A-ARE YOU SURE...?
BUT... WHAT IF IT FAILS...? THAT'D BE SOOO EMBARRASSING!
おほほ giggle
COME ON, YOU GIRL.
うわぁ。 hey
FOR ME, THE JOY ISN'T THE INVENTION...
...BUT THE DELIGHT ON YOUR FACES WHEN I SEE YOU USE THEM.
PROFESSOR...
じーーん quiet

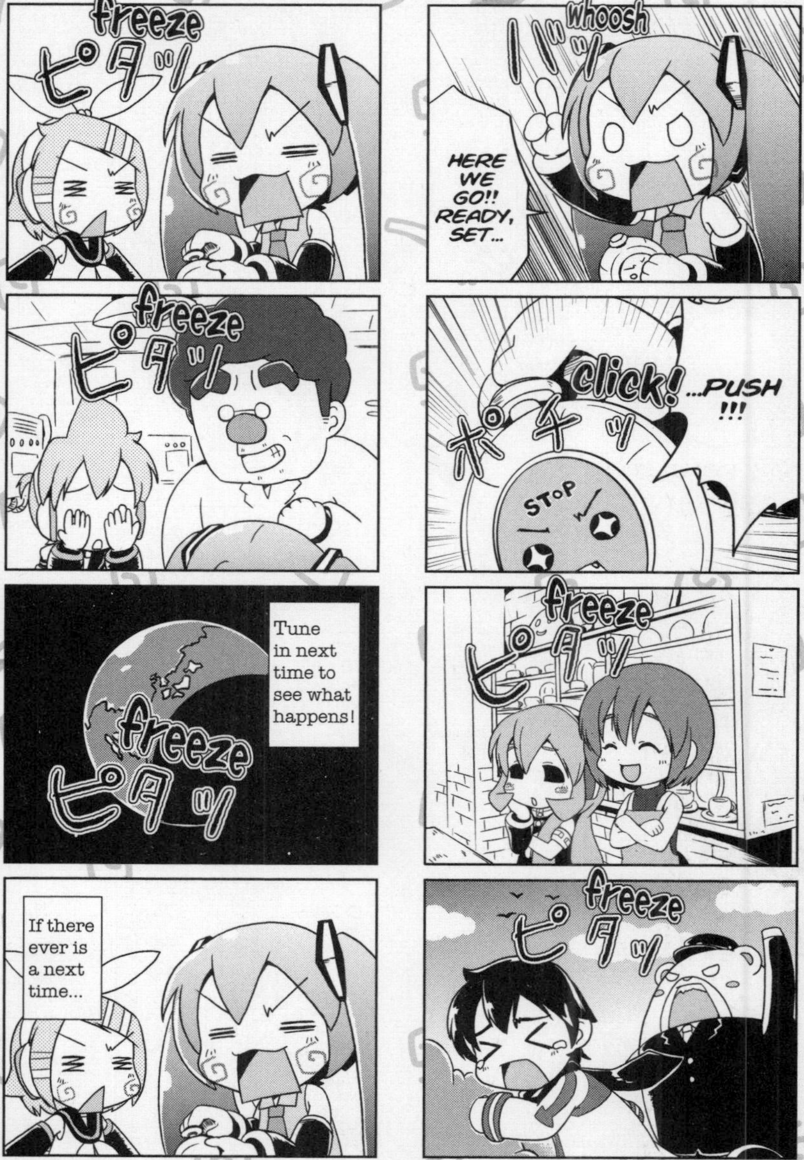

whoosh
バッ
HERE WE GO!! READY, SET...
freeze
ピタッ
click!
ポチッ
...PUSH !!!
STOP
freeze
ピタッ
freeze
ピタッ
Tune in next time to see what happens!
freeze
ピタッ
freeze
ピタッ
If there ever is a next time...

**Tales from the
making of...**

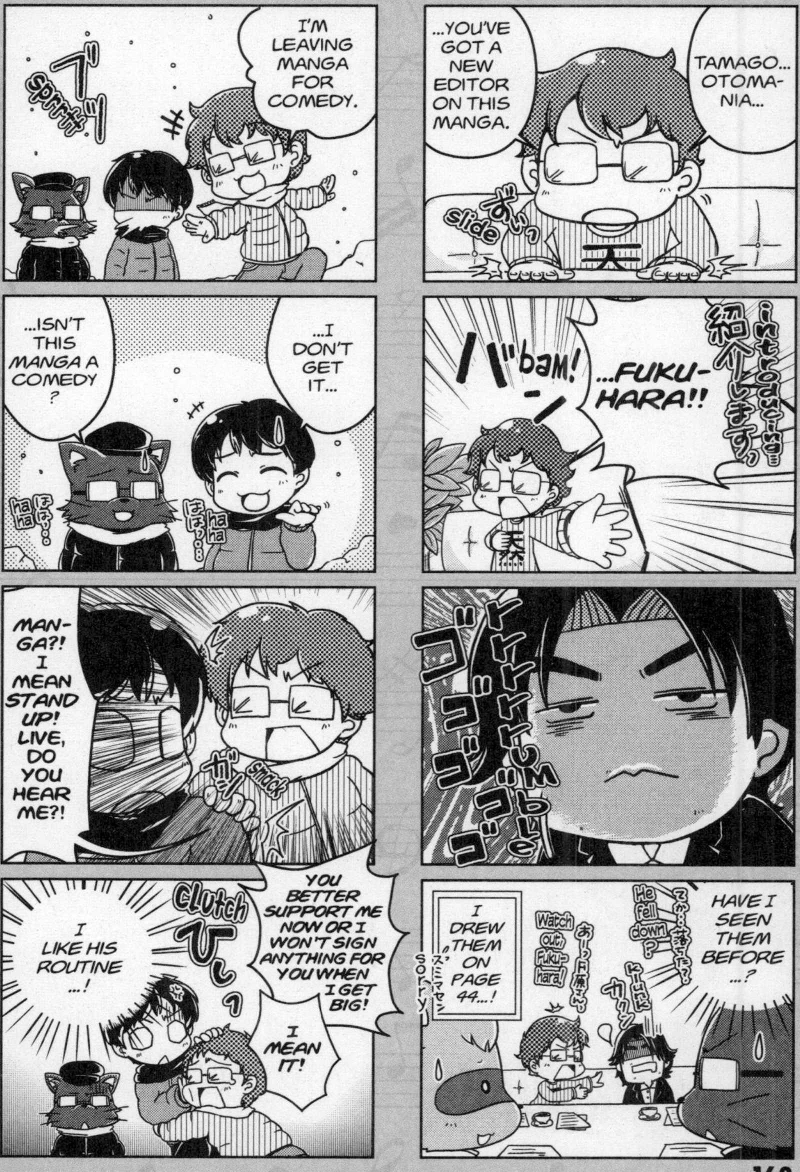
TAMAGO... OTOMANIA...
...YOU'VE GOT A NEW EDITOR ON THIS MANGA.
ずいっ
slide
I'M LEAVING MANGA FOR COMEDY.
ブッ
sprrrt
紹介します
introducing
...FUKUHARA!!
バッ
bam!
...I DON'T GET IT...
...ISN'T THIS MANGA A COMEDY?
ははっ...
haha
ははっ...
haha
ゴゴゴゴ
rumble
MAN-GA?! I MEAN STAND UP! LIVE, DO YOU HEAR ME?!
ガッ
smack
HAVE I SEEN THEM BEFORE...?
He fell down?
Watch out, Fukuhara!
I DREW THEM ON PAGE 44...!
スミマセン
sorry
YOU BETTER SUPPORT ME NOW OR I WON'T SIGN ANYTHING FOR YOU WHEN I GET BIG!
I MEAN IT!
I LIKE HIS ROUTINE...!
ひしっ
clutch

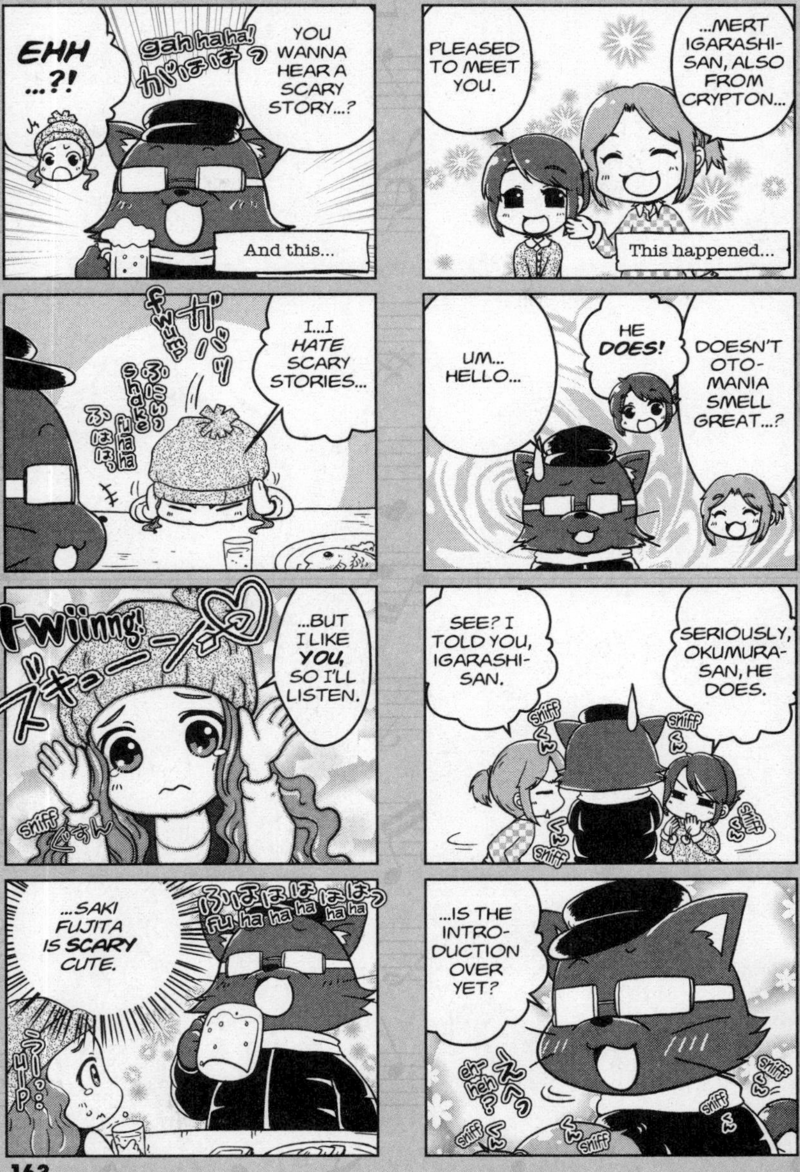
...MERT IGARASHI-SAN, ALSO FROM CRYPTON...
PLEASED TO MEET YOU.
This happened...
DOESN'T OTO-MANIA SMELL GREAT...?
HE DOES!
UM... HELLO...
SERIOUSLY, OKUMURA-SAN, HE DOES.
SEE? I TOLD YOU, IGARASHI-SAN.
sniff
sniff
sniff
sniff
...IS THE INTRODUCTION OVER YET?
sniff
eh-heh?
sniff
sniff
sniff
YOU WANNA HEAR A SCARY STORY...?
gah ha ha!
EHH ...?!
And this...
I...I HATE SCARY STORIES...
fwump
shake
fu ha ha
...BUT I LIKE YOU, SO I'LL LISTEN.
twiinng!
sniff
fu ha ha ha ha ha
...SAKI FUJITA IS SCARY CUTE.

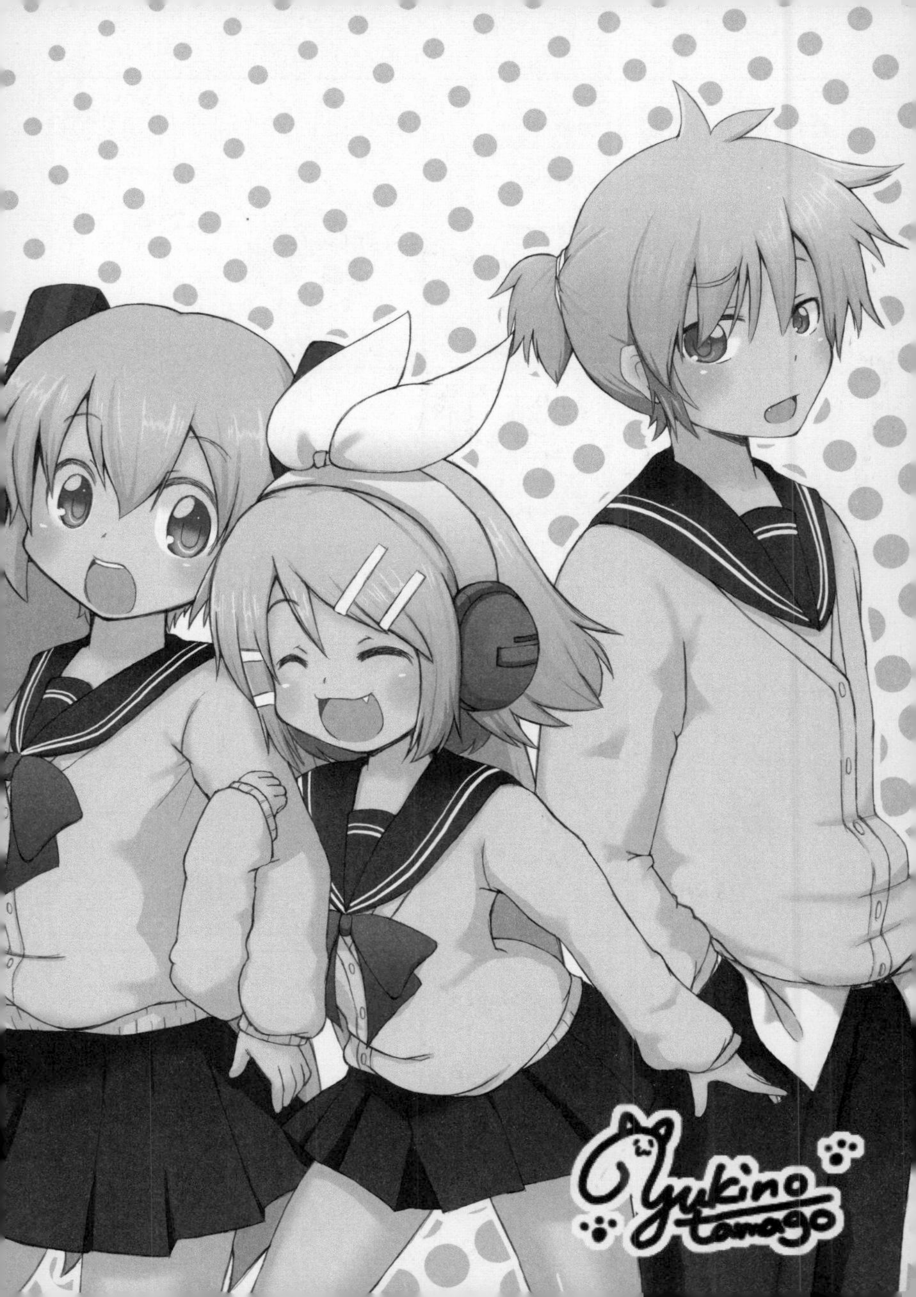
Yukino
tamago

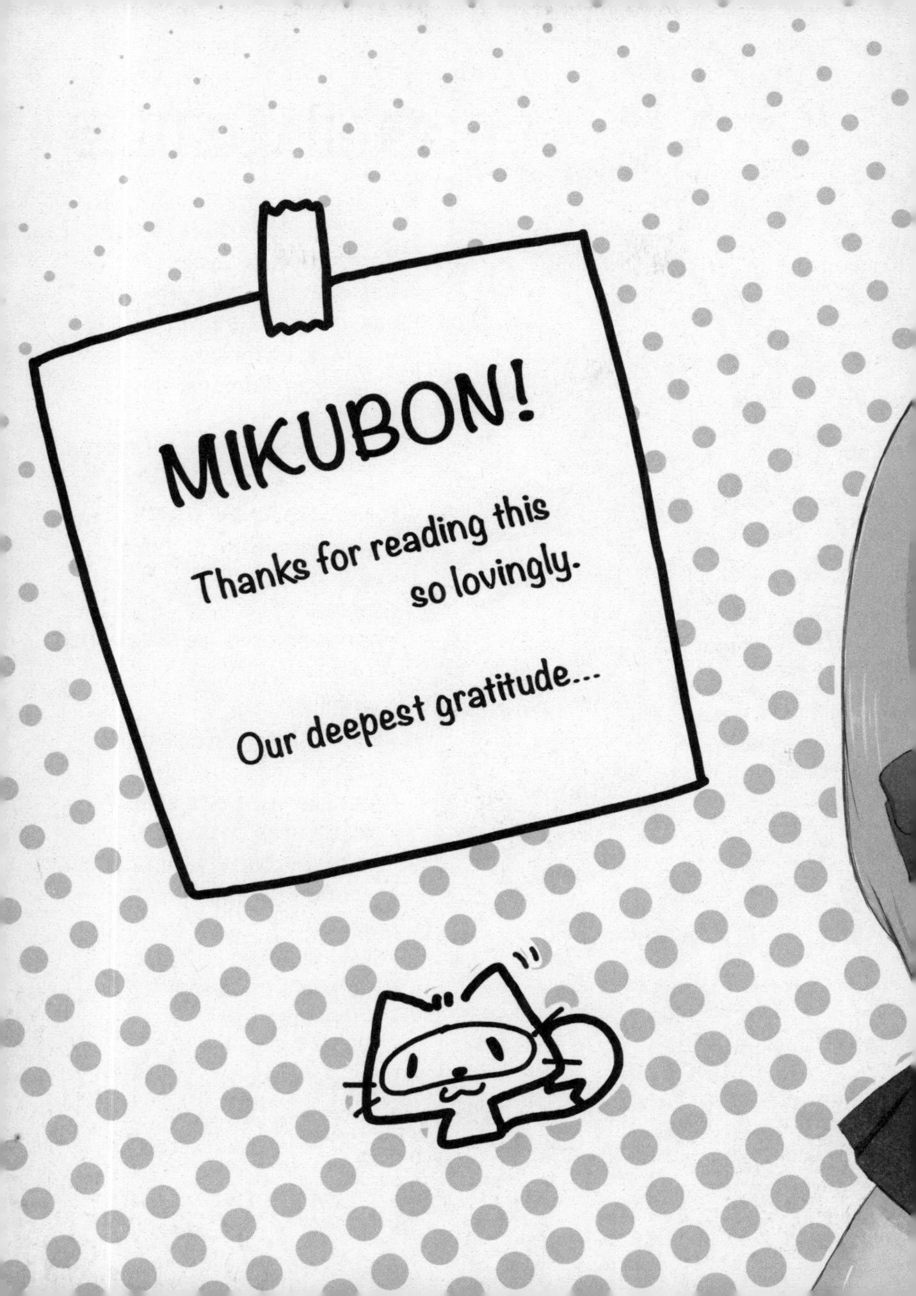
MIKUBON!
Thanks for reading this so lovingly.
Our deepest gratitude...

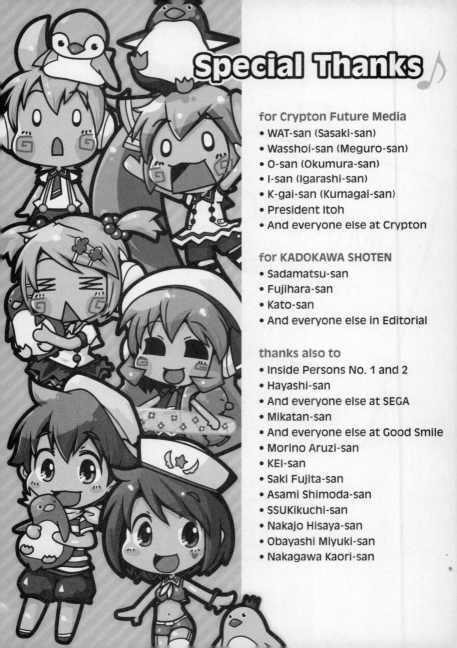

Special Thanks ♪

for Crypton Future Media
- WAT-san (Sasaki-san)
- Wasshoi-san (Meguro-san)
- O-san (Okumura-san)
- I-san (Igarashi-san)
- K-gai-san (Kumagai-san)
- President Itoh
- And everyone else at Crypton

for KADOKAWA SHOTEN
- Sadamatsu-san
- Fujihara-san
- Kato-san
- And everyone else in Editorial

thanks also to
- Inside Persons No. 1 and 2
- Hayashi-san
- And everyone else at SEGA
- Mikatan-san
- And everyone else at Good Smile
- Morino Aruzi-san
- KEI-san
- Saki Fujita-san
- Asami Shimoda-san
- SSUKikuchi-san
- Nakajo Hisaya-san
- Obayashi Miyuki-san
- Nakagawa Kaori-san

Learn about
Miku, Rin, Len, Luka,
Meiko, Kaito, and all the
other Vocaloids, concert
dates, software updates,
and more!

piapro.net

TAMAGO　　　　　**OTOMANIA**

ABOUT ONTAMA

This manga was written and drawn by Ontama, a pen name for a duo consisting of music producer Otomania and graphic designer Tamago. On September 4, 2007, just a week after the original release of the Hatsune Miku Vocaloid software, Ontama created what is probably the most famous Miku music video of all time, a remix of "Ievan Polkka" ("Eva's Polka"), an old Finnish song revived by the folk-pop group Loituma. The animated video has over 14 million views on YouTube alone, and introduced the popular leek-swinging (actually, *negi*-spinning ^_^) caricature of Hatsune Miku known as Hachune Miku—"Hachune" being how a young Japanese kid might pronounce "Hatsune."

PRESIDENT AND PUBLISHER
MIKE RICHARDSON

DESIGNER
SANDY TANAKA

DIGITAL ART TECHNICIAN
CHRISTINA McKENZIE

Special thanks to Michael Gombos.

English-language version produced by Dark Horse Comics

HATSUNE MIKU: MIKUBON
MIKUBON © ONTAMA 2013 © Crypton Future Media, INC. www.piapro.net piapro First published in Japan in 2013 by KADOKAWA CORPORATION, Tokyo. English translation rights arranged with KADOKAWA CORPORATION, Tokyo, through TOHAN CORPORATION, Tokyo. Dark Horse Manga™ is a trademark of Dark Horse Comics, Inc. All rights reserved. This English-language edition © 2016 by Dark Horse Comics, Inc. All other material © 2016 by Dark Horse Comics, Inc. All rights reserved. No portion of this publication may be reproduced or transmitted, in any form or by any means, without the express written permission of the copyright holders. Names, characters, places, and incidents featured in this publication either are the product of the author's imagination or are used fictitiously. Any resemblance to actual persons (living or dead), events, institutions, or locales, without satiric intent, is coincidental.

Published by Dark Horse Manga
A division of Dark Horse Comics, Inc.
10956 SE Main Street
Milwaukie, OR 97222

DarkHorse.com

To find a comics shop in your area, call the Comic Shop Locator Service toll-free
at 1-888-266-4226

First edition: October 2016
ISBN 978-1-50670-231-5

1 3 5 7 9 10 8 6 4 2
Printed in the United States of America.

NEIL HANKERSON Executive Vice President • TOM WEDDLE Chief Financial Officer • RANDY STRADLEY Vice President of Publishing • MICHAEL MARTENS Vice President of Book Trade Sales • MATT PARKINSON Vice President of Marketing • DAVID SCROGGY Vice President of Product Development • DALE LaFOUNTAIN Vice President of Information Technology • CARA NIECE Vice President of Production and Scheduling • NICK McWHORTER Vice President of Media Licensing • KEN LIZZI General Counsel • DAVE MARSHALL Editor in Chief • DAVEY ESTRADA Editorial Director • SCOTT ALLIE Executive Senior Editor • CHRIS WARNER Senior Books Editor • CARY GRAZZINI Director of Specialty Projects • LIA RIBACCHI Art Director • VANESSA TODD Director of Print Purchasing • MATT DRYER Director of Digital Art and Prepress • MARK BERNARDI Director of Digital Publishing • SARAH ROBERTSON Director of Product Sales • MICHAEL GOMBOS Director of International Publishing and Licensing

東京 TOKYO BABYLON

CLAMP

CLAMP's early epic of dangerous work —and dangerous attraction!

It's 1991, the last days of Japan's bubble economy, and money and elegance run through the streets. So do the currents of darkness beneath them, nourishing the evil spirits that only the arts of the onmyoji—Japan's legendary occultists—can combat. The two most powerful onmyoji are in the unlikely guises of a handsome young veterinarian, Seishiro, and the teenage heir to the ancient Sumeragi clan, Subaru—just a couple of guys whom Subaru's sister Hokuto has decided are destined to be together!

"Tokyo Babylon is CLAMP's first really great work."
—Manga: The Complete Guide

Each omnibus-sized volume features over a dozen full-color bonus pages!

VOLUME ONE
ISBN 978-1-61655-116-2
$19.99

VOLUME TWO
ISBN 978-1-61655-189-6
$19.99

CLAMP オキモノ キモノ
Mokona's
OKIMONO
KIMONO

CLAMP artist Mokona loves the art of traditional Japanese kimono. In fact, she designs kimono and kimono accessories herself and shares her love in *Okimono Kimono*, a fun and lavishly illustrated book full of drawings and photographs, interviews (including an interview with Onuki Ami of the J-pop duo Puffy AmiYumi), and exclusive short manga stories from the CLAMP artists!

From the creators of such titles as *Clover*, *Chobits*, *Cardcaptor Sakura*, *Magic Knight Rayearth*, and *Tsubasa*, *Okimono Kimono* is now available in English for the first time ever!

ISBN 978-1-59582-456-1

$12.99

AVAILABLE AT YOUR LOCAL COMICS SHOP OR BOOKSTORE
To find a comics shop in your area, call 1-888-266-4226
For more information or to order direct: • On the web: DarkHorse.com
E-mail: mailorder@darkhorse.com • Phone: 1-800-862-0052 Mon.–Fri. 9 AM to 5 PM Pacific Time.
CLAMP MOKONA NO OKIMONO KIMONO © 2007 CLAMP Mokona. Original Japanese edition published by Kawade Shabo Shinsha, Publishers. English translation copyright © 2010 Dark Horse Manga. Dark Horse Manga™ is a trademark of Dark Horse Comics, Inc. All rights reserved. (BL 7089)

CLAMP

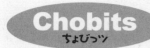

Chobits
ちょびッツ

IN NEAR-FUTURE JAPAN, the hottest style for your personal computer, or "persocom," is in the shape of an attractive android! Hideki, a poor student, finds a persocom seemingly discarded in an alley. He takes the cute, amnesiac robot home and names her "Chi."

But who is this strange new persocom in his life? Hideki finds himself having to teach Chi how to get along in the everyday world, even while he and his friends try to solve the mystery of her origins. Is she one of the urban-legendary *Chobits*—persocoms built to have the riskiest functions of all: real emotions and free will?

CLAMP's best-selling manga in America is finally available in omnibus form! Containing dozens of bonus color pages, *Chobits* is an engaging, touching, exciting story.

BOOK 1
ISBN 978-1-59582-451-6
$24.99

BOOK 2
ISBN 978-1-59582-514-8
$24.99

Cardcaptor Sakura

カードキャプターさくら

Story and Art by

CLAMP

Fourth grader Sakura Kinomoto has found a strange book in her father's library—a book made by the wizard Clow to store dangerous spirits sealed within a set of magical cards. But when Sakura opens it up, there is nothing left inside but Kero-chan, the book's cute little guardian beast . . . who informs Sakura that since the Clow cards seem to have escaped while he was asleep, it's now her job to capture them!

With remastered image files straight from CLAMP, Dark Horse is proud to present *Cardcaptor Sakura* in omnibus form! Each book collects three volumes of the original twelve-volume series, and features thirty bonus color pages!

OMNIBUS BOOK ONE
ISBN 978-1-59582-522-3 $19.99

OMNIBUS BOOK TWO
ISBN 978-1-59582-591-9 $19.99

DARK HORSE MANGA
DarkHorse.com

AVAILABLE AT YOUR LOCAL COMICS SHOP OR BOOKSTORE!

To find a comics shop in your area, call 1-888-266-4226

For more information or to order direct: • On the web: DarkHorse.com

E-mail: mailorder@darkhorse.com • Phone: 1-800-862-0052 Mon.–Fri. 9 AM to 5 PM Pacific Time